D1498141

The Creation
of Elisabethville
1910-1940

The Creation
of Elisabethville
1910-1940

Bruce Fetter

HOOVER COLONIAL STUDIES
Edited by
Peter Duignan and Lewis Gann

HOOVER INSTITUTION PRESS
Stanford University, Stanford, California 94305

Hoover Institution Publications 155

© *1976 by the Board of Trustees of the*
Leland Stanford Junior University
All rights reserved
International Standard Book Number: 0-8179-6551-3
Library of Congress Catalog Card Number: 76-26774
Printed in the United States of America

To Vicky, David, and Manou
who know me better than I know the city

CONTENTS

TABLES

TABLES

ILLUSTRATIONS

Hoover Colonial Studies Series

Cities are of ancient origin in Africa. Precolonial settlements included the traditional Hausa towns, dependent on handicraft and overland trade, and the "agrotown," a type of city represented by such centers as the *kibuga*, the royal seat of
Buganda. Such communities, however, housed but a tiny proportion of the population of precolonial Africa. Their economies
rested, in varying proportions, on handicraft, commerce, tribute,
and on local agricultural production supplemented by food im-
ports. Ancient East Africa developed a maritime civilization
founded in large measure upon the transoceanic commerce in slaves
and luxuries such as gold, cloves, and ivory.

Western colonization and Western technology brought about a
major change. In many parts of Africa, agriculture became more
productive and created a surplus of victuals that could be used
for feeding great urban agglomerations. Steamships, railways,
and motor trucks facilitated the movement of people, of manu-
factures, of food, and of industrial and mining equipment. Medical science and new urban techniques concerned with the supply
of power, water, and the disposal of sewage gradually reduced
some of the more serious health hazards. The new rulers had the
means to deliberately plan new settlements; they imported new
techniques of urban technology and urban architecture, city
building, road making, draining, and so forth. They could also
supply communities over long distances. The colonial era thus
saw a swift expansion of urban settlements both along the coast
and in the hinterland. The majority of modern African cities,
then, are of colonial origin. Modern imperialists, like the
ancient Romans, were among the world's foremost city builders.

The new cities can be divided into several types. There
were military stations like Fort Beaufort in the Cape Province,
established to defend the settlers' frontier against intruders.
King William's Town began as a mission station. There were
trading settlements like Dakar, developed by the French to become the greatest maritime city in French colonial Africa.
There were administrative posts like Lusaka in what used to be
Northern Rhodesia (Zambia), a backveld Canberra whose main industry was government. Finally there were mining communities

whose importance arose from the proximity of ore bodies in pay-
able quantities; these included vast cities like Johannesburg,
dependent on gold mining, or Elisabethville (Lubumbashi), linked
to the development of the Kantangan copper industry.

Bruce Fetter's work makes an important advance in the field
of urban history in Africa. It is one of the first book-length
accounts of a colonial African city by a professional historian.
The author traces the development of Elisabethville from a rough
camp to a city housing some thirty thousand permanent residents
and a much greater number of migrants. The city began as an
outpost of the South African mining frontier, but after its initial phase of development, the settlement was purged of Anglo-
South African influence and was effectively "Belgianized." It
became the center of an all-pervading colonial complex that
transformed the entire region of Katanga. During the second
period, Belgian influence was consolidated under the aegis of
what the author calls "the colonial trinity" of missions, government, and corporations.

Scholars have differed vastly in their particular assess-
ments of urbanization during the colonial era. Traditional
historians of empire have regarded the colonial impact with its
urban orientation as one of pure gain. As an academic of the
early 1920s put it in relation to British West Africa:

Inaccessible places . . . have been rendered accessible. Diverse and scattered communities have been
bound into large administrative and economic units.
Civilisation has spread into the heart of the Jungle
Forest. . . . By means of improved transport, mining
of gold, tin, coal and manganese has become important, and exchange cultures have arisen, bringing
increased wealth to the natives and multiplying the
trade of the region. The standard of life and comfort has been heightened for many of the natives,
and the Revenue of the Administration has been augmented, permitting the rendition of a number of public utilities to the community as a whole, in the
way of education and sanitation and agricultural
aid. . . . In the matter of currency and means of
exchange a great revolution has been wrought. Bar-
ter and the old commodity currency ranging from
slaves to cowrie shells have been abolished. . . .
Even the most illiterate native is learning to prize
the coin currency. . . . The Medical Revolution has
altered the entire outlook. . . . Africa has bene-
fitted by the importation of manufactured goods,
and the substitution of law and order for chaos

and barbarism.*

This mood hardly survived World War II. Godfrey Wilson, a British sociologist writing during that conflict, put forward a very different interpretation. Having investigated the effects of urbanization in Broken Hill, Northern Rhodesia, Wilson argued that the existing imbalance in colonial capitalism could be resolved only by a radical transformation. Northern Rhodesia, as he saw it, was a land of darkness:

> The disproportionate withdrawal of young men from the rural areas destroys the balance of the old primitive agricultural systems, without creating a new market sufficient to make any general revolution in agricultural method possible. Of the small market for agricultural produce, moreover, a large part is already occupied by immigrant Europeans employing unskilled African labor at low wages. The distant rural areas are thus left poor and hungry; their poverty drives to town all the men who can possibly find a living there; and this, in its turn, keeps urban wages low. The transfer of gifts from town to country does not and cannot ever make up for the withdrawal of the young men's labour.**

Bruce Fetter follows in Wilson's tradition. The author sees Elisabethville as a city built for Europeans by Europeans to serve European needs. Admittedly, there were some improvements in African wages and living conditions at the end of the colonial period. But, he holds, "Elisabethville was . . . parasitical on its African hinterland, drawing its food and labor and giving little in return." These conclusions are challenging. They do not accord with our own notions. Neither do they conform to the interpretation of a philosopher like Marx who thought poorly of the supposed blessings conferred by rural life on preindustrial people, and who believed that urbanization and modern capitalism—despite the immediate suffering they brought in their train—were beneficent in their long-term consequences. Fetter, however, has marshalled a vast amount of new evidence. He tells a fascinating story. His pioneer work will make a valuable contribution, not only to a particular chapter of

---

   *Allan McPhee, *The Economic Revolution in British West Africa* (London, 1971), pp. 304-7.

   **Godfrey Wilson, *An Essay on the Economics of Detribalization in Northern Rhodesia,* part 2 (Livingstone, 1942), *Rhodes-Livingstone Papers,* no. 6, p. 80.

colonial history, but also to general urban history and to the wider debate on the nature of colonialism and its impact on African society.

Peter Duignan

L. H. Gann

Hoover Institution

August 1976

This is the first book-length description of a colonial
African city written by a historian, and as such it will provide
a building block for filling an important gap in our knowledge.
Given the development of urban history in other parts of the
world, one might well ask why the field has been so long in
reaching African scholars.

There are a number of reasons for the underdeveloped state
of African urban history. From a technical point of view, urban
historians of tropical Africa lack the professional tools which
their colleagues often take for granted. The monographic literature is scanty and the archives are frequently closed or in
ravaged condition. A more fundamental problem is the absence of
a model which explains African urban development in historical
terms. Colonial civil servants, economists, geographers,
anthropologists, and political scientists have all studied
African development from the point of view of their respective
disciplines—which can be very helpful to historians—but their
outlook is not the same as that of someone in the discipline of
history.

Even within the historical discipline, serious problems
arise in translating historical studies from one part of the
world to another. Although there are universal aspects of
urbanization, each city's history is in large part a function of
the experience of the people who created it. The history of
cities in the United States, Latin America, or Asia contains
problems which are not strictly translatable to Africa. The
historian of Africa is thus thrown back on more general resources.
He can select aspects of the other social sciences which seem
to illuminate his particular problem, and he can seek help from
other branches of history. Two historical genres would seem
particularly useful: biography and political history.

The story of a city lies somewhere between biography and
the history of a nation and has a number of elements in common
with both. Like an individual, it has a birth which can be
located in time as well as prenatal circumstances which influence its later growth. Once formed, however, a city's development is infinitely more complicated than that of an individual.
A suitable subject of a biography becomes somewhat more complex

over time as the individual matures and interacts with others,
but a city becomes more complex on an entirely different order
of magnitude since it encompasses the divergent lives of a mul-
titude of individuals. Thus, difficult as it is to write a
thorough biography, it is easier to describe the career of an
individual than to capture the collective growth of a social
unit containing thousands or even millions of people.

The history of a modern city resembles that of a nation in
its development but not in its origins. The birth of a nation
is not so clearcut as that of an individual or a modern city.
National identity develops over a period of years during which
an increasing proportion of the citizenry acquire a national
consciousness. Such collective behavior encompasses not just
political institutions but, as Karl Deutsch and others have
shown, depends on economic and social developments as well. By
the same token, the growth of a city must be explained in terms
of collective behavior and—although certain individuals may
play important roles in decisionmaking—it is the institutions
which tailor the alternatives from among which these individuals
must take action.

Urban history thus must include an analysis of the institutions which contribute to urban development as well as the contributions of those individuals who appeared to dominate the
city. On the basis of these analyses, the urban historian can
construct a synthesis which ties together the city's constituent
parts and which, at least in part, explains their interaction.
In the case of a colonial city this synthesis must explain the
city in relation to other geographic units: its hinterland and
its mother country.

In Elisabethville, the subject of this book, local developments depended on several external factors: European colonization, technology, and capital, and a Central African labor
supply. Europeans from distant lands played a more important
role in the foundation and development of the city than did
local Africans. The city's creation in fact, can be explained
entirely as the result of European political and economic power.
It was built to meet foreign needs—to serve as a center for the
exportation of copper and as the seat of Belgian colonial administration in the copperbelt. And so it would remain until independence in 1960.

This dependence on Europe poisoned the relationship between
Elisabethville and its African hinterland. Europeans viewed the
surrounding countryside purely as a source of labor and, to a
lesser extent, food. Elisabethville was thus parasitical on its
African hinterland, drawing from it food and labor and giving

little in return. The ensuing undernourishment in rural areas, combined with the colonial nation's tax policy which required Africans to pay taxes in European currency, tended to push people from their villages into the city.

This migration from rural areas which already had a low population density impoverished the hinterland but promoted the development of the city. A short ten years after Elisabethville's creation some of the Africans working there began to think of the city as their home and Elisabethville began to acquire a permanent African population which grew in size almost continuously, except during the worst years of the Great Depression. The city's white minority also gradually increased over the years. This minority—the most influential members of which were colonial officials, a few missionaries, and management personnel at the copper industry—continued to dominate the city and its economy. Partly in response to this domination, city Africans began to develop their own organizations which were to play an increasingly important role in history.

The city's early history falls into two periods which are reflected in the two major sections in which this book is divided. The first period, from 1910 to 1920, was the formative one during which European forces totally dominated the scene. During the second period, which ran from 1920 until the outbreak of the Second World War, the city constituted a field of local and external forces in a state of constant interaction. Even in this period, however, local forces never predominated, for the city continued to exist to meet foreign rather than local needs.

Many people helped me with this study. Some of my most valuable information has come from those who are in complete disagreement with me on its interpretation. I therefore thank them for their contribution and lay claim to all sins here included as my own.

Professor Jan Vansina has been a constant inspiration. His qualities as a groundbreaking and enthusiastic scholar are equalled only by his modesty, good humor, and great warmth. Professor Philip Curtin, who created the programs of African Studies and Comparative Tropical History in which I have studied, has always been a living example of scientific rigor and clarity in content and form. Professor Crawford Young has revealed new aspects of my study, thanks to his broad knowledge of contemporary Congo. Without the beneficent concern of Dr. Lewis Gann, this manuscript would never have seen the light of day.

The people in Belgium and in the Congo who helped me with my research are so numerous that I must thank them without reference to their institutional affiliation but only according to the kind of help which they gave me.

In Belgium my thanks go to MM. F. Grévisse, Jean Sohier, A. Decoster, E. Toussaint, and J. Dutron, Mme. R. Toussaint, MM. R. Strijthagen and E. Bourgeois, all of whom now live in Belgium but whose lives are intimately tied to the history of the Lubumbashi, and to Professor J. Stengers, who has begun the enormous task of writing the history of the Congo.

My thanks also go to the following persons associated with Belgian national libraries and archives having materials concerning the Congo for their help and guidance: M. J. Berlage, Drs. M. Luwel and O. Boone, the late M. Walraet, and M. Desneux, Mme. van Grieken-Taverniers and the late M. van Grieken, the late MM. E. Sabbe and E. Neven and MM. E. van der Woude and M. Lorens.

The following representatives of Belgian companies were of enormous help in assembling materials: M. R. Lékime, M. le Baron P. Greindl, Mlle. Thirry and the staff of the Union Minière library. MM. L. Moraux, Barbier, P. M.-C. Cormeau, and R. D. C. Delforge.

The Benedictines of St. André generously allowed me to use their library where le Père Abbé, his secretary and dom J. D. Broeckaert, the librarian, were especially helpful.

Other Belgians with Congolese experience provided assistance at various stages of my work: MM. D. Ryelandt, R.-J. Cornet, Governor A. Lemborelle, MM. P. Montenez, H. Rosy, J. Labrique, M. and Mme. L. Thuriaux, Dr. A. S. Gérard, MM. J. Gérard-Libois, B. Verhaegen, and J. van Lierde.

In England my thanks go to Mr. David Fieldhouse who supplied useful criticism of my current work some years after guiding me through the tasks of an earlier stage in my academic career, and to the Public Records Office and Royal Commonwealth Society for useful materials not available elsewhere.

An even longer list of people helped me while I was in Zaïre. My thanks go first to the officials of the Université Officiele du Congo who offered me hospitality during my first stay in Lubumbashi: to the late Professor J. Dhondt (then the Rector), and to Professors J. Verbruggen, R. Dethier, F. Ngoma (then the Vice-Rector), the Librarian, R. Vrancx, Professor E. Lamy, and Dean A. Déjace. My thanks also go to Mlle. Th.

Centner and the staff of the Centre des Etudes Politico-Sociales Indigènes for their advice and the use of their excellent library.

Certain officials of the provincial and city governments also provided invaluable help in my project: MM. Kyalwe Gilbert, Grandjean, J.-M. Neuville, Kalassa, Kia Alfred, Kalenda Mathieu, Munongo Godefroid, Mwepu Boniface, MM. les Secrétaires des Communes Albert, Kenya, Katuba, and Ruashi, and M. le Procureur de l'Etat Moïse.

The late M. Kasokya Laurent, my assistant, enthusiastically joined me in the search for Lubumbashi's history.

These officials of the companies in Lubumbashi gave me great help: MM. G. van Schendel, G. Heynen, Dr. F. Feuillat, MM. Istace and the late G. Forthomme.

Benedictines and Salesians at Lubumbashi who shared their many years' experience and their books include Mgr. F. Cornelis, the late dom A. Laudé, RRPP. Picron and François.

In addition the following private citizens of Lubumbashi shared their recollections of times past: MM. Antoine Théodore Paul, Berthier Albert, Mlles. G. Dutilleux and de Deurwaarder, MM. Kabwe François, Kalala Joseph, Lunkaba Louis, Mpoyo Victor, L. Sartenaer, and forty retired workers who wrote letters about their lives.

During my second stay in Lubumbashi the Department of History of the National University of Zaïre welcomed me and introduced me to their magnificent work. My thanks go especially to Father L. de St. Moulin, Professors J.-L. Vellut and B. Jewsiewicki, Father L. Greindl, and to the students and former students who have been examining their own history, especially Citizens Yogolelo, Tshibangu, and Malira.

Mr. Bruce Burne of the Zambian National Archives provided a meticulously kept collection, and Professor J. van Velsen offered useful criticisms.

In the United States my thanks go to Miss Marguerite Christiansen and other members of the staff of the University of Wisconsin Memorial Library, and to the staff of the University of Wisconsin-Milwaukee and library; to Professor R. Lemarchand, Mrs. Nelson of the Methodist Church Library in New York; Dr. Arthur Kogan, Chief of the Research and Review Division, Historical Office, State Department, Washington; to the staff of the New York Public Library; and to the University of Wisconsin-

Milwaukee's Cartographic Services Laboratory and to the University of Wisconsin-Milwaukee's Photographic Services. In the revision of my dissertation I received particularly useful criticism from my colleagues Professors John McGovern, Reginald Horsman, Alvin Wolfe, David Healy, and Frank Cassell. Special thanks to Mickey Hamilton, Mrs. Ann Healy, to my sister-in-law, Mrs. Eva Coire, and to Sallie Jaggar Hayes for making my manuscript intelligible. Miss A. Cooper, Miss K. Poplawski, Mrs. A. Schaus, Miss L. Lobotzke, and Mrs. H. Kay competently typed the countless versions of my manuscript.

This study was made possible by grants from the U. S. Department of Health, Education, and Welfare, the State Department, which funded my second stay in Lubumbashi as a Fulbright lecturer; from the Committee on Comparative Tropical History of the University of Wisconsin-Madison; and from my mother, who has been infinitely patient and proud.

Bruce Fetter
Milwaukee, Wisconsin

Photographs

Two Examples of the Earliest European Architecture (pre-1914)

Monseigneur de Hemptinne's Cathedral (1922)

Company Housing (ca. 1940) in the Commune Kamalondo

The Slag Head and Smoke Stacks of the Lubumbashi Smelter

Chapter 1

Elisabethville and its African Hinterland:

A Parasitic Relationship

Elisabethville, known since 1967 as Lubumbashi, was one of the largest cities in colonial Central Africa. Beginning in 1910 it served as the administrative capital of Katanga, the richest province on the copperbelt—a region which stretches from southeastern Zaïre (the Congo's name since 1971) to the Republic of Zambia (formerly Northern Rhodesia). The city was and remains a vital center for the political and economic development of a vast region.

The site on which the governor of Katanga decided to build Elisabethville was singularly unsuitable for settlement by nineteenth-century African standards. No African village had ever been located on the spot. The city sits in the middle of an infertile grassland while the local people build their villages in river valleys, cultivating the richer alluvial soils of the bottom lands. Although a small stream—the Lubumbashi—does run through Elisabethville, the soil on its banks at that point is so infertile that it does not support settled agriculture. Today Elisabethville claims well over a third of a million inhabitants; a hundred years ago the site was too poor even to support an African hamlet.

From a strategic point of view the area has serious shortcomings. Although over four thousand feet above sea level, the land is quite flat. In the older parts of the city the greatest physical relief is provided by ten-foot high termite hills. This openness to attack would have made it particularly vulnerable and unsuitable as a base for military operations.

Nor did Elisabethville's site have any particular advantages from an economic standpoint. The scene of small-scale copper mining by Africans during the nineteenth century, it possessed only one of many similar mines in the region.

Accessible deposits of copper oxides including the beautiful
green mineral, malachite, lay on the Ruashi stream only six
miles from what is today the city center. During the dry season when most Central Africans were freed from agricultural
tasks, bands of men moved to the Ruashi to smelt copper crosses
which were a valuable item in local commerce. But the Ruashi's
copper deposits were not rare; equally rich ores could be found
throughout the region. Consequently, even the Ruashi mine had
little more than local economic value.

In broad perspective, therefore, nineteenth-century Elisabethville was awkwardly situated in comparison with other sites
on which precolonial Africans congregated. Its soil was too
poor to support a dense population, not was it near a more fer-
tile region. Lacking natural defenses and food resources, its
location was not secure from a strategic standpoint. Finally,
its resources were unexceptional copper deposits which could be
found at any of a hundred sites on the copperbelt.

These apparent disadvantages, however, evaporated when the
city's site is evaluated from the perspective of colonial Europeans. By the late nineteenth century they possessed an advanced technology which, for their purposes, made existing
African ways of thinking about the land irrelevant. It was thus
a series of European decisions which brought about the development of Elisabethville in a location which had been of little
value to its earlier inhabitants.

Two distinct European groups played a role in the process
leading to the city's development. Colonial governments had to
extend their authority over the region; colonial firms had to
invest money in transportation and local industries. Only then
could the railroad be built which made possible local urban
development. These decisions were made by white men to satisfy
distant constituencies, the most important of which were metropolitan governments and investors on the international money
market. The city could not have been built without Europeans,
but it was also designed exclusively to satisfy their needs.

The chain of events which led to the foundation of Elisabethville had begun in the last years of the nineteenth century
when European entrepreneurs began to extend the South African
railway system northward toward the Central African copper
deposits. Their activities depended on the adoption of colonial
government policies favorable to the expansion of European rule.
Claiming territory in Central Africa posed no particular problem;
by the 1890s European governments no longer recognized the sovereignty of black African states. Beyond the establishment of
colonial regimes to replace indigenous political units, however,

the Europeans were obliged to make a military decision to
secure the proposed railway track from military attack. In the
case of Elisabethville two governments, the British South
African Company and the Belgian-dominated Comité Spécial du
Katanga, cleared the line of rail in their respective territories. Managers of colonial companies played a vital role in
railway construction since without freight in the form of exportable raw materials and importable manufactured goods the
railways would have been economically unviable.

Although governments and private investors were both essential to the region's development, they did not always act in
harmony. British businessmen spearheaded the capitalist penetration, and by 1908 they had amassed sufficient funds to con-
nect the South African railway system with Belgian territory
nearly two thousand miles away. This communications link posed
a threat to Belgian officials in Katanga who feared that they
would be overwhelmed by a flood of British migrants, and colonial officials in Brussels ordered their agents on the spot to
build a regional capital on the new rail line near an adequate
water supply. By 1909 British engineers were already building
a smelter on the Lubumbashi, so the Belgian chief executive in
Katanga, Major Emile Wangermée, situated the new city adjacent
to the copper company's camp. In that way Wangermée and his
staff could keep a close watch on the English-speakers—Britons,
South Africans, and even a few Americans—who constituted a
majority of the Europeans already developing the mines and the
railroad in the copperbelt.[1]

In 1910 this heterogeneous collection of Europeans were to
witness the rapid transformation of an unsettled African bush
region, a change brought about by arrival of the railroad. A
site which had been unsuitable for settlement in precolonial
times was soon attached to the southern African communications
network. And the first trains brought all that was necessary to
support urban development—food, coal, machinery, and consumer
goods. The colonial administration and local industry, now
abundantly supplied from Europe and South Africa, made Elisabethville the base of operations for forays by tax collectors
and labor recruiters into the surrounding countryside. The
city was developing its own hinterland and becoming the urban
center of a much wider area.

The relationship between Elisabethville and its new hinterland, however, was quite different from that which the city had
with the southern African communications network. With the
latter, the new city functioned more or less on terms of equal-
ity. The inhabitants of Elisabethville consumed the products of
South Africa and the Rhodesias; they also contributed to the

more developed region's economy by providing increased traffic
for the railroads and a market for locally produced consumer
goods.

Elisabethville's hinterland, by contrast, received little
from the new urban center. On the contrary, bands of labor
recruiters and victualers spread from the city to the surrounding
countryside to denude it of its food surplus and siphon off
large quantities of African labor. The Europeans who organized
these activities gave little in return to the Africans of Elisabethville's back country. The colonizers' military might was so
great that they could take what they wanted with impunity. The
confiscation of African resources during the early years of
Elisabethville's history would have many important effects on
the region's later development.

The colonizers' demands on individual Africans, however,
required little local investment. African labor could be brought
to Elisabethville on the existing primitive communications network which consisted of savana paths. There was no need for the
Belgians to build an extensive road network to population centers in rural Katanga. As a result the only efficient transportation medium, the railway, served only long distance commerce:
the exportation of copper and the importation of supplies not
locally available.

The railroad did not even lead to the opening up and subsequent development of the territory through which it passed.
Because of cost, European contractors avoided the more densely
populated river valleys where they would have had to build expensive bridges. Instead they chose a route which followed as
closely as possible the Congo-Zambezi divide. This was indeed
a desolate area. The nearest population centers lay about one
hundred twenty miles to the east of the rail line, in the valley
of the Luapula River which served as a boundary between British
Northern Rhodesia and the Belgian Congo.

Although the railway bypassed these inhabited areas, both
the colonial governments and major European firms had plans to
deal with the rural population. Belgian colonial officials had
two goals in mind: establishing their authority in all of the
territory claimed by their government and finding sources of
revenue sufficient to pay for their administration.

As a first step in the establishment of their authority,
Belgian administrators attacked the African kingdoms which had
ruled Katanga before colonization. Their very claim to Katanga
rested on the death in 1891—at the hands of Belgian agents—of
Msiri, an African empire-builder who had controlled much of the

copperbelt. The Belgians also spent the ten years from 1906 to 1916 in search of Kasongo Niembo, the chief of the Luba-Katanga, and when they finally caught him they proceeded to carve up his kingdom. The same process was repeated dozens of times on a smaller scale. After that, prudent chiefs made peace with the Belgians without first having to be defeated militarily.[2]

The conquest, however, had its positive as well as its negative side. Most important, it put an end to the long distance slave trade and to local wars which had been extremely destructive. This *pax europeana* also augmented the region's productive capacity by freeing men from military obligations to their chiefs. The Europeans, however, would absorb more labor than they freed, leaving rural areas labor-poor.

It was not the intention of the colonizers to impoverish the countryside nor did they seek to eradicate African political organization. Africans were too widely scattered across the countryside to permit establishment of a colonial local government; the cost would have been prohibitive. The Belgians' object was to domesticate African authorities so that chiefs would rule according to the colonizers' bidding. Thus in the Congo as in the rest of Africa, those kings who retained their thrones did so as a part of the colonial hierarchy.

Having made this sacrifice, many African rulers were able to maintain a certain hold over their people. Indeed, Belgian recognition often reinforced a king's political control over previously rebellious districts. In some cases Africans who had been forced to migrate to urban areas retained a measure of loyalty to the rural chiefs who could claim recognition by the colonial power.

Seen as a whole, however, the power of the chiefs was in no way comparable to that of the colonial administrators. The latter were essential links in a political chain of command which conveyed orders from the colonial government to the mass of the vanquished. The chiefs, by contrast, were merely convenient intermediaries in the process of colonization and could easily be replaced if they proved troublesome. The only powers left to them were those deemed innocuous by colonial authorities.

Beyond the domestication of the chiefs, Belgian administrators had a second goal in mind: the acquisition of sufficient revenue to pay the costs of colonial government. By the 1880s it was taken for granted that European colonies in Africa—and for that matter in the rest of the world—should be run as subordinate governments distinct from those of the European

metropole. This practice was based on fiscal as well as political considerations. Politically, the creation of the colony
as a separate administrative entity made it possible to rule
the colonial territory through laws other than those enforced in
the mother country. Thus policies could be imposed on Africans
which never would have been tolerated in the metropole. The
fiscal advantage of creating the colony as a distinct unit lay
in the separation of finances between the dependency and the
mother country. Popularly elected parliaments in Europe strongly
objected to expenditures outside their national territories even
if these were made within their own empires. And although the
creation of separate colonial budgets did not eliminate metro-
politian subsidies, they did give the colonies a strong incentive "to stand on their own feet." More precisely, the existence
of separate colonial budgets impelled colonial administrators to
find local sources of revenue.

At first these colonial treasuries had to be filled with
local products rather than European money. In the early years
of colonization most administrators accepted local goods and
services from their subjects, but this practice was discontinued
as quickly as possible because of the difficulty of transferring
such resources to Europe. In another connection J. S. Furnivall
has described the reasons for demanding payment in European
money almost from the earliest days of British administration in
Burma:

> Burmese officials lived off the produce of the country,
> rice and sesamum oil and fish; but British and Indian
> troops wanted beef and flour and butter. These things
> had to be purchased, and, for other reasons also, the
> collection of revenue in kind, though useful in the
> barter economy of Burma, was unsuited to a commercial
> economy using money as a medium of exchange.[3]

Colonial officials had two possible means of raising the
revenue necessary for their budgets: they could either tax goods
being imported into the colony or tax local production. British
governments, viewing the colonies as markets for British goods,
encouraged the development of taxation systems based on import
taxes. In a recent article on British colonies in tropical
Africa, Cyril Ehrlich has shown that "for much of the period
(between 1890 and 1960) in most territories import duties were
the chief source of revenue, from 30 to more than 60 percent of
the total proceeds."[4]

Africans in those British territories where this policy was
in force benefited at least indirectly from its application.
Since the colonial treasury depended on African purchases of

imported goods, it was in the interest of the colonial government
to see that its subjects earned enough European money to be able
to buy them. Although economic activities not transacted in
European currency were largely ignored by the colonial administration, this fiscal policy stimulated the importation of foreign
goods into the economy which might not otherwise have been purchased at home.

This was not the case in the Belgian Congo (and its predecessor until 1908, the Congo Free State) where the tax system
depended on African production of primary products. The colonial
budget did not depend on African consumption of European goods,[5]
so colonial administrators did little to encourage Africans to
buy them. Moreoever, instead of offering positive incentives to
production they employed the powers of the state to coerce Africans to produce raw materials for export.

Production fed the colonial budget in the Congo through two
major sources: export duties, and taxes on and shares held in
colonial corporations. Export duties as such accounted for a
relatively small proportion of colonial revenues. However,
during the last decade of the nineteenth century and especially
during the first decade of the twentieth the government of the
Free State collected substantial sums from dividends on shares
of stock held in the infamous concessionary companies. These
organizations, having received the right to administer large
sections of the country on the Free State's behalf, extorted
large quantities of rubber and ivory in the guise of taxes from
the Congolese population. Profits from these companies were
then passed on to the government in the form of dividends on
shares of stock which had been given to the state at the time of
incorporation. Most of the concessionary companies lost their
right to collect taxes when the Belgian government assumed responsibility for the country in 1908, and these companies temporarily declined in importance as a source of colonial revenue.
They would regain their importance in the mid-1920s, however,
when the expansion of the copper industry brought unprecedented
profits to Katanga companies, a portion of which reached the
colonial government through its portfolio of stocks and its new
taxes on colonial corporations.[6]

The Africans of Katanga, although contributing to the
colonial coffers through these categories of revenue, were most
directly affected by the hut tax known as the *impôt indigène*
in the Belgian colony. After 1914 every able-bodied African man
was required to pay an annual tax in European currency to the
Belgian administration. Since almost no one in Katanga had products which the Europeans would buy, the taxpayers had no choice
but to sell their labor to European employers.

The hut tax had been instituted at an even earlier date in
the nearby British territories of Nyasaland and Northern Rhodesia
where, as in Katanga, African taxpayers owned little that could
immediately provide revenue to the government except their labor.
Unlike most possessions in British Tropical Africa, in these
territories the hut tax provided a substantial proportion of the
colonial budget. British colonial finances, like those of the
Congo, depended on a tax on what Africans produced—in this case
their labor—rather than on what they consumed.

It was thus on the matter of how colonial revenues were to
be collected that the interests of colonial administrators most
nearly coincided with those of colonial entrepreneurs. By offering the local Africans wages in exchange for their labor,
European employers provided them with European money which could
then be taxed by the administration to fill the colonial coffers.
Of course the relationship between entrepreneurs and officials
was not always harmonious. The former kept wages as low as possible, thus limiting the latter's potential revenues, but most
administrators acquiesced in the prevailing belief that small
salaries were the most gentle means of introducing Africans to
wage labor.

Africans were unaccustomed to wages, but beyond that obser-
vation most colonial Europeans knew little about the indigenous
economy. African men were frequently stigmatized as lazy,
leaving all work to the women. More recent research has shown
that African men were not inactive, only that they did not produce items that were considered valuable by the Europeans.[7]

This misunderstanding of village economies by European
observers seems to have been the result of their underlying
assumption that practically all economic activities had no value
unless they could be translated into money. Of course they
realized the necessity of nonmonetized food production in the
villages, but they did not account for such vital items as the
preparation of land for cultivation in their calculation of the
need for labor in the villages. European observations about
African economies were extremely culture-bound. What could not
be converted into European currency was of little value. Armed
with scientific theories of economic development, Europeans
wrought enormous havoc in the life routines of Elisabethville's
rural hinterland.

Central African economies in the late nineteenth century
were more complicated than the Europeans realized. An individual's labor was not usually sold on a labor market although he
was obliged to contribute some work to his village headman and
to bear arms in times of trouble. Most precolonial families were

basically self-sufficient in the production of foodstuffs; a
long distance trade had, however, developed in certain items
including salt, ivory, copper, slaves, and cloth.[8]

In this precolonial economy trade goods, foodstuffs, and
labor were by no means freely interchangeable in a single market.
Using the terminology developed by Paul Bohannan and George
Dalton, the economy of the region can be described as multicentric—"one in which there are several distinct transactional
spheres," with groups of goods and services rated according to
their value and prestige. Bohannan and Dalton go on to show
that Africans living in multicentric economies were reluctant to
exchange items from one sphere for those in another unless they
were receiving a more highly valued item for a less highly
ranked one. These scholars called the exchange of items from
one sphere to another *conversion.*

In times of great need, however, Africans were sometimes
forced to sell off highly ranked items in order to survive.
Bohannan and Dalton vividly describe this phenomenon which they
call *emergency conversion.* "In such situations treasures are
sold, slaves are given for food, children are pawned and voluntary debt bondage may be incurred." Further describing the
phenomenon, the authors add that emergency conversion "is always
a last resort, a desperate expedient used only when sufficient
aid can be obtained in no other way. Therefore it is done externally with different ethnic groups—outsiders who have no
social obligation to help the disaster-stricken group. It is
done between strangers."[9]

In the view of Bohannan and Dalton, emergency conversion
was practised in precolonial times only in the most desperate
circumstances. During the colonial period, by contrast, emergency conversion became characteristic of most economic transactions between the subject peoples of Central Africa and their
European rulers. This phenomenon was to dominate the economic
relationship between Elisabethville and its African rural hinterland. Not only did the Europeans dominate all commerce, they
severely and permanently disrupted the hinterland's precolonial
economy to a degree which was by no means compensated for by the
pax europeana.

The direct European agent in this breakdown of the rural
economy was the colonial government whose fiscal policies, supported by military force, obliged Africans to convert highly
ranked economic resources into money in order to pay taxes to
their new European masters. Since most Africans in Elisabethville's hinterland could not pay their hut tax without selling
their labor, they were faced with a continuing emergency. In

order to satisfy the administrations' demands, more and more
young men had to go to European centers to work. The conse-.
quences for rural areas were enormous. The production of foodstuffs in the villages declined leaving the women, children,
and old people undernourished since the men's labor was essential for food production. A vital element of the precolonial
economy had thus been confiscated in order to provide revenue
for the colonial administration and cheap labor for European
employers. Labor recruiters frequently accompanied the tax
collectors on their rounds through the villages.

Once recruited, African labor migrants found themselves in
a particularly disadvantageous position in the newly created
European labor market where they had no bargaining power. Most
sought paid employment simply in order to earn tax money for
themselves and their extended families. Tax levels were, more
often than not, tied to salaries. Administrators generally
decreed that Africans should be obliged to work one month a
year to pay taxes. When salaries increased, administrators
decreed a corresponding rise in taxes; this meant that for those
Africans who worked only long enough to earn tax money salary
increases did not result in a speedier return to the village.

Short-term labor stimulated by the hut tax was also wasteful of the Africans' time. Africans usually were paid only for
the days spent at work, not for the time spent walking to and
from their villages which were frequently hundreds of miles from
the mines. Thus even more of the labor which Africans would
normally have contributed to the precolonial village economy was
consumed by Europeans.

Confiscation of the labor supply of the indigenous economic
systems of Central Africa was therefore essential to the development of both the colonial economy and the colonial state.
Without these colonial entities the city of Elisabethville
would never have come into being.

Seen in this perspective, Elisabethville as a city fits
into a pattern of urban development first suggested by the
economist Bert Hoselits. The city was *parasitic* rather than
generative as it had an unfavorable rather than a favorable
impact on the economic growth of its region.[10] While it might
be argued that Elisabethville was simply the cornerstone of a
new economic system which ultimately grew up on the Copperbelt,
the rural areas around the city played little part in the
development of the mining region's economy. Given the basic
infertility of the local soils, the area could not serve as
efficient sources of staple for the urban population. Within
a five hundred mile radius of Elisabethville only the valleys

of the largest rivers, which provided the city with fish, had
any relationship of reciprocity with the city. The rest were
stripped of their inhabitants and their meager resources while
sinking deeper into economic stagnation.

The creation of a city so immediately destructive of the
economy of the area in which it was built did not result from
the free play of economic forces but from the application of
political pressures which obliged the inhabitants of the Katanga
hinterland to act against their own perceived economic interests.
It might be argued that industrialization and urbanization were
in the Africans' long-range interests; nonetheless, the moderni-
zation process entailed a great deal of suffering.

In political matters, then, as in economic affairs the
Europeans crushed those African institutions which stood in the
way of their colonial objectives. This overwhelming imbalance
of power was the result of the development in Europe of political and economic institutions which, when applied to colonized
Central Africa, transformed the region.

A location which had previously been of little value had
become the site of a new city. In turn that city had quickly
become part of two economic networks, one attached to the mining
economy of southern Africa, the other based on the confiscation
of African labor from the new hinterland of Elisabethville.
Although these networks were quite different in character, both
were essential for the growth of a city which needed both African
labor and the European machinery necessary to convert that labor
into exportable copper.

These two African networks, however, were not sufficient in
themselves to promote Elisabethville's development. The capital
necessary to make the city a part of the southern African economy
came from Europe, as did the political power necessary to push
Africans into wage labor. The city's development also depended
on the transfer of European economic and political institutions
which made it possible to transfer European power to the Katanga
copperbelt.

Chapter 2

Elisabethville's European Origins to 1908

The history of any colony is in its very essence the intersection of two histories, that of the colonizer and that of the
colonized. Understanding the nature of this intersection in-
volves a delicate problem of delimination since the effects of
colonization were unevenly felt in the metropolis and the dependency. Thus some regions of Belgium were little affected by the
existence of the nation's colony in Africa; similarly some parts
of the Congo were changed less than others as a result of the
European presence. The impact varied from one area to another,
but on the whole the process affected the colonized more deeply
than the colonizers. Political power, by its very definition,
is the ability to promote a maximum of change in others with a
minimum of change to oneself. And in the cases when political
power was exerted by technologically and militarily advanced
Europeans over Africans, the changes were greater in the colony
than in the mother country.

The delimination of those areas of Europe and Africa which
were affected by colonization, however, is more than geographical. Certain institutions and social classes in both societies,
for example, were far more profoundly affected by the process of
colonization than others. This is equally true for colonizer
and colonized. In this connection chapter one has shown how
colonization in Central Africa affected the allocation of labor
in rural areas more directly than the modes of agricultural production.

The identification of those elements of metropolitan society
which impinged most directly on the colony will make it possible
to see what determined the direction of development in the dependency. The task is somewhat simplified when a colonial city
rather than a whole colony is being considered. Fewer Belgian
industries were involved in Elisabethville's development than in
that of the Congo as a whole. Many Belgian industries which
bought Congolese primary products—played little part in the

city's history, whereas the copper industry was absolutely central to the city's growth.

The fact that some Belgian industries affected Elisabethville more than others does not mean that Belgian inputs into the city's history can be understood simply through an analysis of a few key industries. The role played by the great copper trust, the Union Minière du Haut-Katanga—however dominant—cannot itself be understood without at least a limited discussion of the colonial investment practises on which the company relied for capital. Moreover, the copper company—and for that matter the entire Belgian community in Elisabethville—depended on the peculiar organization of Katanga's administration.

The structure of Belgian colonialism depended, at least in part, on the outcome of European diplomacy both at the time of the partition of Africa and in subsequent years. The history of Elisabethville was always closely linked to the changing pattern of the power struggle in Europe despite the African city's remoteness from those big powers. At the end of the 1890s few parts of the world could have been more unlike the infertile banks of the Lubumbashi River than the capitals of western Europe. Populous, bustling with activity, those cities were the political nerve centers of their nations and of the world; in them the representatives of the leading powers hammered out the rules that were to govern international relations. It was in London, Paris, Brussels, and Berlin that changes in European diplomacy as it affected Africa were developed which would in turn have important repercussions on the growth of Elisabethville.

The rules for the colonization of Africa had presumably been decided upon at the international congresses of Berlin in 1884-85 and Brussels in 1890. At the latter meeting representatives of European countries and of the United States agreed that African lands which had been "effectively occupied" by European colonizers indisputably belonged to the colonizing nation.

In the late 1890s, after the implementation of these rules, diplomatic attitudes toward Africa changed. In the eyes of European diplomats almost all of the continent had been parceled out. Actually this did not mean that Europeans ruled most of Africa—only that they claimed to own it. Nor was the situation as clear cut and simple in Africa as it appeared on the maps of that continent studied in the foreign ministries.

Using the British invasion of Egypt in 1882 as a point of departure, the partition of Africa had been accomplished in less than a generation. The movement to annex new African territory, which had acquired its greatest momentum between 1882 and 1898,

did not simply disappear when European governments had obtained
legal title to most of the continent's land. Borders were
uncertain—which heightened competition, especially for lands
lying in the interior. In 1898 British, French, and Belgian
expeditions converged on the upper Nile from three separate
directions in an attempt to gain control of the continent's most
famous waterway. The lust for African possessions was such that
the European countries nearly went to war in 1905 and again in
1911 over the right to conquer Morocco.

More important than the competition for unclaimed lands—at
least as far as the history of Elisabethville is concerned—was
an unstated assumption that the stronger states of Europe had
the right to seize colonial territory from their weaker neighbors, of which Belgium was a good example. This was not an ex-
plicitly stated principle adopted by an international congress
such as those held earlier in Berlin and Brussels; it was the
result of a series of diplomatic understandings and secret
treaties concluded among the superpowers of the day—Great Britain, France, and Germany. Such machinations kept the smaller
colonial powers in a state of constant uncertainty. Thus the
Belgians were never sure that they could retain control of the
Congo since they did not have the force to hold a colony should
a larger power decide to intervene.

Nor were the Belgian fears unfounded; there had been cases
where stronger powers had menaced or annexed African territory
controlled by weaker states. Beginning in 1898 formal agreements were drawn up for the redistribution of the territory of
weaker European states; in that year the British and Germans
drew up a tentative partition of the Portuguese African empire.
Since the Portuguese monarchy appeared to be on its last legs,
representatives of these two governments agreed to partition the
Lusitanian empire in Africa in the event that the mother country
should be paralyzed by civil strife or be unwilling to continue
the enormous annual subsidies required by the colonies. These
plans were never put into effect, however; the Portuguese maintained control of their empire despite the fall of the monarchy
in 1911. In 1913 the British and Germans worked out a second
partition plan in anticipation of future Portuguese inability or
unwillingness to rule.

The first European political entities in Africa actually to
change hands were the Afrikaner republics conquered by the
British during the Boer War (1899-1902). Although the Orange
Free State and the Transvaal (known officially as the South
African Republic) enjoyed the friendship and moral support of
Britain's rivals on the continent, neither the French nor the
Germans came to the aid of the embattled Afrikaners. Instead

they stood by as waves of British troops overran the republics, devastating the land and confining women and children to concentration camps where they died by the tens of thousands. The European superpowers thus acquiesced in the conquest and colonization of weaker states, even when managed by people of European ancestry.

However, the Belgian's struggle to maintain their title to the Congo was different from that of any of the other European colonizers because of the Congo's unique legal status. Before 1908 the Congo (known at the time as the Congo Free State) belonged to Léopold II, King of the Belgians, and not to the Belgian state. This peculiar status had been recognized by other European nations and by the United States as well as by the Belgian Parliament. As a result Léopold's rule over the Congo was particularly vulnerable to international pressure and at the same time was insulated from forces which in other colonies might have led to administrative reforms. Since Léopold's title to the Congo rested at least in part on international agreements, there was the constant danger that some future international accord might take the territory from him. Meanwhile, the great powers of Europe could take no sanction against the king short of dispossession, so they had no effective ways of influencing his day-to-day policies.

The Belgian government was also limited in its effective control over the Congo. In 1884, when Parliament had voted to allow the king to rule the Congo without financial help from the Belgian government, it had abdicated all authority over its administration. Parliament's attitude was that the monarch could do what he wished in the Congo as long as he made no demands on the Belgian taxpayers. Belgium and the Congo were simply a union of crowns, the Belgian government having no legal right to interfere in the administration of the Congo.

This made it possible for the king to realize long-standing ambitions to create a colonial empire. A constitutional monarch by birth but an autocrat by nature, his personal empire in the Congo afforded him a unique opportunity to establish a colonial administration entirely free of metropolitan controls. In all other African colonies the colonial governments were responsible to a member of the mother country's cabinet which in turn was ultimately responsible to the metropolitan electorate. By contrast Léopold decreed laws, spent money as he saw fit, and hired and fired colonial staff without accountability to anyone. For two decades he ruled as an absolute monarch over his African dominions until his powers and policies were called in question by other European states as well as by members of the Belgian parliament.

Policies developed during the period of Leopold's abosolu-
tism were nonetheless destined to have a long-lasting effect on
the government of the Congo. Although the king ceded the territory to the Belgian state in 1908, the Belgian government found
it impossible to create an entirely new administration. This
continuity was particularly important in the administration of
Katanga, the province of which Elisabethville was to become the
capital. Two of Léopold's policies in particular were to make
an indelible imprint on Elisabethville's history even though the
city was founded after the king's death: the maintenance of an
administration in Katanga separate from that of the rest of the
Congo, and the policy of strong state interference in the economic development of the copperbelt.

Léopold's special treatment of Katanga began long before
any of the European nations questioned his right to rule the
Congo. His claims to the province date back to the earliest
days of the Congo Free State. On Christmas Eve in 1884 the king
had added Katanga to his Central African dominions by a stroke
of the pen in compensation for territory lost to the French in
what is today the Congo-Brazzaville.[1]

For the rest of the decade no European agency questioned
Free State claims to Katanga because of the area's remoteness
from the established lines of penetration into the African continent. In 1889, however, the British began to eye the region
from South Africa; Cecil Rhodes obtained an imperial charter for
his British South Africa Company authorizing him to govern un-
specified territories north of the Limpopo River.

Léopold feared that the foundation of Rhodes' Chartered
Company was but a first step in the eventual takeover of Katanga
by the British. The king's troops had never even visited the
region so he could not claim to be governing it, and by this
time the British government was advocating the principle that no
country should claim land which it did not occupy militarily.
This principle of "effective occupation" became part of international law when it was included in the Brussels Agreement of
1890.[2]

Léopold's task, then, was to send in a number of Free State
expeditions to convince the British that he "effectively occupied" Katanga, but this was harder than might appear since the
Free State treasury lacked the funds necessary for such a show
of force in Katanga. Although the king had dispatched one
expedition to the area in November 1889, only a month after the
establishment of Rhodes' Chartered Company, he could afford no
others. In the words of a distinguished Belgian historian, the
Free State in 1890 was "on the verge of bankruptcy." The French

government, which had allowed the sale of Free State Bonds on the Paris bourse in 1886, now refused to allow the king to float any more loans on the French money market. And although in 1890 the Belgian government had rescued Léopold's enterprise from immediate collapse, they did not provide sufficient money to finance further expeditions to Katanga.[3]

In desperation the king turned to Captain Albert Thys, an explorer who had led some of Léopold's earliest expeditions to the Congo. The adventuresome Thys had returned to Belgium full of tales of the riches of the king's African empire. He convinced a few of his compatriots to invest in the development of that part of the colony that seemed the most promising—the Congo River valley and its main tributaries. In 1887 they had created the Compagnie Congolaise pour le Commerce et l'Industrie (CCCI) which financed three trading companies and the vital railroad linking the Stanleypool with the Atlantic Ocean. Unlike Thys' earlier fields of endeavor, however, Katanga had little European trade and was considered a poor location for a trading company.

Meanwhile, recognizing the difficulty of attracting investment to remote parts of the Congo, Léopold was in the process of expropriating African resources in order to provide the Free State government with some attractive collateral. In a decree promulgated in 1889 he had proclaimed state ownership of all lands not currently cultivated by Africans. In 1891 he declared state ownership of the natural products of these lands.[4]

The king was thus able to offer Thys land in exchange for the money necessary to save his title to Katanga. As a preliminary gesture of good will from Thys, the monarch asked the CCCI to finance a Belgian expedition to Katanga. In September 1890 the CCCI sent out a force under Alexandre Delcommune, and in return Léopold granted the CCCI the predominant role in a new Belgian chartered company which was to rule Katanga. This new group, the Compagnie du Katanga, despatched two more expeditions during the course of 1891. They were joined by a third Belgian expedition ostensibly sent out to suppress the slave trade.

The king's strategem had succeeded. Belgian forces outnumbered Rhodes' agents in Katanga, establishing the Free State's claims to the territory and in the process killing Msiri, the most powerful African king in the area. The British South Africa Company, lacking both military power and a strong African ally, could no longer dispute Free State claims. Legal arrangements were concluded on May 12, 1894, when representatives of the Free State and the British Government signed a treaty fixing Katanga's southern and eastern borders.[5] The Berlin Agreement of 1885, as modified by the Anglo-Congolese Treaty of 1894 granted

international recognition to a government for Katanga even
though this government existed more on paper than in practice.

In the process of securing the Free State's title to
Katanga, meanwhile, representatives of the Compagnie du Katanga
had discovered that the territory possessed no resources which
could be immediately exploited. Reducing expenditures to a
minimum, the Compagnie abstained from further significant activities. Between 1892 and 1900 there were never more than six
Belgians in Katanga at any one time and officials at the nearest
Free State post (in what would become the Kasai province) often
forgot about their existence. Isolation combined with economic
and military difficulties in the Congo itself to prevent the
more rapid development of Katanga. Wars against the Swahili
slave traders and the renegade Tetela soldiers who revolted
against their Belgian officers in 1895 made communications between Katanga and the rest of the Free State extremely difficult.
By 1898 the isolated Belgian posts could no longer be supplied
from the Free State and had to depend for supplies on a British
firm which brought goods from the east coast by way of Lake
Malawi to the Anglo-Belgian frontier on Lake Mweru.[6]

Despite the weakness of the Compagnie du Katanga on the
ground, the Belgian firm became an important precedent for the
future government of Katanga, which already enjoyed a political
status different from that of the rest of the Congo. The Compagnie du Katanga, unlike the infamous concessionary companies
which were to cause so much misery in the rest of the Congo,
enjoyed full proprietary rights over a third of the area which
it administered. This ownership of the land, rather than just
the right to collect taxes from its inhabitants, set Katanga
apart from the rest of the Congo.[7] Its special status can be
traced to the conditions under which the Compagnie du Katanga
began. If Léopold had not been so frightened lest the British
seize Katanga, he would not have felt obliged to offer such
favorable terms to Thys and to the CCCI—terms which no other
investor in the Congo had ever received.

Within a few years a renewed British threat would again
force Léopold to alter Katanga's government, but the principle
would remain that Katanga should have a special status. By this
time, moreoever, the Free State's financial position had improved
dramatically since, beginning in 1895, receipts from the collection of rubber had strengthened considerably the king's bargaining position.[8] Thus in 1900, when a new British menace
forced him to overhaul Katanga's administration, he was able to
install a more elaborate—and more costly—government with Free
State money rather than being obliged to rely on Belgian investors.

The new British enterprise had its origins in the patriotic
efforts of a British noblewoman to promote British expansion in
Central Africa. In 1895 the Countess of Warwick, an intimate
acquaintance of the Prince of Wales (later Edward VII), began
looking for a suitable investment in lands claimed by the British South Africa Company north of the Zambezi River. She
entrusted her interests to Robert (later Sir Robert) Williams, a
Scottish engineer who was a friend of Cecil Rhodes and had a
thorough knowledge of this region. Williams had serious doubts
about the possibility of developing such a remote area and refused to accept financial backing from the countess and her
friends until he had been assured that the copperbelt would be
linked by rail with South Africa. Proof was soon forthcoming
and early in 1899 Williams obtained permission from the British
South Africa Company directors to form a new company, Tanganyika
Concessions, Ltd., (TCL), to develop lands at the southern end
of Lake Tanganyika. In the same year Williams's firm received
more limited prospecting rights in lands north of the Congo-
Zambezi divide from the Compagnie du Katanga.

If the presence of an associate of Rhodes and an intimate
of the Prince of Wales in a company designed to explore the
mineral resources of Katanga aroused the suspicions of Leopold
and his advisors, the man chosen to head Tanganyika Concessions'
operations in Africa must have confirmed them. George Grey,
Williams's chief lieutenant in Africa, was a close relative of
some of the most important men in British politics and finance.
His brother, Sir Edward Grey, was to serve as Foreign Secretary
from 1905 to 1916, while his cousin, the fourth Earl Grey—
Governor General of Canada in 1904—was an important shareholder
in the British South Africa Company. Besides his powerful connections, George Grey was an extremely capable leader—despite
a severe stammer. During his first few months in Central Africa
he organized efficient prospecting operations which brought to
light alluvial deposits of gold as well as many copper deposits
that had already been worked by Africans.[9]

These discoveries led Williams to press the Belgians for a
share in the exploitation of Katanga. Although Léopold would
have preferred to keep all the British Tanganyika Concessions
operations out of the Free State, he was bound by the terms of
the Berlin Agreement which called for equal treatment of all
Europeans in the Congo Basin. Even a strategy of forcing Williams to take Belgian partners for his operations in the Free
State territory was excluded, at least for the immediate future,
since Belgian investors were still extremely reluctant to invest
in the Congo; what capital there was available for the area went
to concessionary companies operating in rubber-producing regions
of the country. In the absence of any alternative, Free State

officials allowed Williams into Katanga, in 1900 granting his
company exclusive prospecting rights and almost unlimited freedom of action in the copperbelt.[10]

As a counterweight to Tanganyika Concessions, Léopold
created a new government agency to supersede the Compagnie du
Katanga. Although Thys and his associates had done little to
administer Katanga, they were in a strong bargaining position
with the king because of the terms of their original concession.
In exchange for their title to a third of the land within the
original domain of the Compagnie du Katanga and a fresh investment of only twenty thousand pounds they were able to obtain a
substantial interest in its successor organization, the Comité
Spécial du Katanga. The CSK, chartered in June 1900, provided
the first real Belgian administration in Katanga. In the early
days, however, the Belgian presence was by no means overpowering
since before 1910 the CSK's European staff never numbered a
hundred. These men were divided among the three branches of the
Free State government: the administration, the army, and the
magistracy.

The CSK's civil administration, which was entirely distinct
from that of the Free State, was expected to guard the Congo's
border with British territory and to collect rubber where conditions permitted. Company officials established their headquarters on Lake Mweru at Lukonzolwa, about midway along Katanga's
eastern border with British territory. Katanga was divided at
first into four zones, later into three. (In the rest of the
Congo the analogous units were called districts.) In all but
one of these zones administrators were concentrated along the
British border to remind the British and any other Europeans of
the Belgians' "effective occupation" of Katanga. The only exception to these border zones was the Lomani, located in northwest
Katanga adjacent to the rest of the Free State. There administrators behaved more or less like Free State administrators,
extorting rubber from the African inhabitants. Their colleagues
on the border, disappointed at being stationed in the one region
of the Congo where it was impossible to amass a personal fortune,
almost invariably resigned at the end of their first year of
service.

Like the civil administration, the CSK's military force was
entirely distinct from that of the Free State. Called the Katanga police force, it consisted of a handful of European officers and their African subordinates, a unit really too small to
protect the country; thus its officers undertook no large projects without the support of the Free State's more significant
army, the Force Publique.

The third branch of the CSK administration, the magistracy, although theoretically a subsection of its Free State counterpart, also developed an identity of its own. Courts in Katanga, like those in France and Belgium, tended to limit their activities to the interpretation of statutes without considering their constitutionality. In these legal systems judges are more strictly subordinate to legislative bodies than in the United States. Judges and prosecutors, called respectively the sitting magistracy and the standing magistracy, come under the authority of the Ministry of Justice. Judges in criminal courts are usually chosen from among senior prosecutors. In Belgium, the Congo Free State, and Katanga the corps of prosecutors consisted of a hierarchy of officials headed by the *procureur du roi*, the chief prosecutor. Below him were the other magistrates and the judicial police. The job of the former was to ascertain whether a crime had been committed and afterwards to prosecute those people who, according to their investigations, had committed criminal acts.

In most of the Free State magistrates had acquired a reputation for ineffectiveness. Few of them were Belgians, and as foreigners they lacked the personal authority to bring Belgian offenders into line. Moreover the civil administration, seeking to increase revenues from the forced collection of rubber, discouraged magistrates from prosecuting Europeans who abused Africans.

Rubber did not grow abundantly in CSK territory outside of Lomani, however, so magistrates outside of that region were freer to follow their consciences and the law. Frequently their severity in dealing with European offenses against Africans intimidated CSK employees. Needless to say they were even sterner where British subjects were concerned.[11]

Therefore the magistrates, like the civil administrators and the Katanga police, had acquired an identity quite distinct from that of their counterparts in the Free State administration as a result of the circumstances of their employment and of the problems which they were called upon to face. Beyond its initial capital the resources of the CSK were extremely limited, since the chartered company did not have nearly as much revenue as the Free State. Members of the CSK staff stationed on the borders therefore considered themselves underpaid as well as militarily ill-equipped to deal with their British rivals. Because of this disadvantage from the start the Katanga administration developed a strong anti-British element, a resentment more easily projected on local English-speakers than on company directors in Brussels.[12]

The CSK officers' animosity against the British was to a certain extent founded in fact as far as the copperbelt was concerned since Williams's men were actually a rival group with more power in the region than the Belgian company. The British based their authority on the agreement concluded in December 1900 which gave Williams's company, Tanganyika Concessions, Ltd., exclusive prospecting rights in Katanga for a five-year period; these rights were later extended to 1909. The agreement also gave Williams the right to participate in companies later formed to exploit the minerals discovered.[13]

Williams entrusted the development of the copperbelt to George Grey with personal responsibility for planning railways and recruiting labor for the mines. Grey established a network of labor camps at the most promising mine sites—Ruwe for gold, Busanga for tin, and Kambove, among others, for copper—all linked together by bicycle paths. His small staff of Europeans recruited in London increased from eighteen at the end of 1906 to forty by the end of 1909.[14] Therefore although the Tanganyika Concessions crews numbered only half the size of the CSK staff, they did nevertheless constitute a recognizeable British presence in Katanga.

This small British community aroused increased Belgian suspicions during controversy over the Congo scandals 1903-8, which Belgians believed to be part of a British plot to take over the colony. Since the turn of the century certain British missionaries and commercial agents in the Lower Congo had complained about the atrocities which accompanied the collection of rubber. Léopold, in accordance with his policy of delegating government powers to private companies, had conceded large blocks of land to concessionaries as well as to his own personal representatives whose only concern was the extraction of rubber for export. The brutal methods used by the concessionaries' European and African employees to force local Africans to collect rubber caused an international scandal in 1903 when the British consul in Boma, Roger Casement, revealed the extent of the Free State atrocities after an inspection tour. In 1903 the British government published Casement's report and the resultant British Congo Reform Association organized an effective campaign against continued Free State rule in the Congo.

By 1906 Congo reformers, who had gained great influence with the governments of Great Britain and the United States, suggested an international congress to consider the future government of the Congo. Léopold, fearing that his colony might be partitioned among the great powers, rallied his cohorts for a defense of the Congo. As far as Katanga was concerned he ordered a temporary halt to rubber collection by the CSK, while at the same time he sought the support of Robert Williams and his associates. The directors of Tanganyika Concessions, appreciating the free hand granted them in Katanga, became Léopold's staunchest defenders in London.[15] Thus the king reaped political dividends in Europe for the special privileges which he had granted to Tanganyika Concessions in Katanga.

Meanwhile CSK officials in Africa as well as in Brussels found that their situation had taken a turn for the worse. They had lost the right to collect rubber, their only important source of revenue, while the king was cementing his relations with the hated British. Those who remained in Katanga became more anglophobe than ever.

Things looked quite different from the king's point of view. In 1906 his life's work was being called into question. Even the Belgian Parliament was restive and Léopold desperately needed help. He therefore sought new allies in the world of finance. His plan included the establishment of three new industrial consortiums, each backed by Belgian and foreign capital: the Société Internationale Forestière et Minière (Forminière), the Compagnie du Chemin de Fer du Bas-Congo au Katanga (BCK), and the Union Minière du Haut-Katanga (UMHK). By offering attractive investments he hoped to gain the support of financiers and, through them, to gain sympathy from their governments.

Indeed he did manage to get influential foreigners on the boards of directors of each of the companies. Five Britons joined the Union Minière board, including Robert Williams and Lord Arthur Butler (later Marquis of Ormonde). A French banker active in colonial affairs, L. Villars, President of the Union Parisienne, served as Vice President of the BCK and another administration of the same institution, the Marquis de Frondeville, served on the railroad's Board of Directors. To Forminière the king attracted an American, Thomas Fortune Ryan, a promoter who had amassed a considerable fortune by organizing urban transit companies.[16] Unfortunately for Léopold, none of these men seems to have had sufficient political influence to save the king's venture.

Nor could Belgian financiers who invested in the new consortiums save the king from Belgian parliamentarians, although some of these financiers were destined to play an important role in shaping the future economic development of the Congo which up to that time had been in the hands of relatively small scale investors. Belgian financiers being notoriously discreet, few accounts have been published on the methods and arguments used by the king in 1906 to obtain the investment of important Belgian capital in his proposed consortiums.

One of Léopold's most likely sources of capital was the Société Générale, the largest bank in the country. The Société Générale early had been a party to his Congolese ventures, but in its capacity as a deposit bank—which limited its activities to such fields as commercial credit and the sale of securities— rather than as an industrial bank. Thus beginning in 1888 the Société Générale had been involved in the emission of Free State bonds. In these earlier transactions the bank had only helped market these securities.[17] In 1906, however, the king was asking the Société Générale to act as an industrial stock-issuing bank, involving the riskier activities of promoting and financing enterprises which seemed far less promising than the usual rail- road companies in Czarist Russia and Imperial China. In the end the Société Générale managers agreed to buy—or at least to place among their business associates—stock in two of the three corporations, the BCK railway and the Union Minière. Forminière seemed so unpromising that the king eventually had to dip surrep- ticiously into Free State funds for 50 percent (₤59,250) of the initial offering to insure that the issue was floated.[18]

Of the other two new corporations, the Union Minière du Haut-Katanga seemed the more attractive and the Société Générale had already found half the necessary capital. The mining com- pany had no difficulty raising foreign capital, since Williams and his London backers were eager to put up the other half of the company's foundation capital because his men had discovered abundant supplies of exploitable copper and even some gold in Katanga. Transportation was no problem because the rail network from South Africa had already reached Broken Hill (now Kabwe) and plans were underway to extend the line another hundred miles to the Congo frontier. Having gained the support of both the Société Générale and Tanganyika Concessions, the Union Minière received its charter of incorporation on October 28, 1906.

The creation of the Union Minière and its sister corpora- tions did not save Léopold's personal empire but it did help prevent the Congo from falling into foreign hands. Given the greater Belgian stake in the territory the Belgian parliament assumed responsibility for the colony. And once the Belgian parliament had passed the act of annexation, ratified by the king's signature on October 18, 1908, the other countries of Europe granted the Belgian government time to establish colonial order in the Congo.[19]

Even though the creation of the consortiums did not have the political effect desired by the king, his strategy became the basis for later Belgian economic policies toward the Congo in general and Katanga in particular. The major problem facing Léopold, his successor, the Belgian parliament—and, for that

matter, other colonizers in Central Africa including Cecil
Rhodes—was a shortage of capital. In the early years the king's
main source of capital was his own private fortune. According
to most recent estimates, he diverted approximately 19,500,000
francs of his own money to the Free State budget before 1890,
to which he added ten million francs in the following decade.
At thirty francs to the pound this amounted to a total of one
million pounds sterling, which was then a large personal fortune
but could not be compared with contemporary huge corporations
such as United States Steel, capitalized in 1901 for two hundred
million pounds.[20]

Unlike the capital amassed by corporations, however, Leopold's money was all his to dispose of as he saw fit. And so
was the Free State Treasury. Accountable to no one, the king
lavished state securities—as negotiable as checks—on his favorite project.[21] The consequences of this freedom of action,
however, went beyond the satisfaction of royal whims; the king
spent Congolese revenues when he thought it was in the colony's
interest—for example, he invested in public works when the
money could not be raised on the open market.

In this respect he was a good deal freer of control than
his British rival, Cecil Rhodes. Like Léopold, Rhodes had
obtained authorization from a European government—in this case
the British government—to create an empire in Central Africa.
In 1889 Rhodes raised one million pounds—equal to Leopold's
lifetime investment—when his British South Africa Company
floated its stock on the London market. Responsible to a board
of directors which carefully scrutinized his accounts, Rhodes
lacked the freedom of action enjoyed by his royal counterpart.[22]

Still, when compared with the size of Belgian companies
operating within his domains, Léopold's management of the Free
State was a relatively large enterprise. The concessionary companies, for example, were ludicrously undercapitalized. ABIR,
the notorious Anglo-Belgian India Rubber Company, was floated on
an initial investment of less than eight thousand pounds. In
the 1890s the king seemed unconcerned about the amount of investment so long as the Free State received its cost-free 50 percent
of the stock which entitled the government to half of the profits. Even the Compagnie du Kasai, an amalgam of earlier trading
companies organized in 1901 when the rubber boom was at its
height, was capitalized at only thirty-three thousand pounds.[23]

Katanga ventures began on an equally small scale although
they were to increase in size as the possibility of industrial
development became more real. In 1891 the Compagnie du Katanga
obtained a third of the land in its dominions for an initial

investment of one hundred thousand pounds. British capitalists
were scarcely more daring; Tanganyika Concessions was capitalized in 1899 for the same amount. Stockholders in the Compagnie du Katanga added only twenty thousand more to convert
their holdings into a one-third interest in the CSK.[24]

What is noteworthy here is the willingness of Léopold to
invest Free State funds in the CSK. Although it might be argued
that the CSK was really an agency of his Free State government,
the king soon proved willing to support more clearly private
ventures when he felt that the interests of the Free State were
at stake. The chartering of the Chemin de Fer du Katanga (CFK)
in 1902 is an example of this policy. The king insisted that
the Free State put up twenty thousand pounds, 60 percent of the
total capital, leaving only a minority share to be raised by the
ubiquitous Robert Williams who was making railroad development
his principal activity. Furthermore in later years the state
became the principal investor in the company. By 1914 it was
estimated that the Free State and its successor, the Government
of the Belgian Congo, had provided seventy of the eighty million
franc (₤ 2-2/3 millions) absorbed by the railroad up to that
time.[25]

Admittedly the state had only guaranteed bonds for part of
that money, but the amount of money raised by the state was
beginning to outpace that provided by private investors. Cer-
tainly this was not the case in all companies, but the Katanga
Railway—like many other railroads in the country—was considered a special case which justified government assistance.

Unlike the Katanga Railway, the Union Minière had employed
no state money in its initial capitalization, although Leopold
had played an extremely important role in the company's creation.
It might even be argued that the state's role was more important
in bringing together the Société Générale and British investors
in a Congolese venture than it would have been in providing the
capital itself. Although British investment did not ultimately
improve the Free State's position with the British government,
Léopold made an effort which he considered vital to the survival
of his regime. By contrast, the first major investment in the
Congo by the Société Générale proved a turning point in the
economic development of Central Africa; it led to the first
significant transfer of investment capital to the Congo, and
incidentally to the creation of a colonial financial empire for
the bank.

Thus, even in the case of the Union Minière, the policy of
state intervention in economic affairs had been consciously
applied. That policy was twofold—investment either directly or

in the form of guaranteed loans to corporations deemed vital to
the country's security, and nonmonetary intervention in company
activities where the government's interests seemed at stake.
King Léopold adopted an interventionist policy in economic
affairs, a policy which was to be maintained by his successors
at the Belgian Colonial Ministry.

These economic attitudes, together with the peculiar character of a Katanga administration haunted by fear of British
takeovers, constituted Léopold's legacy to the city of Elisabethville, founded the year after his death. Thereafter the
king's presence, despite colonial mythology to the contrary,
did not dominate the character of Elisabethville although it did
play an important role in the development of the city. All
three of the Leopoldian bequests affected the city's relations
with the outside world in very tangible ways. The city's first
decade was characterized by Anglo-Belgian rivalry. Its political debates were punctuated by discussions over the question
of Katanga separatism. And the city's economic growth, unlike
that of many other cities in colonial Africa, depended in large
part on government commitment to foster the city's economic
development. Thus the policies developed by King Léopold played
an important role in determining the nature of Elisabethville's
relations with the rest of the world. Furthermore, it must be
remembered that Léopold frequently acted in response to maneuvers
by his rivals on the chessboard of international power politics
which were also to influence Elisabethville throughout its
history.

Chapter 3

The Building of Elisabethville, 1910-1914

In its early years Elisabethville was an extremely fragile
creation—like Jonah's gourd which grew in a single night and
was destroyed in an equally short time. Except for the nearby
copper desposits and water supply, which were by no means unique
in the region, the city had no resources of its own. Its
growth depended entirely on the importation of capital and
labor, both of which were in short supply and could be diverted
to another location on short notice. But the effects of capital
importation and labor migration being cumulative, the longer the
city endured the more likely it was to survive. In the early
days, however, the city could have been deserted quite easily
had its resources been cut off.

Before the arrival of the railroad in November 1910
neither British miners nor Belgian administrators had made much
of an impact on the local environment. The largest settlement
in the area was the Union Minière's Star of Congo mine located
on the Ruashi stream six miles east of the future location of
Elisabethville. Although sixty Europeans and a few hundred
Africans lived at the mine, operations were limited to prospec-
tion as mining could not begin without the railroad to bring in
machinery and to export the finished product.

The copper ore extracted at the Star of the Congo mine was
to be purified at the Union Minière's Lubumbashi smelter which
was still in its earliest stages of construction. Consisting
of a few earthworks and ditches, the smelter site looked more
like an African village than a mining camp. Europeans and Africans alike lived in huts built on the African model out of
sticks and mud with thatched roofs made from long savanna grass.
Soil from the huge local termite hills made fine bricks, but
with the virtual absence of sand no concrete could be mixed to
hold them together.[1] Without the materials necessary for

construction of more permanent buildings the nearby town of
Elisabethville was subject to the same constraints.

Colonel Emile Wangermée, the Belgian Vice Governor-General,
had the taxing job of directing construction of the town while
keeping an eye on the British miners. At the beginning of 1910
he had moved his headquarters from the British border on Lake
Mweru to a temporary site on the Kafubu stream just south of
both the smelter and the location he had chosen for the town of
Elisabethville. From these temporary headquarters Wangermée
supervised the grading of the new city's roads during the dry
season of 1910. Even in this respect Wangermée did not escape
British influence. On the advice of technicians sent out by
the new Ministry of Colonies in Brussels the colonel laid out
Elisabethville on a rectilinear grid pattern copied from the
street plan of Bulawayo in Southern Rhodesia.

Wangermée and his superiors in Brussels saw the British as
a military threat to Belgian rule in the copperbelt. To reinforce Wangermée's position the Colonial Ministry sent a thousand
well-armed troops from Kivu to Elisabethville under the direction of Commandant F. V. Olsen. These troops reached Wangermée
in October 1910, only a month before the arrival of the railway
from South Africa. Wangermée stationed the troops on the main
road running between the Star of the Congo mine and the Lubumbashi smelter. Thus the town site and the military camp lay
strategically between the two Union Minière camps (see Map
3.1).[2]

The Belgians were not worried about the hundred Britons
already resident in the mining camps; they feared that the railroad from South Africa would bring a massive influx of rowdies
and subversives. Indeed the railroad transformed the city.
First came the subcontractors with their crews of unskilled
Africans who cleared and graded the trace of the rail line.
Then, under the direction of the South African contractor George
Pauling, came skilled crews of Africans and Europeans who laid
down the track—at the almost miraculous rate of six miles a
day. Accompanying Pauling on his steady march north were artisans, merchants, fortune seekers, and prostitutes, who together
constituted the first wave of new immigrants to Elisabethville.
The European population of the town, which numbered scarecely a
hundred at the beginning of November 1910, rose to three hundred
and sixty by the end of December; a year later it was over a
thousand.[3]

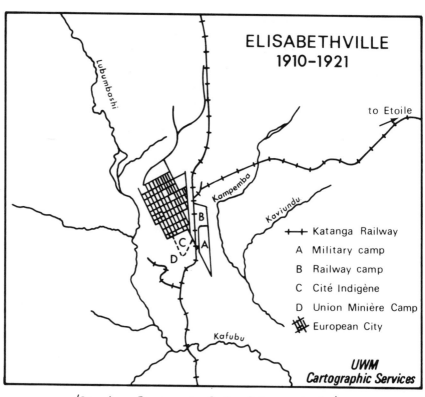

ELISABETHVILLE
1910-1921

to Etoile

Lubumbashi

Kampemba

Kaviundu

Kafubu

+—+ Katanga Railway
A Military camp
B Railway camp
C Cité Indigène
D Union Minière Camp
European City

UWM
Cartographic Services

(Based on Grevisse, Le Centre Extra-coutumier)

Demand for previously unavailable bulk goods soon exceeded
the supply. Each train that arrived was loaded with building
supplies, mining machinery, and fresh settlers. In the first
year merchants who could obtain flour, cloth, or whiskey had no
trouble finding buyers. New buildings seemed to grow out of the
termite hills lining the streets of Wangermée's grid: the
governor's mansion, offices for the government and for the Union
Minière, hotels, stores, and a few houses.

Many of the first settlers, expecting quick profits and a
rapid return to "civilization," were willing to put up with
great discomfort. Conditions were at their worst during the
1910-11 rainy season immediately after the arrival of the railroad. A few lucky Europeans lived in mud and straw huts on the
African model, but most of the others had to be content with
floorless tents which were often washed away by the tropical
downpours. Two enterprising men even dug out a shelter inside
a ten-foot-high termite hill.[4]

It is hardly surprising that in the earliest days the city
did not offer a very rich cultural or spiritual life. Two
priests served the Roman Catholic community; a hundred and fifty
Jews attended High Holiday services held in 1911. However, most
of the population spent their leisure time in more earthly
amusements. For example, at Christmas in 1911 the British Vice
Consul counted no less than forty-seven bars in Elisabethville
and the surrounding areas. Doing an equally booming business
were twenty-five prostitutes out of a total European feminine
population of one hundred and forty.[5]

In 1911, in order to compensate for this cultural void, two
young Belgian officials—Robert de Meulemeester, a magistrate,
and André van Iseghem, secretary to Governor Wangermée—founded
the Cercle Albert-Elisabeth. Located in the center of town just
opposite the courthouse, the Cercle Albert became the focal
point of social life in the European community—for those for-
tunate government officials and mining engineers permitted to
join. Although primarily a men's club where tired members met
for a gin and tonic at the end of a hard day's work, the Cercle
Albert also sponsored formal dinner parties where the few wives
who had accompanied their husbands to the copperbelt held court
and could forget, if only for a few hours, their primitive
housing and cultural isolation.

The Cercle Albert also had a more serious purpose. As a
select club which appealed to the snobbery of Britons and Belgians alike, the Cercle Albert gave a certain leverage to the
Belgians who ran it. Governor Wangermée, appreciating the club's
prestige, made it a *de facto* adjunct of the provincial government.

In 1913 he appointed five of its charter members to serve on his first advisory council.[6]

Poorer Europeans, deprived of political power, wealth, and comfort, found Elisabethville harder to bear than their wealthy neighbors in the Cercle Albert. There were no gold and diamond deposits like those in South Africa and Southern Rhodesia which could bring immediate riches. Business had to be done through the existing major corporations: the Union Minière, the Katanga Railway, and the CSK. Since the last firm retained title to the land, no entrepreneur could make a killing in real estate speculation. In the first years, moreover, there was a good chance of a quick death from frequent epidemics of typhus, dysentery, and typhoid fever. In 1911 forty-three Europeans died in town, a very high rate indeed from a settler population of about one thousand. Such statistics were not lost on many of the earliest arrivals who soon left for more healthy settlements in South Africa and Southern Rhodesia.

At the beginning of 1912 Belgians constituted the single largest national group of the settler population (42 percent), but they were not a majority. They were followed in relative importance by the British, Italians, South Africans, Greeks, Russians, Germans, and Turks (see Table 3.1)[7] Later on in 1912 the Belgians became the majority of Elisabethville's white population, the non-Belgian fortune seekers who left the city in 1912 having been replaced by Belgians. The city's European population as a whole declined by seventy-seven; so by 1913 Belgians constituted over half of Elisabethville's Europeans.

Except for the Belgians each of the national groups tended to specialize in one or two occupations. The Greeks, for the most part men from the islands of the Dodecanese, were merchants and labor recruiters. So were the Jews, who comprised most of the Russian and Turkish residents, as well as a scattering of some of the other national groups. Most of the Italians were artisans who had moved north with the railroad from the Rhodesias. The Germans, on the other hand, were recently arrived skilled workers who supervised smelting operations for the Union Minière. Most of the Britons and South Africans (English-speakers as well as Afrikaners) worked for the Union Minière and the railway. Some Belgians worked for the Union Minière—in 1911 they comprised one third of the company's white force in Africa—or for other local firms, but the largest number seem to have been government employees including administrators, clerks, soldiers, and policemen.[8]

So by 1913 Elisabethville had become a predominantly Belgian city with a white population of just over one thousand.

Table 3.1

THE EUROPEAN POPULATION OF ELISABETHVILLE BY NATIONALITY

AT THE END OF 1911 and 1912

Nationality	Population 1911 (Percentage)		Population 1912 (Percentage)	
Belgian	430	(42)	557	(58)
British	127	(12)	85	(9)
Italian	100	(10)	58	(6)
South African	86	(8)	27	(3)
Greek	81	(8)	55	(6)
Russian	57	(6)	45	(5)
German	41	(4)	26	(3)
Turkish	33	(3)	28	(3)
Others	74	(7)	75	(8)
Total	1031	(100)	956	(101)*

*Percentages rounded to the nearest whole percent.

SOURCE: *Journal du Katanga*, February 13, 1912 and February 11, 1913.

Seen in a broader perspective, however, these Europeans constituted only a tiny minority of the city's total population
which included at least seven thousand Africans. These Africans, most often villagers who had been forced to work in the
city against their will, were not considered as part of the
city's permanent population. They were faceless sojourners who
lived in Elisabethville for brief periods, only to be replaced
by other equally faceless sojourners.

This depersonalization of Africans was by no means unique
to the white community in Elisabethville, although the extent
to which rich and poor whites shared these racial attitudes is
noteworthy. Depersonalization was the result of the white
people's belief in their superiority, Africans being considered
a benighted lot unfit to rule themselves. European settlers
were convinced that they had the right to treat Africans as
they saw fit, employing them—in the case of Elisabethville—as
a source of cheap labor for the economic development of the
copperbelt. And most important, the colonizers had sufficient
military might to force Africans to do their bidding.

Accordingly, in order to obtain the necessary labor,
colonial governments in Africa had from the outset established
tax policies forcing Africans to leave their villages to obtain
European currency, available only from European employers. This
resulted in a profound transformation of the African countryside
and the beginning of European-imposed urbanization in the
copperbelt. Thus African migration to the city began primarily
as a result of the "push" of European demands on rural Africans
rather than by the "pull" of the city.

From the African standpoint this meant that during the
period before the First World War few Africans living in Elisabethville had chosen to go there. They had in most cases been
forcibly recruited by Europeans who often worked hand in hand
with the local chiefs. Village headmen would designate single
young men and older men of low status to earn tax money for the
whole village. Those selected had no choice but to leave their
families and way of life and go off to a totally new environment.[9]

Once in the city Africans were assigned to various employers who housed them in work camps where the laborer's first
task was often the construction of his own hut. From 1910
onwards most Africans lived in four such work camps situated on
the periphery of the European city. Three of these camps
belonged to the three major employers in the area: the Union
Minière, the Katanga Railway, and the Force Publique. The
fourth was a cooperative venture established to house African
employees of smaller firms in the area (see Map 3.1, p. 30).

Conditions were primitive at best; sanitation was poor and housing frequently crowded.

The Africans who were herded into these company labor camps were also dependent on their employers for food. At the end of a long working day, during which they had been given no rations or time off, the workers lined up to receive their daily rations of *tukutuku*, an industrially processed maize meal which produced a much coarser flour than the manioc and sorghum meal to which they had been accustomed. Instead of fish, the traditional village protein, the African received meat and instead of palm oil, peanuts.[10]

It was also necessary to adjust to a new kind of labor and an imposed European time schedule which was much more rigorous than the less structured work patterns of village life. For example, one might be chosen to dig up copper ore by hand with pick axes at the Union Minière. The work day began before sunrise when a loud mine whistle woke the men. Shortly after rising they had to line up to be divided into work crews, each of which was assigned a specific task for the work day which lasted between eight and twelve hours—longer if the day's assignment was not completed.[11]

Conditions in the camps varied with their size. Major employers such as the Union Minière could afford to buy large quantities of supplies from the South, thus assuring adequate weekly rations for their employees, while greater financial resources also enabled them to provide better housing and medical care. Smaller employers, on the other hand, had to buy supplies on the unstable Elisabethville market. Although all camps had primitive hygiene facilities, the smaller camps were less crowded, had fewer epidemics, and therefore a lower deathrate.

Elisabethville's camps soon acquired a reputation for pestilence and death. In the first year after the opening of the railway, the head of Katanga's medical service estimated that the annual death rate for Africans in the city was 24 percent. And even though the death rate at the Union Minière would fall to about 10 percent per annum by the last years of the First World War, Africans continued to be afflicted with epidemics of typhoid fever, tick fever, and pneumonia, not to mention the pandemic of Spanish influenza which decimated the popuation in the last two months of 1918 (see Table 3.2).[12]

The prevalence of sickness and death frightened Africans, causing them to flee in great numbers. Exact statistics for the early years are rare, but the few which we have are eloquent. In the last three months of 1912, for example, 45 percent of the

Table 3.2

DEATH RATE PERCENTAGES AT UNION MINIERE CAMPS

IN ELISABETHVILLE AND IN THE CONGO AS A WHOLE, 1914-1927

YEAR	LUBUMBASHI	ETOILE-RUASHI	ALL UNION MINIERE CONGO
1914			6.5
1915			5.2
1916			9.2
1917	8.8	10.0	10.6
1918	16.0	13.6	20.2
1919	6.1	2.1	5.1
1920	1.3	1.7	3.3
1921	2.1	3.1	2.7
1922	[a]	[a]	3.1
1923	4.4	4.1	3.3
1924	2.5	4.0	3.0
1925	3.5	8.0	5.0
1926	2.2	9.1	5.1
1927	3.8	3.7	4.3

[a] Not available.

SOURCE: Union Minière du Haut-Katanga, Medical Service, Annual Reports 1921-27, Congo belge, *Rapport aux chambres* 1925, pp. 24-25, and L. S. Waterall, "Report on Rhodesian Labour in Katanga, April to September, 1914," in Zambian Archives, BS 3/72.

Africans sent to the Union Minière by a semiofficial recruitment agency, the Bourse de Travail du Katanga, ran away and an equally large proportion abandoned the city during the outbreak of influenza at the end of 1918.[13]

In the camps the Africans usually lived with members of their own ethnic group. Sometimes the chiefs who collected laborers for the mines sent their own overseers to the camps to supervise their subjects. Union Minière managers recognized these overseers' authority in the hope that the chiefs would then continue to provide a steady supply of labor, but the workers refused to become part of this new arrangement. The unwilling labor conscripts used two methods to show their hatred for their former leaders and their resentment of their working conditions.

As desertion figures attest, they ran away in great numbers. A second and more effective form of resistance in the copperbelt were closed associations, a device through which commoners had resisted chiefs in late precolonial times. These closed associations were religious cults which operated independently of the precolonial political hierarchy. Initiates swore obedience to the officers of the cult who thereby acquired a certain political authority. The cults were often so strong that royal officials sent out to enforce the king's orders felt obliged to become members of the local closed association. Once initiated, the king's agents were subject to the very people they had been sent out to rule.

Most of the Africans forced to work in Elisabethville resented the chiefs and headmen who had sent them from the villages; in the camps closed associations, transferred from the villages to the urban environment, provided an effective means of protest. Instead of obeying the chiefs' representatives in the camps they followed their cult leaders, who organized the lives of the men in the hours after work and on Sundays. The cult's responsibilities were not confined to the organization of dances, burial of the dead, and other religious rituals; they also organized cooking, food sharing, and care of the sick.

Before the First World War *butwa* was the most powerful closed assocation in Elisabethville. While the root -*twa* refers to the pigmies, who were nearly extinct on the copperbelt, the association was actually found among most of the peoples living between the Lualaba River and Lake Malawi—almost all of Elisabethville's hinterland. Thus, in addition to providing an outlet for protest, *butwa* also provided a common bond for many of the men who had been forced to work in the mines. And

although the *butwa* groups in Elisabethville were almost invariably confined to members from a single work gang, adepts of the
sect from other regions were able to understand the significance of the ceremonies performed by their coreligionists.
Many of their ceremonies were open to the camp populace in
general.

Butwa also provided a means of expressing hostility against
Europeans. One of its most important public rituals was an
unmistakably erotic dance whose popularity was enhanced by the
scowls of disgust evoked in straitlaced European spectators.
Another more private ceremony was specifically anti-Christian.
A *butwa* official, the *Kakonge*, performed a ritual of ablution
on initiates during which they solemnly swore to refuse baptism
from the missionaries. The Katanga provincial government responded to this hostility by imposing curfews and banning dances
in the camps. Henceforth, lives of the camp residents were even
more rigidly controlled than they had been before.[14]

One group of African migrants, however, seems to have
remained aloof from *butwa*, since they preferred more European
forms of organization. These were the Malawians, known then as
Nyasalanders, who constituted Elisabethville's first African
elite. Former inhabitants of northern Malawi, especially the
Lakeside Tonga, they had had the good fortune to be proselytized
by the Livingstonia Mission of the Free Church of Scotland which
provided the best education then available in Central Africa.
Young men who had attended Livingstonia Mission schools in
Nyasaland frequently migrated throughout Central and Southern
Africa in search of work. Since many of them spoke English in
addition to being good workers, the Anglo-Saxon staff of the
Union Minière often made them *capitas* ("boss-boys" in the term
of the day) of the work crews.

Many of the Malawians believed that their Christian educa-
tion set them apart from the mass of Africans in Elisabethville.
Frequently they scorned the closed associations, looking instead
for missions similar to those which they had known at home.
Indeed the first European Protestant mission in town, run by
American Methodists, moved to Elisabethville in response to a
letter from twenty-four Malawians who had been full members of
Presbyterian mission churches in Nyasaland.

The smatterings of culture acquired by these Africans
enabled them to get a greater share of the white man's material
benefits. The houses of the *capitas* were the best in the camps.
They were better paid and better dressed. Some bought their own
bicycles—quite a status symbol at a time when no local European
owned an automobile. A few even became independent of the Euro-

peans for employment. For example, in 1915 twenty-five
Malawians retired from the camps and became market gardeners
on plots leased on the outskirts of town.[15]

These Malawians represented an elite minority among Africans in early Elisabethville. Table 3.3 gives a rough estimate
of the origins of the mass of other Africans working in Elisabethville in 1914. Linguistically the largest single group
spoke Bemba and related languages; this included all of the
Zambians, those Zaïrois from the Haut-Luapula district, and
perhaps a third of the Zaïrois from the Tanganika-Moëro district.
The other Zaïrois spoke some form of Luba while the Malawians,
since they came from the north of their country, spoke some form
of Tonga.

This ethnic distribution is a direct reflection of recruitment policies of the Belgians and British in the copperbelt.
The latter obtained workers solely through Robert Williams and
Company, a subsidiary of Tanganyika Concessions. Its recruiters
operated an efficient recruitment system, concentrating on the
area in Northern Rhodesia within two hundred miles of Elisabethville. Robert Williams's main operation was at the British administration's district headquarters, Fort Rosebery (known now
as Mansa). Africans destined to work in the Katanga mines often
walked first to Fort Rosebery in order to be able to join a
group which was travelling to Elisabethville. The Aushi people
who lived in the Fort Rosebery subdistrict preferred this organized migration, while the Lunda and Bena Chishinga people from
the Kawambwa subdistrict to the north of Fort Rosebery preferred
to travel on their own.

After July of 1910 the Belgian counterpart of Robert Williams and Company was a semiofficial recruitment agency called
the Bourse de Travail du Katanga. BTK agents usually worked
directly with the chiefs, sharing with them the per capita fee
paid by the companies for each recruit. Despite the cash incentive provided to the chiefs, they were unable to round up enough
recruits, partly because Belgian territory within a month's
march of Elisabethville simply did not have enough men to meet
the demands of Katanga employers. Thus the later had to rely
on the British recruiting company for a large part of their
workers.[16]

Differences between the bookkeeping practices of the BTK
and Robert Williams and Co. prevent an exact comparison between
the two sources of labor, but it is possible to indicate the
dimensions of their operations. Between April 1, 1913 and March
31, 1914 Williams brought 2,913 Zambians to Katanga. Between
June 1, 1913 and May 31, 1914, the BTK recruited only 3,513

Table 3.3

THE ORIGIN OF AFRICANS FROM THE BELGIAN CONGO

AND NORTHERN RHODESIA RECRUITED FOR WORK IN KATANGA, 1914

Katanga districts (June, 1914-May, 1915):

Haut-Luapula	979
Tanganika-Moëro	2,817
Lomami	4,384
Total	7,649

Northern Rhodesia districts and subdistricts (April, 1913-May, 1914).

Mweru-Luapula:		
Chiengi	376	
Kawambwa	696	
Fort Rosebery	971	
Mweru-Luapula Total		2,043
Awemba:		
Luwingu-Nsumbu	806	806
Volunteers		64
Total		2,913

SOURCE: Northern Rhodesian district and subdistrict notebooks, National Archives of Zambia, Lusaka; Fetter, "Immigrants to Elisabethville, Their Origin and Aims," *African Urban Notes* III, 2 (1968): 17-38.

Zaïrois. If the hundreds of Malawians who flocked on their own
to Elisabethville after a 1912 edict forbidding recruitment in
Nyasaland for the South African mines are added to these figures
it is evident that fully half of Katanga's labor supply before
World War I came from British Central Africa.[17]

Obtaining workers was a highly competitive affair since
Katanga employers were not the only Europeans seeking the services of the Zambians; Southern Rhodesian settlers and mine
owners also wanted the lion's share. As far back as 1907 the
British South Africa Company had created a recruitment agency
known as the Rhodesian Native Labour Board which was to furnish
Northern Rhodesian labor for Southern Rhodesia. This agency
would have taken potential labor away from the Katanga mines
which were already employing large numbers of Zambians for por-
tage and prospecting operations. In 1908 the hopes of the
Southern Rhodesians were temporarily buoyed by a ban against
migration from Northern Rhodesia to Katanga, a ban imposed by
the British because of an outbreak of sleeping sickness in the
Luapula Valley. The colonial administration, however, soon
lifted this ban when it discovered that the mines as well as
some of the access routes were free of the disease. Thereafter
Africans from the Luapula flocked to Katanga where they could
earn their tax money far more easily and with less travel time
than in Southern Rhodesia.[18]

The 1911 decision to allow Northern Rhodesian Africans to
continue working in Katanga was made after the Union Minière had
demonstrated that it could provide good conditions for its African employees. In May of that year Robert Williams and Company
signed an agreement with Northern Rhodesian officials authorizing migration to Katanga and establishing the first specific
standards for the treatment of Africans in Elisabethville.
Thereafter the recruitment company built supply stations along
the paths to the mines. Williams's officials also agreed to give
Africans specified rations, a minimum wage, medical services,
and cash compensation for work accidents. The Administrator of
Northern Rhodesia retained the right to limit recruitment in any
area that was becoming depopulated; Africans were required to
return home at the end of their terms (six months, renewable for
three more). In a supplementary agreement reached in 1913 the
Katanga government allowed the Northern Rhodesian government to
appoint an Inspector of Rhodesian Natives with headquarters in
Elisabethville.[19]

This series of agreements ultimately had far-reaching consequences for both Africans and Europeans living in Elisabethville. Migrants from the Luapula Valley henceforth enjoyed the
best working conditions in Central Africa and the benefits which

they obtained eventually percolated to the Zaïrian community. The Union Minière had obtained a reliable supply of labor, albeit at an increased cost. However, despite the boost for the Katanga economy which the agreements made possible, Belgian officials were extremely dissatisfied, the presence of a British labor inspector being in their view an encroachment on their sovereignty in the Belgian Congo.

Since this official had the power to hear the complaints of African residents in Belgian territory, the Belgians felt that the British were extending their jurisdiction into Katanga. The Foreign Office defended the arrangement by showing that the British allowed a Portuguese officer to inspect workers from Mozambique at the South African mines, but the Belgians remained unconvinced. The British had been a threat for too long to be trusted. Indeed the Belgians had a case, for the British labor inspector did actually acquire considerable authority over the Zambians and Malawians who came to work in the Katanga mines.[20]

Disputes between the Belgians and the British over the powers of the latter's labor inspector in Elisabethville were but one of many sources of friction between representatives of the two European nations in Central Africa. Indeed anglophobia dominated much of Belgian colonial policy both at the Ministry in Brussels and on the spot in the Congo. Nor was this anglo-phobia—which had its origins partly in the British humanitar-ians' campaign against King Léopold's Free State—simply the result of irrational Belgian nationalism; the Belgians rightly realized that the British government had the power to oust them from the Congo if this were perceived as being in Britian's national interest. Belgian awareness of these political reali-ties colored the attitudes of both the government in Brussels and of the first Belgian settlers in Elisabethville.

At the time that Wangermée was laying out the new city the major issue between the two colonial powers was over the refusal of the British government to recognize Belgian annexation of the Congo enacted by the Belgian Parliament in 1908. For the next five years the British cabinet, yielding to humanitarian pres-sures, withheld recognition of the new regime, awaiting proof that the Léopoldian abuses had been brought to an end. More-over, in order to supervise the Belgians, the British Foreign Office maintained a staff in the Congo composed of a consul and three vice consuls, one of them stationed at the Star of the Congo mine near the future Elisabethville. Their presence implied a clear threat of British intervention in case of further scandal; furthermore, unknown to the Belgians, these consuls were seeking increased judicial powers from the British Foreign Office.[21]

Recognition was still withheld at the beginning of 1910 when fears of a British takeover had seized the highest levels of the Belgian government both in Brussels and Katanga. Léopold's successor Albert I, who had visited Katanga in 1909, wrote to the Belgian Foreign Minister that South Africans saw Katanga as "a promised land" and that the Britons of the Union Minière "had no intention of sharing their authority with us." Even more pessimistic than the king, Commandant Léon Tonneau, who alternated with Wangermée as head of Belgian operations in Katanga, remarked to the British Vice Consul that "his body (would) be found at the southern frontier."[22]

The British threat led the Belgian government hasten already projected changes in the Congolese administration of Katanga. After the annexation of the Congo in 1908 a Belgian parliamentary commission had begun negotiations for the transfer of Katanga from the jurisdiction of the Belgian chartered company, the CSK, to the Colonial Ministry. The British danger hastened the process. Attacks on the CSK's governmental authority during the winter of 1909-10 in the Belgian Parliament were the final blow and the company agreed to surrender its authority on September 1, 1910, two years earlier than had been anticipated.[23]

This action, even though it removed governmental power from the last of Léopold's concessionary companies, was not followed by British recognition of the Belgian annexation of Katanga. This fanned Belgian anglophobia still further. Belgians in Brussels and Elisabethville feared that British settlers at the mines might stage a *coup d'état*. Belgians remembered the ill-fated Jameson Raid on Johannesburg in 1896 when friends of Cecil Rhodes had attempted to dislodge the Afrikaners from the gold-fields. The Belgian hold on Katanga appeared even less sure than that of the South Africans; Paul Kruger, president of the South African Republic, had at least provided a government for Johannesburg, but the copperbelt—between 1901 and 1909—had been left to the British miners. Powerful forces were aligned against the Belgians: E. D. Morel, the spearhead of the Congo Reform Association, was urging English-speaking South Africans to go to Katanga. Dr. L. S. Jameson, the leader of the earlier raid, was president of the British South Africa Company which governed the Rhodesias.

A spark was enough to kindle Belgian panic and in April 1910 the Belgian Consul in Johannesburg, Pierre Forthomme, reported that adventurers were indeed organizing a raid on Katanga.[24] The government in Brussels undertook immediate diplomatic and military action. In June at the funeral of Edward VII, King Albert personally approached the British Foreign

Secretary Sir Edward Grey about the report. Grey, who was a
key figure in Anglo-Belgian relations, proved surprisingly sym-
pathetic. Perhaps his attitude toward the Belgians had been
favorably influenced by his brother, George Grey, who had
directed Tanganyika Concessions' operations in Katanga.

Whatever the reason, Grey and the Foreign Office had championed the Belgians, leading the fight within the British Liberal Government for British recognition of the Belgian annexation of the Congo. When asked by Albert about the possibility
of a British *coup d'état*, Grey personally assured the monarch
that his government had no plans for a raid and would disown any
that might occur.[25]

The Belgian government was pleased but not entirely reas-
sured: Colonial Minister Jules Renkin ordered his largest
available body of troops to Katanga from the Anglo-German border
near Lake Kivu. A regiment under Commandant Olsen reached
Elisabethville in October 1910, just a month before the arrival
of the railroad from South Africa. Fortunately for the Belgians
the plot never materialized; it had sprung from the imagination
of a South African alcoholic who claimed to be a defector from
the Natal Security Branch. The arrival of Olsen's troops
prompted the British Administrator for Northwestern Rhodesia to
request a similar dispatch of British troops but the British
High Commissioner in Cape Town refused to allow an arms race to
develop between Britons and Belgians in Central Africa.

Thus when the railroad arrived in Elisabethville the Belgians there were protected by some of their best colonial troops
and by the good faith of the British government. But fears of
a British takeover were not permanently allayed, partly because
some adventurers who had worked for the Union Minière actually
did have a plot in mind. These men, however, were turned away
by the British government, as were the humanitarians, so that
their plans did not materialize. Thus at the time of Elisabethville's foundation in 1910 Belgian control of Katanga was not in
real danger.[26] What is important, however, is that many Belgians
remained certain that it was.

Fears of British designs on Katanga continued to haunt the
Colonial Ministry. To counter the possible British threat, the
ministry created a provincial government for Katanga different
in many ways from that of other parts of the Congo. The new
regime in Katanga, however, remained an integral part of the
Belgian colonial system, subject to the same controls as other
parts of the Belgian African empire.

Since 1908 the Brussels headquarters of Belgian colonization had undergone substantial changes. Both the Congo Free
State and the CSK had surrendered their governmental powers to
the Belgian government which henceforth controlled the Congo
through a complex hierarchy. At the top was the king, whose
decrees still formed the main body of colonial legislation.
After 1908, however, no colonial decree could be enacted without
consultation with the Colonial Council, a body consisting of
some members appointed by parliament and others appointed by
the king. In addition to Colonial Council deliberations each
colonial decree required the countersignature of the colonial
minister. The colonial legislative process was thus subject to
scrutiny by parliament through the colonial minister who was a
member of the cabinet, which could be dismissed by a majority
vote of the Chamber of Representatives.

In administrative affairs, the colonial minister was the
real head of the Congo's government, since he was responsible
for the annual colonial budget—henceforth subject to parliamentary approval—and supervised all appointments to Congo
posts. The colonial minister commanded two groups of subordinates. The vast majority were the civil servants who had been
transferred more or less automatically from the government of
Leopold's Congo Free State to the new Colonial Ministry. The
other group, much smaller in number, were the colonial minister's personal cabinet of political protégés who, like the
cabinet of other ministers, were responsible to him personally
rather than to the ministry's permanent officials.[27]

A large proportion of the minister's staff, both personal
appointees and higher level civil servants, were lawyers.
Minister of Colonies Jules Renkin was himself in private practice but most of his appointees, including the director of his
personal cabinet and most of his section heads, were magistrates
who were civil servants. Magistrates—unlike many other lawyers
at that time—were university graduates who had completed the
doctor of law degree which quaified them for jobs in the Ministry of Justice. Having obtained their civil services appointments, most magistrates worked in the administration of criminal
justice as public prosecutors. The presence of so many magistrates put an unusual mark on the new Belgian Colonial Ministry
which became extremely meticulous in its operations, paying
great respect to the letter of the statutes which it wrote and
administered.

Indeed the Colonial Ministry was more effective in its
law-making capacity than in decision making, subject as it was
to a number of direct outside influences—namely the king, the
cabinet and Parliament, and the Colonial Council. Structurally

this was a far cry from the decision-making process in the Congo
Free State where every decision had lain within the powers of
Léopold. In practice, however, during Elisabethville's early
years power tended to gravitate to the Minister of Colonies
Jules Renkin who, between 1908 and 1918, did much to perpetuate
Leopoldian policies within the new administration.

    Renkin, a man of humble origins who had acquired a good
legal education, had begun his parliamentary career in 1896 on
the left wing of the Catholic Party when he had been elected as
the champion of Catholic workers. During the next eleven years
he acquired a measure of power and money, becoming at the same
time socially acceptable and adopting more conservative views
than those held in his younger days. One important·step along
the way was his election in 1902 to the board of directors of a
colonial railroad, the Chemin de Fer des Grands Lacs (CFL), which
operated a rail and river network in eastern Congo. He was to
remain one of the line's directors until his death in 1934.
Thanks to this "colonial" experience, in 1907 Renkin was appointed
to the parliamentary commission which negotiated the transfer of
the Free State to parliamentary control. After devising a com-
promise which satisfied both his colleagues and King Léopold,
Renkin became Minister of Justice and in 1908 Belgium's first
Minister of Colonies.[28]

    In the years immediately preceding the outbreak of the First
World War Renkin made a number of decisions affecting Elisabethville. His actions seem determined both by his patriotism and
by his financial outlook as a director of a Belgian colonial
corporation. The two roles were, in fact, interrelated in that
he was willing to use government resources to help private companies while at the same time being prepared to use private
companies in order to help the national interest. In this respect he was the spiritual heir to Léopold II, who had profited
from colonial enterprises while at the same time investing his
own and the Free State's money in colonial corporations whose
advantages were more strategic than pecuniary.

    As colonial minister,.Renkin undoubtedly worked out his
policy for the relationship between the colonial government and
colonial companies by drawing on his experiences with his own
Chemin de Fer des Grands Lacs. The Free State had granted the
CFL its original charter in 1902 for an initial capitalization
of twenty-five million francs (₤833,333). Under terms of an
agreement between Léopold and the railroad's main backer, the
banker Edouard Empain, the company would in good times give the
state 47.4 percent of its profits, but in bad times the Free
State would guarantee shareholders a minimum dividend of 4.0
percent a year. Renkin continued this practice of guaranteeing

interest on new emissions of stock; the company's guaranteed
capital rose from fifty million francs in 1911 to one hundred
million in 1913. According to Article 14 of the Charte Coloniale the Belgian Parliament had to approve such guarantees, so
Renkin had the approval—or at least the acquiescence—of the
Belgian cabinet for this continuation of Léopold's policy.
Since the railroad company's real resources were siphoned off
through a subsidiary, the CFL never earned the profits necessary
to pay dividends. Thus the colonial government was liable to
pay over four million francs a year in interest—amounting to
approximately 10 percent of colonial revenues in the years before
1918.[29]

Renkin's willingness to divert colonial revenues to the
CFL in order to attract additional capital was not lost on Belgian directors of the Union Minière. In 1911 they were engaged
in a board room battle with British directors for control of the
copper company and desperately sought Belgian government support.
The circumstances under which they received state aid, however,
cannot be understood without a look at the development of the
Union Minière in the years immediately after the company's creation in 1906.

Between 1907 and 1911 the Union Minière had two European
offices, a "headquarters" in Brussels and a "technical committee"
at Robert Williams's chambers in London. Although the board of
directors met in Brussels, Williams's office exercised real control of operations in Africa since it was responsible for the
administration of the mining camps and almost all recruitment.
The Brussels office stll retained the right to appoint the director of African operations. This division of authority in
Europe created discontent in Africa, partly because the predominantly British staff had little respect for their first two
Belgian directors, Armand Bertholet (1907-09) and Eugéne
Hallewijk (1910-12), who were not men of towering authority.[30]

On the other hand the Belgian directors of the Union Minière
were dissatisfied with the British management for economic as
well as nationalistic reasons. Between 1906 and 1911 the company had exhausted its initial capital and borrowed heavily from
the Société Général to buy mining and smelting equipment—without repaying any of its debts or yielding a penny in dividends.
The Union Minière's financial status reached a crisis in April
of 1911 when the mining company, in accordance with the terms of
an earlier agreement, was called upon to provide new funds for
the construction of the Katanga Railway. Needless to say the
Union Minière was unable to meets its obligation. This shortage
of capital for railway construction threatened the entire copper
industry with bankruptcy, for at that time the CFK served only

one mine, the Star of the Congo, which was proving to be much
less rich than originally anticipated. The Union Minière's capital shortage, however, did not prove fatal since the rail construction contract provided for other sources of capital. When
the mining company could not raise the needed capital, its
obligation was transferred to its parent corporatins, the
Société Générale and Tanganyika Concessions.

This gave the directors of the Belgian bank great leverage
over the British managers at the Union Minière, for Williams
could not raise the money for the CFL construction. The Belgians accused the British of being too slow to make the mines
run a profit and of not having the capital necessary to sustain
the company through the period of delay. On the basis of these
British shortcomings the Société Générale refused to keep its
side of the bargain. They had already invested too much of
their clients' money in the Katanga mines to risk any more funds
on such a doubtful venture.[31]

This line of reasoning may have simply been a ploy on the
part of the directors of the Société Générale to rid themselves
of their British partners and at the same time to obtain government aid. They realized that the government could not allow
the railway construction to be terminated so they approached the
Colonial Ministry to help raise the additional capital. Since
the colonial treasury was guaranteeing profits to bondholders in
Renkin's CFL railway, the colonial budget could also be tapped
to buy stock in the Katanga Railway. Renkin agreed in 1911 and
by 1914 the colony's holdings in the Katanga Railway were worth
fifty-five million francs—nearly two million pounds sterling.[32]

By providing capital from the colonial treasury for the
Katanga Railway Renkin and his ministry were not simply helping
a Belgian enterprise at a critical moment; they were also
enabling Belgian managers to gain control of the Union Minière.
The latter took advantage of the demonstrated weakness of Robert
Williams to force his men out of their positions of power at the
Union Minière. They attacked Williams on economic grounds,
claiming that his crews were not properly running the mines. To
investigate these assertions the Union Minière's Board of Directors sent out an investigating team to Africa composed of a
Briton, two Belgians, and an American: Dr. Sheffield Neave of
Tanganyika Concessions; Jules Jadot, brother of the Société
Générale director, Jean Jadot; Edgar Sengier of the same bank;
and an American engineer named Vigeon.

The commissioners dealt first with a relatively minor problem. The first shipments of Katanga copper reaching Europe had
sold for less than the cost of production because they had been

smelted with coke imported from Europe. The commissioners
quickly discovered that cheap coke could be obtained from the
Wankie colliery in Southern Rhodesia thereby clearing the way
for profitable copper production.

Beyond this relatively trivial change in provisioning, the
commissioners recommended sweeping reforms in the Union Minière's
organization. Most important, they condemned the division of
company headquarters between Brussels and London, recommending
that the London office be closed. This was anathema to Williams
but he was so over-extended financially that he could not fight
back. His Tanganyika Concessions had even turned over its
shares in the Union Minière to its creditors as security for
other debts.[33] Williams had no choice but to agree with other
members of the Union Minière board of directors that the company
be reorganized and that technical operations be transferred to
the Brussels office. An American engineer, P. K. Horner, considered political.ly neutral, was then appointed to head all
Union Minière activities in Africa. Although outwardly a com-
promise, the new arrangement was a victory for the Belgian management. Proof that this was so can be seen in the sharp increase in the proportion of Belgians employed in the Katanga
mines after hiring operations were transferred to Brussels; an
increase from 23 percent of the white employees in January 1912
to 53 percent in August 1914.[34]

With control of the mining company moved from London, the
Colonial Ministry was also able to find more Belgian investors
for the Union Minière. Late in 1911 the Board of Directors
voted to augment its capital from ten to twelve and a half million francs. Once again the question arose as to where the
needed capital could be obtained. Renkin had reason to fear
that private investors would not adequately defend Belgian national interests. The original stock of the Union Minière had
been bought, not by the CSK, but by the Société Générale and a
number of smaller companies including the Compagnie du Katanga,
the Compagnie Congolaise pour le Commerce et l'Industrie, and
the Banque d'Outremer. These smaller Belgian investors had
begun to sell their stock on the open market. If their holdings
came on the market at the same time as Williams's mortgaged stock
some foreign power might possibly gain control of the Union
Minière. To avert the danger of losing control of the Katanga
copper company Renkin applied pressure on the directors of the
CSK, a majority of whom were permanent officials of the Colonial
Ministry. The CSK capitulated and in May 1912 bought most of
the Union Minière's new issue, thus assuring the continuation of
Belgian control of the mining industry.[35]

Once again the Colonial Ministry under Renkin resorted to the policy of intervention in economic affairs inaugurated by Léopold. Renkin tapped the colonial treasury for increased capital for the Katanga Railway and obliged the CSK to invest its own capital in the Union Minière. This interventionism would characterize other projects relating to the development of Katanga, some involving substantial sums of money, others of a relatively cheap nature.

This same principle was involved in the Belgianization of a British firm, Pauling and Company, which had built most of the rail network linking Katanga with South Africa. In April 1911, when the Colonial Ministry was debating whether or not to buy stock in the Katanga Railway, it was also forcing changes in Pauling's construction company. No contractor in Central Africa could lay rail better than Pauling's crews, so the Ministry could not dispense entirely with his services; they could, however, force him to accept Belgian investment in his business. Thereafter Pauling continued to build the railway as part of a new company, the Société Coloniale de Construction, which gave the Belgian banks Nagelmaekers and Josse Allard a share of the contractor's profits.[36]

Financial projects involving the Union Minière and the construction and operation of the Katanga Railway seem to have been organized by Jules Renkin personally while other projects for the promotion of Belgian interests in Katanga can be traced to his subordinates. The most economically important of these was the project of Edmond Leplae, director of the Colonial Ministry's agricultural service, to establish an agricultural colony on the copperbelt. Leplae planned a series of villages to be located along the rail line between Elisabethville and the Northern Rhodesian border, where Flemish peasants would grow maize to feed the African labor force. The costs proved astronomical: in 1911 the government financed the migration and settling on land of a score of families at an ultimate cost of eight million francs, almost as much as the initial capitalization of the Union Minière! The settlers were too few in number and unwilling to bear the hardships of colonization; many left the Congo after a short time. Those who remained made their living as truck farmers, selling their produce to Elisabethville Europeans for—unlike better equipped farmers in Northern Rhodesia—the Belgians were not able to produce staple foods such as beef and maize for African consumption.[37]

The Colonial Ministry's expert on religious affairs, E. Kervyn, also tried to solve the agricultural problem. During the Middle ages monasteries in Belgium had served as centers for the dissemination of advanced agricultural techniques. Monastic

Catholicism was undergoing a great revival and Kervyn hoped to convince the powerful Benedictine order to establish an agricultural colony in Katanga. In 1911 the Abbey of St. André near Bruges agreed to build a monastery in the bush. The African soil, however, was too poor to sustain intensive European agriculture and the monks, who were of upper and middle class origin, knew little about farming. The only long term result of this experiment was the presence in Katanga of dom Jean Félix de Hemptinne who would become the driving force behind Belgian colonial Catholicism after the First World War.[38]

Beyond these projects intended in part to support the Belgian presence in the copperbelt, the Colonial Ministry created a special form of government for Katanga. Many writers, notably Réné Lemarchand, see the special administrative status of Katanga as an important stimulus to later Katanga separatism. Before this proposition can be tested, however, it will be necessary to analyze the relationship between the Belgian administration in Elisabethville and the Colonial Ministry in Brussels.

Theoretically the governor general in Boma was the head of the Belgian administrative hierarchy in the Congo. Boma, however, was at the mouth of the Congo River some twelve hundred miles from Elisabethville, so in 1910 colonial minister Renkin introduced a series of laws creating a vice governor general for Katanga whose powers were similar to those of the governor general. Until 1914 the vice governor general of Katanga dealt directly with the Colonial Ministry in Brussels rather than taking orders from his theoretical superior in Boma.[39] In later years serious problems would develop over the relationship between the vice governors general and the governor general.

However, the Charte Coloniale granted neither official substantial powers. According to Article 22, the power to make laws remained in Belgium. Although law-making was theoretically the monopoly of the king, these powers in fact rested in the Colonial Ministry and the Colonial Council. The only legislative authority given to Belgians in Africa were emergency powers granted to the governor general which allowed him to make ordinances having the force of law for a period of six months. Aside from these emergency powers the governor general could promulgate ordinances only in those matters where authority had been specifically granted by the king or the Parliament.

The governor general and the vice governors general were similarly handicapped in budgetary matters. According to Article 12 of the Charte Coloniale, authorities in Brussels retained ultimate control over the budget, which was submitted annually to the Parliament by the Colonial Ministry. Thus the allocation

of resources to the individual provinces depended on decisions
made in Brussels. Furthermore neither the governor general nor
his subordinates could undertake projects without the ministry's
approval and a specific appropriation of funds.

Both of these restrictions on local initiative severely
limited the powers of the administration in Katanga. And although the vice governor general was at the head of a large
hierarchy, he was always subject to the supreme power of the
Colonial Ministry which could easily undo local projects. For
long periods of time, of course, it was in the ministry's interest to bolster local authority—there was no need to air differences between provincial authorities and the ministry—but in
times of crisis the minister and his staff showed no compunctions
about asserting central authority.

Between 1910 and 1914 relations between the governments in
Brussels and Elisabethville were dominated by common fears of
the British. The Colonial Ministry therefore established a
formidable set of colonial government institutions, most of them
located in Elisabethville, to give the Katanga administration an
appearance of strength. The vice governor general received his
own subordinate staff consisting of a commissioner general, a
secretary general, and six heads of departments—more subdivi-
sions than in the Colonial Ministry itself. The Katanga magistracy, already known for its honesty and reliability, had
special status. To foster local autonomy in judicial affairs,
the Colonial Ministry detached the Katanga judiciary from the
appeal court in Boma and created an autonomous magistracy linked
to a new court of appeal at Elisabethville.[40]

In addition to the provincial and judicial hierarchies, the
vice governor general directed a territorial service which consisted of district commissioners, newly created territorial
administrators, as well as agents responsible for individual
outposts. Theoretically this new administration was a great
improvement over that provided by the CSK, but in reality there
were few changes in either personnel or the total number of
officials. The Belgian government offered jobs to all CSK
employees in Africa while the CSK's head of African operations,
Emile Wangermée, became vice governor general. The territorial
administration increased its staff positions from forty-six in
1910 to ninety-six in 1922, but the government had great difficulty in finding suitable officers to fill these posts. Thus
in 1922 sixty-seven men were doing the work of ninety-six.

New employees in the colonial administration were often
Belgian soldiers. According to one source, the Colonial Ministry
announced that any lieutenant could become a territorial admini-

strator and any captain, a district commissioner. Despite the
fact that high colonial offices were easy to obtain—the only
legal requirement being a year's training—vacancies were difficult to fill. Many of the appointees were incompetent: in 1914
one colonial official confided that "outside of Brussels, a
career in the colonial service is for men who are not good for
anything else."[41]

Officials on the spot thought their remunerations—and
their pensions in particular—incommensurate with the difficulty
of their jobs. Thus in January of 1914 lower level government
employees in Elisabethville founded their own trade union, later
known as the AFAC (Association des Fonctionnaires et des Agents
de la Colonie) which soon spread to the rest of the Congo.

The Katanga magistracy, which had already acquired a reputation for competence and integrity, had similar staffing problems to those of the territorial administration. Colonial
magistrates, being administratively distinct from the Belgian
magistracy, could not transfer their seniority to the home
service; if they wanted to return to the Belgian magistracy,
which was directed by the Ministry of Justice rather than the
Colonial Ministry, they had to begin their careers again at the
very bottom. Together with the rigors of African life, these
professional disadvantages caused an enormous turnover in personnel; between 1914 and 1924 twenty-six men passed through five
career positions in the Elisabethville magistracy. This turnover is all the more surprising given the role played by the
Elisabethville magistracy during this period to keep the city
Belgian.[42]

The frequent personnel changes in the colonial administration reflected many of the difficulties still a part of life in
the newly founded Belgian outpost on the copperbelt, although
for Africans as well as Europeans, Elisabethville by 1914 was
becoming a more comfortable place to live. Yet no one could be
called a permanent resident of the city. The area's original
inhabitants, five hundred Lamba of the Kikwesa and Seba chiefdoms who had formerly lived on the Luiswishi stream, had been
forced off their land by European and African farmers.[43] Even
privileged newcomers thought primarily of making a quick killing
and returning to their homes. No one had permanently broken ties
to his old home with the intention of living permanently in
Elisabethville.

For the mass of African workers, residence in Elisabethville was even less a part of their long-term life plans than
it was for the Europeans. The Africans had been recruited as a
result of European conquest, driven to seek revenues to pay the

taxes levied by their colonizers. By 1914, however, even they
received certain material compensations for their work. A man's
first wages were often spent on European clothes. Domestic
servants in the city were in a particularly favored position in
this respect since they often received their masters' cast-off
clothing and were permitted to ride their bicycles. Teenaged
girls who flocked to Elisabethville from nearby villages sometimes received bicycles from European paramours. Attracted by
material goods, some men even began signing up for additional
terms of service in the mines.[44]

Elisabethville, then, was no man's permanent home; but
once there, many people—black and white alike—found that the
city had something to offer. For both groups the attraction
was primarily economic: manufactured goods for African workers,
wealth for European merchants, advancement in governmental service or the Union Minière for members of the European elite.
The city began to constitute a new society in itself—segregated
by color and wealth but nonetheless a social network—each of
whose members could define his place in relation to the other
members.

In the early days, however, Elisabethville was less important as a society in itself than as a projection of European
power into the lives of the people of Central Africa. This
power took two distinct forms: economic and political. Of the
two emanations, the economic is the better known because it is
the more easily recognizable. European economic institutions
brought the railroad, the mines, the smelter with its growing
slag heap, and the mining camps in which the mass of Africans
passed their terms of servitude.

But behind the economic development of Elisabethville lay
the political factor of Belgian power, dominated as it was by
Belgian nationalism. From the time of the city's origin, political decisions determined the allocation of economic resources,
in particular the city's inputs of capital and labor. These
decisions were directed largely against the British who were
correctly feared as Belgium's major rivals in Central Africa.
Just as this power had a well-defined target—the British—it
operated through well-defined channels of communications. It
was manifested in specific policy decisions made by a limited
number of men in positions of authority who lived in two distinct
geographical locations: Brussels, the seat of Belgian government and finance, and Elisabethville itself. These key individuals determined the future of the city and the people who lived
in it.

Thus the history of Elisabethville between 1910 and 1914 was largely determined by a small number of men in government, finance, and the copper industry. Such overwhelming power over the development of a city is rare, occurring only when a city has grown up as a result of political decisions rather than local economic resources. In the course of time Elisabethville came to attract resources without political coercion, but in its earliest years the city's attractions were almost entirely provided from the outside.

Chapter 4

The War and its Aftermath: Economic

Development and Belgian Nationalism

In August 1914, when news of the Great War reached Elisabethville, the city was in the grip of a major recession. Four
years after the great copper rush the economy had cooled off.
Construction had subsided and business was slow. Many of the
original settlers, having failed to make an easy fortune, had
returned to South Africa. Those who remained dug in for a slow
development of the copper industry.

News of the outbreak of hostilities, moreover, came at the
midpoint of the dry season in Katanga when the weather is beginning to warm up but the rains are still months away. Under ordinary conditions August in Elisabethville is set apart from
the rest of the year. The chilly season—when temperatures may
drop as low as 35°F. during the night—has passed, but it is
still too early to prepare the fields for the next rainy season. Life takes on a slower pace.

In 1914, however, August was a month of frenetic activity.
An American missionary described the scene graphically, if a bit
ungramatically:

        The financial upheaval and chaos produced by the
    war meant that the Railroad Construction must be dis-
    continued, and business throughout the whole country
    suffered greatly. Native troops were hurried through
    to Lake Tanganyika, and all unemployed natives about
    town were impressed into service as carriers and hun-
    dreds of others engaged for this service. Belgians,
    Britishers, and Russians who were residents of the
    country enlisted in local defense corps, and were
    drilling both at Kambove and at Elisabethville to be
    prepared for any emergencies, and contingents went

forward to Lake Tanganyika, and scores went south
some to join other forces in South Africa, others to
proceed to Europe to rejoin their regiments or to
enlist in favorite corps.[1]

Located as it was in a tropical area where people resist such an
accelerated tempo, Elisabethville did not remain—if it had ever
been—quite as hectic as this missionary's breathless account
would have it. After August of 1914 life soon settled back to
something more normal, although repercussions from the war in
Europe would be felt in the Congo throughout the war years.

When World War I broke out about eight thousand people
lived in Elisabethville of whom approximately 12 percent were
white and 88 percent black. Since the city's foundation its
European section had taken on a surprisingly permanent air.
Brick houses, paved streets, stores, even a beauty salon had
sprung up in what a few years previously had been a desolate
savanna. In the center of town clusters of government buildings
and the headquarters of the Cercle Albert silently buttressed
the Belgian colonial presence.

In marked contrast to the permanent-looking buildings of
the Europeans were the African huts of the company camps and
the *cité indigène*. Africans who had to work in Elisabethville
shared few of the amenities enjoyed by the Europeans. New recruits built their own huts out of sticks, mud, and savanna
grass as they would have done at home, but living was less comfortable than in the villages. No wives did the cooking. No
children gathered firewood. At the end of the day the exhausted
workers returned to their huts with unfamiliar rations which
they often lacked the strength to cook.

The *cité indigène* and the company camps alike were merely
clusters of huts, but already differences between the two forms
of African settlement were beginning to emerge. In the early
days the *cité* was situated next to the European town while the
camps of the Union Minière, Katanga Railway, and Force Publique
were located on the other side of the railroad tracks. The war,
moreover, would accentuate differences between *cité* and camp.
In the former, construction and commerce would stagnate and as
a result the *cité* would remain about the size it had been in
1914. By contrast, the Union Minière camp would undergo a great
expansion due to Allied demands for copper. Although European
employees received a share of the company's prosperity, the company's African work force did not. On the contrary, African
employees suffered when the company expanded the size of its
operations because the camps became even more crowded and unhealthy.

For a time the deterioration of African living conditions in the Union Minière camps went largely unnoticed in the European community. The copper company was enjoying an unprecedented boom; its output of refined copper rose from 10,000 metric tons in 1914 to 27,000 in 1917. This increased output in turn necessitated expansion of the Lubumbashi smelter and a doubling of its African work force. To carry away the fumes from expanded operations, the Union Minière built a huge chimney which, together with a growing slag heap, came to dominate Elisabethville's landscape.

As in prewar times, the development of the copper industry depended on capital from Europe, but wartime conditions complicated the acquisition and transfer of that capital. Belgian banks which had begun to invest in Katanga after years of mistrust were now in the German empire and cut off as a source of capital. The Colonial Ministry, which had persuaded the banks to invest in Congolese companies, was itself in dire straits. Thus the managers of the Union Minière had lost both their investors and their most effective promoters.

With Belgian government and finance in such disarray, the Union Minière returned to its traditional purveyor of British capital, Sir Robert Williams. The Scottish engineer was fully aware that the Belgians were coming to him as a last resort. Between 1911 and 1914 they had attempted to force him out of the company in favor of the German copper trust. But the war had wiped the slate clean. Williams saw new opportunities to support the company on one hand and to improve his personal fortunes on the other.[2]

Even with Williams's aid, however, the Belgians encountered difficulties in raising money on the wartime London market. In order to promote the war effort, the British government had imposed tight controls on the economy, including restrictions on overseas investment and on the export of strategic materials.[3] These wartime measures posed no particular difficulty for the Union Minière whose copper was strategic to the war effort, and under Williams's guidance the company easily raised the money necessary for expanding its production facilities. Less vital to the war effort than the Union Minière, the Katanga Railway found the British obstructive.

In 1914 the Belgians had suspended construction of the railway, leaving the last fifty miles of track unfinished for want of capital. The Belgian government was in exile and the Union Minière argued that the railway's completion was in everyone's interest and in 1916 the Belgians obtained permission to float a loan on the London market. Even with the money in hand,

however, the railway company could not obtain needed rails and
rolling stock. One British ministry forebade the export of
such strategic goods to Katanga while another ministry prevented
the Belgians from spending their sterling balance on American
supplies. Thus the British wartime bureaucracy had prevented
the completion of the railway. In the end the Belgian army
"liberated" the missing track from an unfinished line in
Allied-occupied German East Africa and the management bought its
rolling stock from Rhodesian Railways. Thus the Belgians completed their railroad in 1918 but only with considerable difficulty.[4]

The Union Minière also had trouble obtaining supplies from
British sources. Between 1914 and 1917 the company increased
production by 70 percent due to new equipment and to an expanded
African work force which grew from 2,500 to nearly 5,000. These
operations naturally required increased supplies of food which
British colonial officials in southern and central Africa refused to provide. On the contrary, shipments of food from the
Rhodesias and South Africa were frequently diverted to meet
local needs or to supply British troops in East Africa. Resultant shortages forced the Belgians to impose tight controls on
the sale to Africans and the consumption by Africans of foodstuffs. Thus the variety and quantity of food available to
Africans in Elisabethville was diminished during the war.[5]

The quality of life for African workers also deteriorated
as a result of Belgian immigration restrictions resulting from
the wartime emergency. Anticipating food shortages, Belgian
managers attempted to reduce African consumption by curtailing
the migration of "nonproductive natives." Although recruiters
had discovered that African men were more willing to work in
the mines if they could bring a female companion, mineward-
bound caravans from 1916 onwards could have no more than one
woman for each ten men. The scarcity of female companionship
discouraged younger men from staying in town beyond their initial
contract of service, although some sweetened their lives through
liasons with the wives of African soldiers who had been sent to
the Tanganyika front.[6]

For the mass of Africans in Elisabethville, however, the
unhygienic conditions in the camps posed even greater problems
than the absence of feminine companionship. The situation was
most visible at the Lubumbashi smelter, which doubled its work
force from one to two thousand between 1914 and 1917 without
modernizing its housing. As it had done before the war, the
company simply asked newly-arrived work teams to build their own
huts out of trees and other local materials, and the task became increasingly difficult as the local countryside was cut over.

The great influx of workers to the smelter also put great pressures on existing sanitation facilities which would not be expanded until 1918. This inaction resulted in a terrible health problem in the camp which became an even worse pest hole than it had been in the earliest years. The deathrate rose precipitously and by 1917 it had reached 9.5 percent per year in Lubumbashi, still higher at the Kambove mine. Thus the expansion of the copper industry led to increasingly unhealthy conditions in the camps.[7]

As descriptions of these camps reached the villages, more and more Africans began to hide from the European labor recruiters. And had more attractive means of earning money been available, even fewer would have gone to the mines. During the war, however, rural Africans in Katanga had to choose between copper mining and service at the front as porters. The deathrate for the latter was even higher than for the miners, and so the falloff in industrial labor which began in 1916 was less precipitous than it might otherwise have been.

Between 1914 and 1917 recruitments by the Bourse de Travail du Katanga fell by nearly a third, from 7,649 to 5,248. In the same period Robert Williams and Company compensated for some of this loss of Zaïrian labor by increasing the recruitment of Zambians from 2,913 to 4,339. Meanwhile pressure developed within the British administration in Northern Rhodesia to cut off this recruitment.[8]

During the first two years of the war British officials deliberately avoided military conscription in the Luapula Valley where Robert Williams and Company did most of its recruitment for the mines. By 1916, however, the British colonial government saw no option but to recruit porters in that area for the East Africa campaign. In Kawambwa subdistrict, for example, the government recruited 3,104 men between April 1916 and March 1917, at the same time allowing Williams only 584 men. Restrictions became even more stringent the following year. Between April 1917 and March 1918 the British government took 8,540 porters out of the Fort Rosebery district which included Kawambwa, while allowing Williams only 548 recruits.[9]

These restrictions, however, were not based on military grounds alone; some Northern Rhodesian officials opposed recruitment for the Katanga mines because of the high deathrate in the mining camps. In 1915 Dr. Aylmer May of the Northern Rhodesian Medical Service visited the camps in Elisabethville and, finding an annual death rate of over 7 percent, recommended suspension of recruitment. May had previously opposed migration to Katanga on the grounds that it took away potential labor from Southern

Rhodesian settlers and was not an impartial observer, but the
deteriorating condition in the mining camps gave added weight
to his recommendations.

Manpower shortages rather than May's exhortation gradually
brought the Northern Rhodesia government to change its recruitment policies. Between April 1916 and March 1917 the administration substantially cut the number of Luapula Valley people
(Fort Rosebery district) recruited for the Katanga mines,
replacing them with Lozi people from the more distant valley of
the Zambezi. Not only did these Lozis have to walk farther to
the mines, but many of them were too weak to perform industrial
labor and many others had formerly been rejected on physical
grounds by recruiters for the South African mines. Not surprisingly these Lozis proved equally unsuited for the Katanga
mines; of 2,461 Lozi recruits sent to Katanga in 1916-17, 436
were repatriated as medically unfit, 696 deserted, and 173 died
on the job. This dismal record was far worse than that of the
Luapulans: out of 1,751 recruits from that group in the same
period only 59 were declared unfit while 13 deserted and 60
died. On the basis of the combined statistics, however, in
April of 1917 the Northern Rhodesian administration and the
British Colonial Office concluded that the Katanga mines were
too unhealthy and dangerous, and sharply restricted recruitment.[10]

By 1917, then, the managers of the Union Minière had
attained their goal of making the company profitable only to
encounter a new problem of supply. The British colonies to the
South which provided industrial Katanga with most of its food
and labor had shown themselves to possess a stranglehold on the
new copper industry. For the duration of the war the company
could do nothing to free itself from dependence in the British
colonies, although plans could be made for future economic
independence. Such hopes, however, provided little consolation.
Instead the vulnerability of the copper industry fed the Belgians'
resentment of their British ally. Many believed that British
restrictions on the shipment of food and labor were part of a
British plot to bring Katanga to its knees so that the territory
could be incorporated into the British Empire. These suspicions
were unfounded, but are understandable in light of the wartime
isolation and weakness of the Belgian community in Elisabethville.
Cut off from the homeland by the war, from the rest of the Congo
by poor communications, and surrounded by a sea of Africans, the
Belgians of Elisabethville developed a kind of collective para-
noia.

The Belgians' sorest spot was the conduct of the war in
East Africa. From 1914 onwards officers of the Force Publique—
the colonial army—had hoped to invade German East Africa in

order to avenge the occupation of their fatherland. British
officers in Africa, lacking this incentive to attack, preferred
a more cautious approach to the well-defended German colony.
This difference of approach provoked a number of incidents
between Belgian officers and their British counterparts. The
Allies finally took the offensive in 1916 and the Belgian
colonial forces won a rapid series of victories. The commander
of the Belgians in Africa, General Tombeur, personally led the
occupation of the German colonal capital, Tabora.[11]

These victories only led to a greater disappointment.
After the Germans had abandoned most of their territory to the
Allies, the British pressed the Belgians to withdraw from most
of their conquests and to allow the British army to administer
them. The Belgian government at Le Havre was in no position to
resist this demand and ordered the Force Publique to withdraw.
General Tombeur handed Tabora over to the British and returned
to the Congo.

To compensate Tombeur for this humiliation, the Belgian
Colonial Ministry in August 1917 named him vice governor general
of Katanga. Tombeur's presence in Elisabethville reinforced
anti-British sentiments already present in the local European
community. Although the new governor was not personally an
anglophobe—his wife was British—his wartime experiences
typified Belgian colonial frustrations. The very sight of Tombeur was enough to remind patriotic Belgians of the need to get
back at the British.

During the first five months of Tombeur's governorship, the
leader of anti-British activity in Elisabethville was Attorney
General Martin Rutten who had gone to Katanga just after the
turn of the century and had witnessed almost every skirmish in
the Belgian battle to retain control of the copperbelt. In the
days of CSK rule he had accompanied Belgian patrols of the British border near Lake Mweru to prevent the British from en-
croaching on Belgian lands. South Africans in the mining camps
feared him because of his readiness to expel any foreigner who
made trouble. A prominent lay Catholic, Rutten had strengthened
his reputation for patriotism and tact by skillfully mediating
a dispute between Belgian administrators and the Scheut Fathers,
the largest Belgian Catholic order in the Congo. Rutten almost
was the only high colonial official to remain in Elisabethville
during the entire war, when many Belgians went to the front and
when vice governors general were being replaced once a year.
In 1915 he because president of the Cercle Albert and thus
unofficial head of the Belgian community. Given his long record
of patriotism and his central position as Attorney General,
Rutten was the ideal man to organize the struggle against the
British.[12]

Rutten drew first blood a few months before Tombeur's
arrival in an encounter with an American Methodist missionary,
Bishop John McKendree Springer. The bishop and his wife had
come to the Katanga copperbelt in 1913 supposedly as the van-
guard of an industrial mission which would bring Christianity
to Africans in the mining camps. Their first clientele, the
English-speaking Malawians, had already been evangelized by
Scottish missionaries who had also provided them with a good
school system. Thus the Malawians, who had come to associate
Westernization and social advancement with Protestant missions,
welcomed the Methodists as bearers of new educational opportunities. Their enthusiasm encouraged the Springers, who returned
to Elisabethville after a home leave in 1916 with a new plan for
building a series of schools around the city. The Springers
saw these schools as the core of a larger Protestant educational
system which would eventually stretch from the Atlantic to the
Indian Ocean.

The Springers's grandiose ideas alarmed many in the local
Belgian community, who feared that the Methodists were trying to
subvert Belgian influence by luring students away from the trade
school already built in Elisabethville by the Salesian Fathers.
Championing the Catholic schools, Rutten convinced the then
acting vice governor general, Baron de Rennette de Villers
Perwin, that the American Protestant missionaries constituted a
danger to Belgian supremacy in Katanga. De Rennette thereupon
refused to grant the Springers any land near the Union Miniere
camp. To bolster the Belgian forces in the Congo, de Rennette
then wrote to the home government for spiritual reinforcements.
The home government responded by arranging for six Salesian
priests to pass through enemy lines to protect Belgian culture
in Katanga.[13]

Another target of Rutten's displeasure was P. K. Horner,
the American hired in 1910 and named African director of the
Union Minière in 1912. Horner adopted an extremely condescend-
ing attitude toward Belgians whom he considered inexperienced in
colonial affairs and in the management of Africans. Since
Horner took no pains to disguise his feelings, he gradually
accumulated a list of enemies which included the highest ranking
Belgian at the Union Minière, Jules Cousin, and the head of the
Katanga Railway, L. Scraeyen, along with Rutten.[14]

The showdown between Horner and Rutten began at the end of
the rainy season in 1917. In March of that year the Northern
Rhodesian government, citing the mounting deathrate in the Union
Minière camps, placed a virtual ban on recruitment for the
Katanga mines. In order to maintain the copper industrial labor
supply, the Belgian wartime government at Le Havre ordered a

thorough investigation of the camps which Rutten, in his capacity as head of the Katanga standing magistracy, was named to
lead. Already predisposed to suspect Horner's methods, Rutten
launched his investigation of the camps at Kambove where conditions were the worst. On the basis of the high deathrate
there, Rutten invoked the 1911 and 1913 industrial inspection
laws,[15] threatening to close all the Union Miniere camps unless
conditions were rapidly improved.

     Rutten had two goals. First of all he wanted to mollify
the Northern Rhodesian administration by doing all in his power
to improve conditions in the camps. As a result, he hoped, the
recruitment ban would be eased—as it was in fact. His second
objective was to focus the blame for poor conditions in the
camps on P. K. Horner whom the local Belgians detested. Beyond
Horner as an individual, Rutten was articulating his community's
long smoldering resenting of Anglo-Saxons.

     At first the Belgian Colonial Ministry did not know what to
make of Rutten's recommendations which seemed on the surface to
be still another threat to Katanga's most profitable industry.
To gain time Colonial Minister Renkin in November 1917 sent out
a public health specialist, Dr. A. Boigelot, to recommend improvements in facilities for industrial workers. In an effort
to mollify the British Renkin kicked Rutten upstairs, transferring him to Boma as vice governor general.

     Meanwhile, in order to reinforce their case against the
Anglo-Saxons, the Belgians of Elisabethville sent a set of
statistics to the Colonial Ministry which demonstrated the
degree to which the copper industry had fallen into British
hands: between August 1914 and June 1917 the European work
force had more than doubled but the proportion of Belgian
employees had dropped from 53 to 22.5 percent. The prospect of
British control, always a horror to Belgians in Elisabethville,
seemed a distinct possibility. Moreover, the statistics convinced many Belgians in Europe. The Le Havre government therefore authorized emergency recruitment among Belgian mine workers
in England; they would be supplemented by Americans where absolutely necessary.[16]

     Meanwhile a new development in Europe further convinced
many Belgian officials and financiers alike that Belgian control
of the mines was indeed in danger. In September 1917 an agent
for Thomas Fortune Ryan, the American promoter who had invested
in the capitalization of Forminière in 1906, proposed to buy a
large number of Union Minière shares. This offer, which was
conveyed to Société Générale officials both in London and the
Hague and to the Colonial Minister in Le Havre, provided what

seemed to be conclusive evidence that English-speakers as a group intended to take over the copperbelt. This insight brought Renkin back into line with Belgian directors of the Union Minière who had been fighting their British colleagues for over a decade.

The question next arose as to how the Anglo-Saxon could best be dealt with. Edgard Sengier of both the Société Générale and the Union Minière's London office recommended trying the tactics used successfully against the British in 1911. He suggested that the Union Minière send out another investigating team to Katanga, led by Sengier himself, to substantiate Rutten's report on conditions in the mines. Rutten's transfer to Boma would allay British suspicions. Then Sengier would make a summary inquiry, fire Horner, and reestablish Belgian control of the Union Minière camps. All went according to Sengier's plan. Having obtained the consent of the English members of the Union Minière's board of directors, Sengier set out on his mission of inquiry. Reaching Elisabethville in March of 1918, Sengier immediately instituted a new regime. After cursory investigation he fired P. K. Horner, personally assuming the latter's title as director general in Africa, and took the responsibility for the care of African workers out of the hands of Robert Williams and Company.

In his new capacity, Sengier then launched a construction program for new housing in the camps with a view to improving the workers' health; although little was actually done, the publicity for the program convinced the British that the new management was concerned with African employees' health.[17]

Meanwhile death rates continued high, higher in fact than before all the furor. For example, between April and June of 1918 Africans at Kambove died at an annual rate of over 14 percent. Also in 1918 Africans in Elisabethville were particularly hard-hit by the outbreak of Spanish influenza. Its victims lay suffering in a hospital which had neither running water nor sufficient beds to accommodate the sick. It was not until after the end of World War I that government standards for the treatment of copperbelt workers were finally raised and enforced to some degree. A 1919 law secured for Congolese workers many of the benefits that the Northern Rhodesian government had obtained for its subjects eight years earlier; the laws in both cases, however, remained far in advance of practise.[18]

While not causing much real change in the conditions of African workers at the mines, Rutten's report and Sengier's management of the Union Minière did mark the beginning of a successful Belgian counterattack against the British in Elisa-

bethville. The next target would be the mass of English-speaking
workers in Katanga industry who were hated both as Anglo-Saxons
and as union organizers and corrupters of honest Belgian work-
men. Although most of these English speakers worked at the
Union Minière, the issue of their role in Katanga industry first
rose at the Katanga Railway, a firm which already had other
labor difficulties to complicate the problem.

Labor problems had begun well before the First World War in
the rail company. Finding that the Europeans who had migrated
northwards from South Africa were not particularly reliable
workers, the Katanga railway in 1913 began employing black
engine-drivers from Senegal. European personnel became still
more scarce during the war so the railway considered hiring
additional Africans, this time from Sierra Leone and the Bas
Congo. This proposal outraged the white workers who argued that
the railway would find ample staff among Europeans if only it
paid decent wages. Some of the white workers, most of them
English-speaking, considered forming a trade union, but they
lost heart—rather quickly it would seem—when the company sum-
marily fired three of their leaders in 1915. Although the
dismissals put a temporary end to trade unionism in Katanga,
white railway workers in British territory continued to press
for improved salaries and working conditions. In 1916 firemen
at Bulawayo struck; when the stoppage spread to Northern
Rhodesia, the Rhodesian workers promptly formed a union and ultimately got their demands for higher wages and better working
conditions.[19]

The successes in Northern Rhodesia furthered anti-trade
unionist sentiment in Katanga. This feeling was exacerbated by
a wave of strikes by Europeans in 1919 and 1920. The immediate
stimulus for the workers' action was the rapid devaluation of
the Belgian franc. The management of the Union Minière ordered
wage increases to compensate for the currency depreciation, but
prices rose even faster than the number of francs to the pound.
Angry workers seemed ready to strike when in April of 1919 the
then Vice Governor General Tombeur appointed a commission of
inquiry to investigate the cost of living.

Although this action appeared to demonstrate the administration's sympathy for the European workers, it was simply a
ruse to gain time. Tombeur still hated the British for depriving
him of the fruits of his victory in 1916. His cost of living
commission brought in a report issued in May 1919 which outraged
the British workers in Elisabethville. The commission found
that prices had indeed risen by 25 percent, but claimed that the
companies provided the workers with everything that they needed.
The report also reproached the white workers for spending too

much on entertainment, which was precisely the item showing the greatest rise. Outraged Union Minière workers at the Lubumbashi foundry went on strike, but they were not joined by workers at any other Union Minière establishment or at the Katanga Railway. Some of the strikers returned to work after an appeal by the management, while the rest gave up the strike in disgust after British extremists tried to blow up the office of the new Attorney General, Antoine Sohier.

The settlement of this first strike did not, however, put an end to the copperbelt strike movement because of the continued depreciation of the franc which was at the base of the workers' grievances. However, instead of attributing the inflation to the war, Vice Governor General Tombeur blamed the unrest on the British. To his thinking, the white workers in Elisabethville would have been content with their wages had they not been gouged by the city's British merchants.

In February 1920 Tombeur issued a stringent antiprofiteering ordinance which tied prices ot their original purchase cost in francs and which gave the magistracy the right to confiscate merchants' records and wares while cases were being adjudicated. The magistracy intervened energetically, forcing a number of British shopkeepers to the point of bankruptcy. In May 1920 British Vice Consul Denton Thompson wearily summed up the situation: "After five years' residence here....I am very reluctantly forced to the conclusion that there is a very determined effort being made to prejudice the Foreigner, and particularly the Britisher in every possible way."[20]

In spite of these measures the franc continued to depreciate and white workers of all nationalities continued to complain about the inadequacy of their salaries. Officials of Belgian companies alike, however, refused to admit that a problem existed, complaining that the fault lay with the British trade unionists who continued to set a bad example for solid Belgian employees. In April 1920 the association of government employees (AFAC) went on strike to be followed by the railway workers. Both strikes ended quickly, but South African syndicalists rekindled the agitation by sending an organizer to establish a general organization called the "Union Générale des Ouvriers du Congo." The South African was deported, but not before leaving his mark on a series of demands which the union presented to the Union Minière and the CFK: exclusion of Africans from skilled jobs, wages tied to the pound sterling, and participation of workers in company profits. To obtain these demands unionists at the Union Minière and the CFK went on strike on September 1, 1920.

Expecting trouble, the government declared a ten o'clock curfew on bars, forbade the carrying of arms, and sent troops to the Union Minière works. The management of the CFK, annoyed at this second strike in one year, tried to keep the trains running with a small force of willing Europeans and trained Africans. These measures so enraged the strikers that on October 2nd they dynamited a freight train as it passed over a trestle just south of Elisabethville. The management of the two companies then changed tactics; on October 5th they agreed to union demands and the strikers went back to work a day later.

The workers' victory proved short-lived, however; those employees involved in the strike were sent back to South Africa by a simple device—the employers simply refused to renew the contracts of anyone considered a troublemaker. Thus at the expiration of each striker's contract, a man without other visible means of support could be expelled as an undesirable by the government. The companies then replaced the South Africans with Belgians who, being so far from home, were too vulnerable to make trouble. Between 1917 and 1922 the proportion of Belgians at the Union Minière rose from 22.5 to 58 percent. Thereafter any English-speakers who continued to work for the Union Minière did so on the company's sufferance.[21]

In effect, a private war between the Belgians and Anglo-Saxons in Katanga—which was as old as the Union Minière itself —had finally been settled. Led by Edgar Sengier and Jules Cousin, Belgian managers had routed P. K. Horner and his minions. Workers of Belgian origin once more formed a majority of the company's white work force. The fearsome Springers had not taken over the Congolese schools. The Africans were back in their camps—a bit more crowded and insalubrious—but they were where they belonged. Moreover, new laws governing conditions in the camps would soon bring some improvement into the lives of workers lodged there.

The sense of triumph following the defeat of the Anglo-Saxons at the Union Miniere spilled over into the Belgian settler community in Elisabethville, its effect potentiated by the Allied victory in Europe. Local leaders of industry, government, and the church felt increasingly confident of their ability to run their own affairs. In their minds Elisabethville was becoming a special place—an improved version of the mother country; a society which defeated the enemy instead of being conquered by it; a society where even unskilled workers had servants; a society which questioned neither the Catholic Church nor the French language. The Belgians of Elisabethville entered the 1920s with great self-confidence, feeling that they were better Belgians than their compatriots in the metropole.

This superior attitude soon brought the settlers into conflict with the Belgian colonial administration which defended
quite another variety of Belgian nationalism. For the ministry
in Brussels, the colony was strictly subordinate to the mother
country. By law the Belgian colonial administration held virtually unlimited legal power over the colonial community. Such
power had existed since the city's creation but had fallen into
abeyance during the war. On the very eve of hostilities, as a
matter of fact, the limits of local initiative had been clearly
defined.

In the eyes of the Colonial Ministry, Vice Governor General
Wangermée, the founder of Elisabethville, had begun to exceed
his delegated authority when in 1913 he had created a consultative committee intended to give Katanga settlers a voice in
government decisionmaking. Neither Léopold II nor the Belgian
Colonial Ministry had ever created such a body, which resembled
more than anything else a British legislative council. In
British colonial practice legislative councils had limited law-
making powers and were seen as a first step in the creation of
a colonial parliament.

Such a development was anathema both to the Colonial Ministry and to the Belgian Parliament, both of which had consciously refrained from assigning lawmaking powers to officials
in Africa—even to the governor general. To scotch any suggestion that such powers could be exercised outside of the ministry,
in the Arrêté Royal of July 28, 1914, the government severely
cut back Wangermée's powers. Thereafter the chief executive of
Katanga was placed on a par with the three other vice governors
general, all of them strictly subordinate to the governor general. Abolishing Wangermée's consultative committee, the ministry created for each of the provinces a new body called a
Regional Committee which had more limited powers. Angered at
this restriction of both regional autonomy and his own authority,
Wangermée precipitously resigned from the colonial administration.[22]

At the end of the war Wangermée returned to Elisabethville
in the specially created position of "Representative" of the
Union Miniére—a title which gave him more weight than a private
citizen or even a vice governor general who had been forced to
leave the administration. He added his voice to a growing settler chorus demanding greater autonomy for Katanga. The economic benefits of a devolution of power to the Katanga settlers
would be real and immediate. The Union Minière paid dividends
for the first time in 1919, then again in 1920, and out of the
proceeds the colonial government received twelve million francs.
The settlers wanted this money to be reserved for Katanga alone

rather than passing it into the general budget. Wangermée and
the higher echelons of the Katanga civil service supported
settler demands because the money would have reinforced local
autonomy.

At first the coalition of officials and settlers acted with
a certain restraint, framing their request so that it seemed
less an innovation than a return to earlier practises. The
Katanga Regional Committee, which had replaced Wangermée's
Consultative Committee, met for the first time in April 1919.
On that occasion official and unofficial members alike joined in
petitioning for a return to provincial autonomy as it had existed
before the war. This plea ignored, the committee resubmitted
its petition a year later.

Meanwhile a settler group led by Monseigneur de Hemptinne,
head of the Benedictine mission who had recently returned to
Elisabethville after ten years in the bush, suggested more radical changes in the colonial administration. In a plan submitted to the ministry the settlers proposed to abolish the
administrative headquarters in Boma, leaving Katanga directly
subordinate to the central administration in Brussels. The
province would have its own budget to be funded by the government's holdings in the copper industry, of which only a small
percentage would go to the central treasury in the Congo.

At this point the interests of the Colonial Ministry clearly
conflicted with those of the Elisabethvillois. Had the settlers'
plan been adopted the central administration and the poorer
provinces would have been deprived of a rich source of revenue
simply to satisfy the demands of the settler community. Without
a moment's hesitation the ministry overruled the settlers'
demands, thus maintaining the integrity of its hold on the Congo
as Parliament had originally intended.[23]

The rebuff put an end to this particular demand for provincial autonomy, but the question was by no means closed.
Monseigneur de Hemptinne and his associates remained convinced
that they, as patriotic Belgians, had a legitimate right to
control the government of Katanga. As Katanga developed, its
industries would bring increasing revenues to the colonial treasury, revenues which settlers in Elisabethville and officials
of the provincial government wanted to control. The province's
revenues would remain a growing treasure which Belgians in
Katanga wanted for their very own.

The groundwork thus was laid for a new controversy involving Belgian nationalism. For the defenders of Belgian law at
the Colonial Ministry the First World War had simply replaced

one set of enemies with another. Having withstood the challenge
of the British and the Germans, they now faced a band of Elisabethville settlers who championed a Belgium that was disappear-
ing in Europe. Francophone, Catholic, and capitalist, the city
was to become the last outpost of the Belgium of Léopold II.

The First World War had provided the founders of Elisabethville with opportunity to realize many of the plans which they
had made for the city. Between 1914 and 1917 the managers of
the Union Minière increased production and made the company
profitable for the first time in its history. Between 1917 and
1920 officials of the Belgian colonial administration realized
a dream of their own: the dislodgement of foreigners from
their positions of power in Katanga. In both cases, however,
the solution of one problem simply led to the discovery of
others. From this perspective the war years were less a water-
shed in the young city's development than a period during which
the forces involved in the city's creation had sorted themselves
out.

Chapter 5

Capital and Labor, 1920-27

The men who served as governors general of the Congo seldom visited Elisabethville during their term of office, even though the city was the second largest in the colony. Before the completion of the Bas-Congo Katanga Railway in 1928 the journey from Boma to the copperbelt took a minimum of three months. Even after communications had improved, however, governors general did not undertake the trip lightly because of fear of the reception they would receive from the local settlers. Thus it was a rare occasion when, just after the rainy season in 1921, Governor General Maurice Lippens visited Elisabethville.

Unlike his predecessors, Lippens came to his office through Belgian politics rather than African military service. A French-speaking Liberal from Ghent, Lippens had served as Governor of East Flanders and as a director of the oldest Belgian colonial company, the CCCI, before his appointment to the Congolese governor-generalship. His tour of the Congo, of which Elisabethville was only the first stop, was thus an introduction to the unfamiliar territory under his authority—a vast area which he had influenced but never visited. To broaden his perspective, Lippens had carefully studied the English-speaking territories through which he passed during his slow journey from Cape Town to Elisabethville. As a result of this itinerary, which included stops at several British administrative centers, Lippens was full of British administrative practices when he crossed the border into Belgian territory.[1]

Upon his arrival in Elisabethville Lippens necessarily changed his role from observer to chief executive. His position was enhanced by a vacuum in local leadership. Vice Governor General Tombeur had left Elisabethville definitively in July 1920 and his second-in-command, Commissioner General Léopold de Koninck, was scheduled to depart a month after Lippens' visit.

Thus the Governor General did not even have to contend with his own subordinates.

At first Lippens limited his activities to primarily ceremonial visits to government and private installations. On June 6, 1921, he laid the cornerstone of the Elisabethville cathedral, an edifice built to symbolize the power of Monseigneur de Hemptinne, the Prefect Apostolic. Like the prelate, however, the governor general was not content to play a passive role in his office. During his short stay in Elisabethville Lippens intervened decisively in public affairs with a brusqueness which appeared as almost calculated to offend the local administration.

As governor general, Lippens had no more legislative authority than the vice governor general of Katanga but he was, however, commander-in-chief of the Force Publique. He found his military authority a powerful tool to move the local administration. On one occasion Monseigneur Sak, head of the Salesian mission, asked him for help in completing a road from Elisabethville to the missionaries' farm on the Kafubu. Lippens immediately ordered the dispatch of soldiers from the army camp and prisoners from the local jail to do the job.[2]

The new governor general's initiative regarding the *cité indigène* was even more spectacular and would have long-range effects on the development of Elisabethville. His plans for the *cité* had their origin in his visit to South Africa where Lippens had been impressed by the management of the government locations in Johannesburg. These municipally-owned African quarters were physically removed from the European sections of town—in theory to prevent the spread of disease from Africans to Europeans. Emulating the South African model, Lippens ordered the immediate destruction of Elisabethville's *cité indigène* by the Force Publique and prison labor. In its stead a new *cité* was to be built, scientifically planned, hygienic, and removed from the European settlement.[3]

Katanga civil servants, unaccustomed to such arbitrary interference in their administrative routine, breathed a sigh of relief when the governor general left Elisabethville to visit his other domains, but the construction projects undertaken during Lippens's brief visit were to have a lasting effect on the development of the city. The new *cité indigène*, located a mile south of the old one, housed over three thousand Africans in 1923 (see Table 5.1). Dwellings in the new *cité*, subject to strict standards of construction, were far superior to those allotted to Africans at the time of Lippens's visit. Many of the new houses were built of brick; each block had its own sanitary facilities and water supply.[4] These superior living

Table 5.1

THE POPULATION OF ELISABETHVILLE, 1923-1929

AFRICANS:

Camps	1923	1929
Union Minière	3,290	6,765
CFK	1,300	2,670
Force Publique	1,750	1,672
Police Urbaine		224
BTK	500	
Corréa	500	
Robert Williams	250	
Total	7,590	11,331
Cité Indigène	3,200	11,339
Farming Villages	160	1,800*
Servants & Rural	2,500	5,470
Total	13,450	29,900
EUROPEANS:	2,094	3,535
GRAND TOTAL:	15,544	33,435

---

* Author's estimate

SOURCES: Africans: A. Chapelier, *Elisabethville: Essai de géographie urbaine*,; Administrateur Territorial A. Marquet's estimate of December 10, 1929 in AP, A 32, Dist H-L; Union Minière, Service Médical, Rapports annuels.

Europeans: J. Tasch, "Elisabethville d'autrefois," *Essor du Congo*, May 12, 1943.

The number of servants and semi-rural Africans is calculated on the basis of one servant for each European plus 25 percent for Africans not known to the Administration.

The 1929 figure for farming villages is a rough average of the 1928 and 1930 figures provided by Chapelier.

conditions attracted many Africans to the *cité* and by 1929 that quarter alone had a population of nearly twelve thousand. Thus Lippens's project, although hastily conceived, proved enormously successful.

The other important landmark begun at the time of the governor general's visit, the cathedral, was less a product of Lippens's policies—he was steadfastly anticlerical—but it was also to have an important effect on the lives of the inhabitants of Elisabethville, both black and white. Monseigneur de Hemptinne planned the massive edifice and supervised every stage of its construction, making the cathedral and his Benedictine order a dominant force in local affairs. It was not by chance that he placed his headquarters on Avenue Tombeur which connected with the main government offices and the residence of the vice governor general. And on many occasions in the course of the next twenty years Monseigneur de Hemptinne would appear to be more powerful than the chief executive of Katanga.

Strong men such as de Hemptinne and Lippens altered the city's physical appearance, but their powers were almost invariably limited to local affairs. Their impact on the physiognomy of Elisabethville, as a matter of fact, tended to conceal the fundamental relationsihps between the city and the outside, which would thus perpetuate the settlers' illusion that individuals on the spot could single-handedly control the copper capital's destiny. In reality, however, its prosperity and very survival still depended on external sources of capital and labor.

In the course of the 1920s Brussels replaced London finally and definitively as the source of capital for the development of the Katanga copperbelt. This shift in the balance of economic power was the result of new conditions growing out of the postwar settlement which ended competition between colonizers for control of African territory. Economically the new conditions fostered the flow of investment from each colonial power to its own colonies. As in the prewar period, political developments cleared the way for economic changes. Most basic to the future of the Congo was the question of whether the Belgians would retain their title to the colony.

During the First World War the possibility of confiscation of the colony by other European powers was finally laid to rest. Although the British government had in August 1914 opposed Belgian plans for the Congo to remain neutral, on September 2nd, they had committed themselves to the "integrity" of Belgian colonial possessions. The French government, which for years had held the right to first option on the Congo in the event it were sold, added its own assurances to the Belgians later in the war. In the "Déclaration de Saint Adresse" issued on April 29, 1916, the French government reaffirmed the Belgian title to the Congo and endorsed the right of the colony to collect an indemnity from the Germans for war damages.[5]

During the entire war only the freewheeling American representative, Colonel Edward House, ever raised any doubts about continued Belgian ownership of the Congo. House had been given wide latitude by President Wilson to find some formula—no matter how unconventional—for ending the war. House therefore suggested, in an interview with King Albert on February 2, 1916, that the Germans be allowed to purchase the Congo as part of an overall settlement of the war in Europe. The king vigorously opposed this suggestion and House let the matter drop. The idea of transferring the Congo to the Germans in order to get them to retire from their conquests in Europe had been characterized by one historian as a "fantastical scheme."[6] By the end of the war Belgian cession of the Congo had become unthinkable to all the major colonial powers.

Moreover, changes were taking place in international finances which discouraged British investment in Belgian colonial enterprise. Before 1918, it will be remembered, most of the capital invested in the Union Minière was raised by Robert Williams on the London market. As early as 1914, however, the British Treasury had restricted British investments in foreign enterprises. During the war these restrictions had been lifted for the Belgian copper industry, given the importance of the Union Minière's production for the Allied war effort. After 1919 the British government applied selective restrictions to the floating of foreign bond issues on the London market, but not on new issues of stock in overseas enterprises. Once again British investors were able to invest in the Union Minière—in this case through Robert Williams' Tanganyika Concessions, Ltd. —but in an atmosphere of official discouragement of investment in foreign enterprise.[7]

Beyond the disapproving attitude of the British government, changes in the European monetary system also discouraged British investment in Belgian colonial ventures. Before World War I the major nations of Europe had all been on the gold standard, and their currencies were thus freely interchangeable at a fixed rate. After the war, however, the Germans, French, Belgians, and even the British went off the gold standard, necessitating a system of variable exchange rates among their respective currencies and with the U. S. dollar, which alone among major currencies remained tied to gold. Of the major European currencies, the British pound fell less in value than the others, returning to its prewar value of $4.86 in 1925 when the British

reverted to the gold standard. The Belgian franc, while not
suffering the disastrous depreciation of the German mark, declined in relation to the pound sterling. Thus the exchange
rate fell continuously from thirty francs to the pound in 1919
to over one hundred seventy in 1927. [8]

This decline in the relative value of the Belgian franc
discouraged British investment in Belgian and Congolese enterprise, because the profits obtained had to be large enough to
offset the depreciation of the Belgian currency. Williams's
Tanganyika Concessions suffered particularly from this depreciation. In December 1920 TCL collected 4.9 million Belgian francs
in dividends on its shares of Union Minière stock for profits
earned during 1919. During the calendar year 1920 the value of
the franc in relation to the pound fell by nearly fifty percent.
As a result the British company received only Ł86,700 for dividends which would have been worth Ł163,000 at the beginning of
year.

By the early twenties, in fact, Tanganyika Concessions had
become little more than a holding company whose main assets were
its stock and purchasing rights in the Union Minière. The completion of the Benguela Railway was delayed until 1931, and up
to that date the railroad was a constant drain on the TCL's
resources. Only the magnitude of the Union Minière dividends
allowed Tanganyika Concessions to remain afloat; in fact, the
company did not pay its first dividend until 1925. Thus Tanganyika Concessions ceased to be an important agency for raising
capital for the Union Minière. In 1922 and again in 1925 the
company itself had to raise new capital on the London market
just to buy new issues of Union Minière stock—and it was able
to do so only with great difficulty. Meanwhile Robert Williams,
once the driving force behind the expansion of the Congo copper
industry, had become merely an exhausted hanger-on whose ultimate
success depended on the eventual completion of the Benguela
Railway. [9]

In the early 1920s, then, the combination of British entre-
preneurship and British capital, which had been so important in
the early development of the Union Minière, had lost its importance. Some money could still be raised on the British market,
but it was more difficult than it had been before or even during
the war to find new investors. British investors avoided enterprises whose dividends were paid in devalued francs and whose
assets were drained by chronically delayed railroad construction
in Angola. So, although British investments were not actually
removed from the Belgian copper industry, they remained static
and constituted a decreasing proportion of the Union Minière's
capital.

Fortunately for the copper industry, this decline in British investment had no adverse effect on the Union Minière's ability to raise capital because it was more than offset by new Belgian investments. The monetary conditions which discouraged the investment of sterling in franc-denomination securities worked to the advantage of Belgian investors. They could invest their rapidly depreciating francs in the copper industry, which sold its product for hard currency on the international metal market. Thus the sale of copper brought two profits: one based on the traditional difference between sale price and total price of production, and the other accruing from the acquisition and sale of sterling against devaluing francs.

This happy condition was not, however, automatic. Without adequate demand in the copper market, the Congolese industry could not have turned a profit. In 1920, as a matter of fact, the prospects for the copper industry seemed poor. Hit by the postwar recession, copper prices slumped from ₤122 per ton in January to ₤70 at the end of the year. In order to raise prices by restricting supply, leading American companies formed a combine. Some even closed their mines for a year to allow consumers to use up their stocks. On the surface, the prospects of the Belgian copper industry looked far from promising.

Taking a different tack from the Americans, the Belgians decided to expand production. The Union Minière, moreover, possessed a number of hidden assets which would help them ride out the slump. The completion of the Katanga Railway to Bukama on the Lualaba (Upper Congo) River had opened new, potentially rich deposits of copper, along with population centers to provide workers for expansion of the company's field of activities. Moreover, the company could count on the active support of both the Belgian and colonial government. Louis Franck, who had become colonial minister at the end of 1918, had promised to continue the Léopoldian tradition of government aid for the development of Belgian private industry in the Congo.

Finally the directors of the Société Générale, Belgium's largest bank as well as the major purveyor of Belgian capital to the Union Minière, had demonstrated their willingness to underwrite the expansion of the copper industry. Immediately after the war, before the fall of copper prices, the bank had already expanded its control of copper refining within Belgium. At the end of the war a subsidiary of the Société Générale had owned only one small plant, while the other two refineries were the property of the German copper trust. In 1919 the Belgian government confiscated the German plants and sold them to the Générale group. The amalgamated industry became the Société Métallurgique de Hoboken and its capital was increased from two million to twenty million francs.

these secondary refineries in Belgium put the
̣ strong position to help meet the slump in
ch hit the world market in 1920. Moreover, the
untapped deposits which were easily accessible
nded railroad; it could count on government
̣s on new investments from the Société Générale.
̣onditions struck Edgar Sengier, the bank's
ho recommended expansion after a tour of the
1921.[10]

̣e the Union Minière's Belgian capital came from
same sources drawn on in 1906 and in 1912, but
much larger scale. The Société Générale lent the
85 million francs, a large amount not withstand-
ing the ԁevᴜᵣᴜᴜtion of the franc—the company's capitalization
at the end of 1921 was only 76 millions. Furthermore, the total
expenditures of the Congo colonial government in that year
amounted to only 94 millions: the CSK, under government orders
as in 1912, subscribed 22 millions to a new issue of Union
Minière stock.

Colonial Minister Louis Franck proposed an ambitious program for the expansion of government activities in the Congo
which would parallel the expansion of the copper industry.
Franck's program envisioned public expenditures of 660 million
francs over a period of five years, including 300 millions to be
raised through colonial bonds and 75 millions of direct subsidies
from the Belgian parliament. Coinciding as it did with the
Union Minière's expansion program, the colonial minister's project stimulated Belgian investor interest in the Congo; capital
which before the war would have come from London was now easily
raised in Brussels.[11]

One indication of the growth of investment is the prolifer-
ation of new industries in Katanga which were partly-owned subsidiaries of the Union Minière. These included a coal company,
Charbonnages de la Luena; a building company, Cofoka; a milling
company, Minotéries du Katanga; a company to generate electric
power, Sogéfor; a company to distribute that power; and a chemical company, Sogéchim. At the end of the decade these subsidiaries had a combined nominal capitalization of 400 millions and
a market value several times that amount.[12]

The real value of Union Minière stock was even greater. At
the end of 1919 shares of common stock nominally worth 100 francs
each were selling for 1600 francs, the lowest price in the postwar period. By 1925 the same shares cost 4300 francs on the
Brussels bourse, forty-three times their book value. Katanga

enterprises, led by the Union Minière, had become a very good investment.[13]

The massive transfer of Belgian capital to the Union Minière and its subsidiaries in the early twenties made possible the vertical integration of the copper industry. By 1927 the company would obtain at least a measure of control over all phases of its African production. Beyond its mining and smelting operations, the Union Minière ran its own power and, as will be seen, recruited its own African staff. With the creation in 1926 of a single holding company encompassing the Benguela Railway, the Katanga Railway, and the BCK, the Union Minière obtained a controlling interest in all routes by which copper could be economically transported to the sea. Given this control of transportation facilities, the Union Minière was more vertically integrated than the American "Big Four" copper producers.

In addition to increased efficiency arising from vertical integration, the company made a concerted effort to improve its output and productivity. The new plants opened as a result of the 1921 decision to expand facilities were much more efficient than their predecessors. Between 1921 and 1922 productivity doubled from 2.5 to 5.2 tons per employee, leveling off at that point for the rest of the decade. New methods developed in the United States for the concentration of copper oxides made it possible to use a lower grade of ore and still get a marketable product. Thus the company expanded its output from 19,000 tons in 1920 to 43,000 tons in 1922 and 86,000 tons in 1924.[14]

Most of the new industrial development took place outside of Elisabethville, although the city benefited indirectly from the copper boom. The Union Minière augmented its African work force in the city and its immediate surroundings from 2,000 in 1918 to 3,500 in 1924 (see Table 5,1). This overall increase in the Union Minière's Elisabethville staff was paralleled by a similar increase in the African population of the *cité indigène*.[15]

The vast majority of workers employed in Katanga, however, worked outside of Elisabethville. Between 1922 and 1924 the Union Minière nearly doubled its work force—it rose from 7,500 to 14,000. The construction of the BCK railway required greater numbers of workers. By the mid-twenties Katanga's employers were in competition with one another for African labor.[16]

Once again growing demands for labor quickly outstripped the local supply. In 1923 recruiters for Northeastern Rhodesia, Katanga, and Angola brought only 12,400 men to the copperbelt— a quantity that fell short of current demand and was woefully

insufficient to meet the demand projected for 1924. For that
year the Union Minière and Katanga Railway alone needed 16,000
men. With the BCK construction, then, Katanga employers wanted
about three times the available supply of workers. The European
colonizers faced a labor crisis which was threatening the new
industries which had attracted so much Belgian capital.

Belgian administrators were anxious to help industrialists
in this emergency, but were constrained by legal limits on the
coercion of Africans after the First World War. By this time
forced labor conscription for the copperbelt had been more or
less abolished, although the practice continued for railway construction. The major stimuli to recruitment were the hut tax,
whose collection involved coercion or the threat of it, and the
more classical economic incentive of consumer goods which could
be obtained in exchange for wage labor.

Both British and Belgian administrators had long used the
hut tax as their principal means of getting Africans to work for
Europeans. In part the administrators wanted to satisfy European demands for labor, but they were even more strongly moti-
vated by the need to add revenue to their colonial treasuries.
For example, the British South Africa Company, which governed
Northern Rhodesia until 1926, was particularly hard pressed for
funds; raising the hut tax seemed the only way of balancing the
territory's budget.

Northern Rhodesian officials raised the hut tax in Northeastern Rhodesia, home of most Zambians on the Katanga copperbelt, from five shillings in 1919 to ten in 1920. After complaints by the territorial administration, the rate was reduced
to 7/6 in 1923. The initial rise in taxes stimulated engagements
for work in Katanga to unprecedented levels in 1920 and 1921,
when approximately 9,000 men a year joined Robert Williams and
Company's work crews at the Union Minière. In 1922 and 1923,
however, the engagement rate fell off to about half that of the
preceding years, rising again to about 7,000 in 1924 and 1925.
Thus except for the years 1920 and 1921 rising engagement taxes
do not seem to have coincided with higher hut taxes. Moreover,
the decline in the hut tax enacted in 1923 actually seems to
have stimulated recruitment.[16]

Another factor which appears more closely related to Zambian
engagement for the mines was the buying power that came from
wages in British currency. Until the end of the war inexperienced workers had received ten shillings for each thirty days'
labor; in February 1919 this salary increased to fifteen shillings.[17] More important than the actual amount was the fact
that the salary was paid in sterling rather than in depreciating

Table 5.2

SALARY OF ZAMBIAN UNSKILLED WORKERS AT THE UNION MINIERE

FOR A TICKET OF THIRTY DAYS, CONVERTED TO FRANCS, 1914-1926

Date	Wages	Exchange	Franc Equiv- alent	Cost of Living	Buying Power
6/1914	10/	30	15	100	15.00
6/1919	15/	30	22.50	125	18.00
6/1922	15/	58	43.50	248	17.54
6/1923	15/	87	65.25	349	18.70
6/1924	15/	95	71.25	407	17.51
6/1925	15/	101.33	76.00	442	17.19
6/1926	15/	158.17	117.13	832	14.08

SOURCES: *Rapport officiel de la Commission du coût de la vie au Katanga* (Elisabethville, 1919); *Renseignements de l'Office Colonial 1924, 160;* and *Congo belge, Rapports aux chambres* 1926, 116-17.

francs, so that the real earnings of Zambians kept pace with
the inflation in the cost of consumer goods on the Elisabethville market (see Table 5.2).

The situation was far more complicated for Congolese
workers on the copperbelt. Unlike the Zambians, Congolese
workers in Elisabethville's hinterland paid varying hut taxes.
Inhabitants of the eastern districts of Haut-Luapula and Tanganika-Moëro, who lived nearest the European employers, paid
higher taxes than inhabitants of the western districts of Lulua
and Lomami. The hut tax in the eastern districts remained at
approximately twelve francs from 1915 to 1924, while the rate
in the western districts was fixed at approximately six francs.
The administration raised the tax rate substantially in all districts but Tanganika-Moëro at the end of 1924. Until the most
critical moment in the labor crisis, the hut tax remained more
or less constant.

Increasingly effective methods of collection greatly wid-
ened the impact of the hut tax in rural Katanga. Before 1920
the best years were 1915 and 1917, during each of which the
Katanga administration collected about a million francs in hut
tax. Then in 1922 the tax collection for the province rose to
nearly 2 million francs; over 4 million francs were collected
in 1924. Considering the lower tax rates in the western districts, which were being exploited with greater intensity than
previously, this means that at least four times as many Congolese were paying their hut tax in 1924 than had done so in the
best years before 1920.

Surprisingly, the increased tax levies were not reflected
in recruitment figures from the Bourse de Travail du Katanga
(BTK) or independent recruiters. Although the Katanga agencies
recruited over 7,000 men in 1920, they did not again attain this
figure until 1923; the number fell off again in the crisis year
of 1924. Thus wider payment of taxes did not stimulate increased
engagement for the copperbelt. The Congolese paid their taxes
from other income, including the sale of agricultural products
and accumulated savings.[18]

The reluctance of Congolese to work on the copperbelt can
be attributed, at least in part, to the falling buying power of
their wages. The salary paid industrial employees of the Bourse
de Travail du Katanga for thirty days' labor remained more or
less constant at 15 francs from 1914 to 1923, despite a three
hundred percent rise in the cost of consumer goods. Some industries raised the wage rate to 18 francs in 1923, but more adequate salaries were not introduced until still later (see Table
5.3).

Table 5.3

SALARY OF CONGOLESE UNSKILLED WORKERS AT THE UNION

MINIERE FOR A TICKET OF THIRTY DAYS, 1914-1926

Date	Wages	Cost of Living	Buying Power
6/1914	15	100	15.00
6/1919	15	125	12.00
6/1922	15	248	6.05
6/1923	15	349	4.30
6/1924	30	407	7.37
6/1925	45	442	10.18
6/1926	70	832	8.41

SOURCE: See Table 5.2.

Between 1919 and 1923 Zambians received substantially higher wages from the Union Minière than the Congolese for equivalent work. Between 1923 and 1926 the gap narrowed a bit, but even in 1926 the Union Minière paid Zambians in sterling, representing twice the real wages which the Congolese received in francs (see Graph 5.1). Is it any wonder that the Congolese showed so little enthusiasm for jobs at the Union Minière?

This economic behavior contradicts the assumption held by most Europeans of a backward-bending labor supply curve. In this line of thinking, Europeans assumed that Africans wanted few consumer goods and would work only long enough to earn a target income, largely determined by their tax obligation. One would therefore expect that the number of Africans employed in European wage labor would increase if tax rates were raised as in Northern Rhodesia in 1920, or if more taxes were collected as in Katanga between 1920 and 1924. With the exception of the two years following the tax increase in Northern Rhodesia, however, this was not the case. For Zaïrian employees in particular, recruitment rates were more closely tied to potential buying power than to tax collection. As workers saw that they could purchase fewer goods with their earnings, they became less and less willing to work. Major stimulus to employment in the mines, however, was the fact that work on railway construction paid even less.

The condition of Africans employed in railway construction was aptly characterized in a June 1927 conversation between Belgian Prime Minister Henri Jaspar, who also held the colonial portfolio, and Sir Edward Grigg, governor of Kenya. Jaspar admitted to the Briton that in the Congo "it was impossible to build railways without forced labour." In 1925, when the minimum salary at the Union Minière had finally risen to forty-five francs for thirty days, the northern branch of the BCK construction was still paying its workers one cloth with a trade value of ten francs for a month's work. Thus, to men conscripted to build the railroads, even work on the copperbelt may have been more appealing than railway work closer to home for such low wages.[19]

Indeed, European employers on the copperbelt also took better care of their workers than did the BCK. Railway employees received low wages as well as poor provisions, since during construction a railway encountered enormous problems of food supply. Railway officials often argued that their crews lived so close to home that they could be supplied from their own villages. In practice, however, this was seldom the case, since the rail line —like that of the Katanga Railway—ran along the divide while the villages were in the valleys.[20] On the copperbelt the food

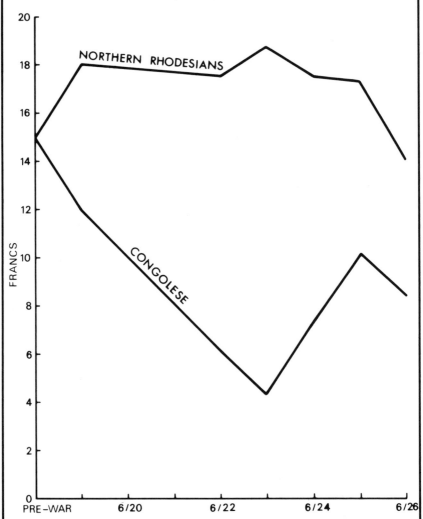

BUYING POWER OF INEXPERIENCED EMPLOYEES OF THE UNION MINIERE, 1914-26 (IN 1914 FRANCS)

NORTHERN RHODESIANS

CONGOLESE

FRANCS

20

18

16

14

12

10

8

6

4

2

0

PRE-WAR   6/20   6/22   6/24   6/26

Northern Rhodesian Wages Are Converted To Francs At The Union Minières Rate. Wages In Francs Are Adjusted By The Elizabethville Cost Of Living (1914 = 100). Neither Figure Includes Food Rations Which Were Provided By The Company.

UWM Cartographic Services

and lodging of work crews was a well-established employer obligation, since colonial law carefully specified the rations and housing conditions which each employer had to supply. Railroad construction workers came to regard the copperbelt as a place where Europeans would better provide for their African employees than on the railroads.

In sum, the inhabitants of rural Katanga had learned by the middle twenties that Europeans were not going to leave them undisturbed in their villages. Since young men had to earn tax money for themselves and their families, it was better to take a job with an employer who provided tolerable living conditions and access to consumer goods than to be mistreated without compensation closer to home by the BCK.

Some Africans avoided European recruiters, taking their employment into their own hands. Those who had worked on the copperbelt knew that they could be hired on the spot, sometimes at higher wages than those offered by the recruiting agencies. Men who had acquired special work skills or a little French could get relatively well-paying jobs on their own initiative.[21]

In 1924 the CSK reported that many of the workers who were hired on their own were earning more than their recruited counterparts. Domestic servants, to take an example, earned from 35 to 100 francs a month plus food and lodging, far more than ordinary BCK recruits. Skilled Africans commanded even higher salaries, earning—according to CSK estimates—from 70 to 500 francs a month. Competition for skilled workers became so keen that the large corporations had trouble holding on to their skilled African employees. Between 1923 and 1926 the desertion rate among seasoned workers at the Union Minière varied from 11 to 18 percent, rates nearly double that of the company employees as a whole. Thus experienced wage earners derived a comparative advantage from the labor shortage, commanding higher wages than their unskilled recruited counterparts.[22]

During these years of labor shortage certain patterns emerged which were to have an important effect both on settlement patterns and later migrations to Elisabethville. A major distinction developed between recruits and volunteers. The former were those who had been brought to town by a large organization; in general they lived in the camps under the close supervision of their employers. The volunteers were usually veterans of the recruitment process who had either remained in the city at the completion of their terms or who had returned to the city on their own. They tended to live in the new *cité indigène*, relatively free of European control.

Certain ethnic groups also began to show a marked preference for either the camps or the *cité*. As far as Zambians are concerned, the Bena Chishinga and the Kazembe's people, both from the lower Luapula Valley, preferred the *cité* while the Aushi from the upper Luapula preferred the camps. Exact statistics are unavailable, but estimates of African migration from the lower Luapula range from two to three thousand per year in the late twenties, compared with about three hundred from the upper Luapula. Recruiters, by contrast, obtained between one and two thousand men a year from the upper Luapula and from one to five hundred from the lower Luapula.

The difference between the two regions seems to have arisen from their divergent economic conditions. The Fort Rosebery subdistrict, which encompassed the Zambian side of the upper Luapula, was substantially poorer than the Kawambwa subdistrict downstream. In 1926, for example, only 40 percent of the able-bodied men in Fort Rosebery subdistrict paid their hut tax as compared with over 75 percent in Kawambwa. When the Aushi of Fort Rosebery subdistrict were compelled to pay their taxes, they were especially receptive to the recruiters who sent them to the mining camps. Most Africans from the lower Luapula could earn their tax money at home, and so those that migrated did so in hope of obtaining greater wealth rather than just a guaranteed source of income.[23]

A similar division appeared among the Zaïrians. The migrants from Lomami district, which later became part of the Kasai province, tended to prefer the camps, while Africans from the rest of Katanga favored the *cité indigène*. This seems to have been a result of their experience in the early twenties. The Kasaians, subjected to forced labor on the BCK construction, saw the camps as havens from harassment. The Katangese, who had not suggered this trauma, drifted to the *cité* where they could command higher wages—if they could find jobs.

In addition to these trends in the pattern of African settlement in Elisabethville during the 1920s, a broad discrepancy emerged between the standard of living in the city and that in the countryside. During the labor crisis of the mid-twenties European employers improved the living conditions of their African staff in order to keep them on the job. By the end of the decade Africans in Elisabethville enjoyed the best food and housing of any blacks in the whole of Central Africa. Rural areas suffered by comparison, as well as absolutely, as a result of excessive recruitment. In the absence of the able-bodied men, the women, children, and old people were unable to maintain adequate agricultural production. Death rates increased and many rural areas were depopulated.

Europeans with a social conscience, who were aware of the
deplorable conditions prevalent in rural areas, had for several
years made efforts to ameliorate this situation. In fact, one
group, originally appointed to find ways of obtaining more labor
from rural areas, ended up in restricting recruitment. Late in
1923 the Katanga government convened a special subcommittee of
the Belgian Commission for the Protection of Natives to look
into the labor shortage. Chaired by the magistrate Antoine
Sohier, it had among its members representatives of the government, of the missions—including Monseigneur de Hemptinne himself—and of Katanga's business community, but not of the BCK
or of the Union Minière. Sohier had served on an earlier commission appointed in 1918 to investigate the labor potential of
those areas of eastern Katanga which had been devastated by the
campaign against the Germans, so he was prepared for the suffering which his committee discovered. Conditions had in fact
deteriorated, and the committee recommended strict limits on
recruitment rather than any increases. Where the earlier committee had suggested that no more than 25 percent of the able-
bodied men in any region be recruited for long-distance labor,
the new committee suggested a maximum of 10 percent.

Their suggestions were reinforced by international pressure.
Reports of conditions in rural Katanga reached the Anti-Slavery
Commission of the League of Nations, which in July 1925 condemned
all administrative practices favoring recruitment. Martin
Rutten, now governor general of the Congo, sympathized with
Katanga employers, but felt that the colonial government had no
alternative but to accede to the commission's demand. Having
lived through the rubber scandals, Rutten was not disposed to
allow the Congo again to become the object of international
opprobrium. To implement the needed reforms, he proposed two
emergency measures: a total ban on recruitment in seriously
depopulated areas, and the termination of all administrative
help for recruiters. Thus in the ten months between November
1925 and September 1926 Governors Bureau and Heenen of Katanga
banned recruitment in most of the Haut-Luapula, Lomami, and
Lulua districts.

The final blow to Katanga industry fell in December 1925
when the government of Northern Rhodesia, now determined to
develop its own mines, restricted the number of Zambians allowed
to work in Katanga. In the early twenties British and American
companies, encouraged by new techniques for processing copper
ores containing sulfides, had decided to develop deposits in
Northern Rhodesia. Aided by veterans of the Katanga industry
such as P. K. Horner who had been chased away by the Belgians,
they persuaded the British administration to prohibit the migration of Northern Rhodesian Africans to the Congo through the
device of setting diminishing quotas.

Fortunately for the Union Minière, Governor General Rutten, who had done so much to promote Belgian control of the copper industry, had already prepared a plan to provide the company with new sources of African labor. Rutten suggested that the Union Minière be given recruitment monopolies in Belgian territories beyond Katanga. Although this would force the company to spend more on labor transportation, the managers readily agreed with Rutten. In 1926 the government granted the company recruitment rights in the Maniema district of Orientale Province as well as in the mandated territory of Ruanda-Urundi. In 1927 these rights were extended to three territories of the Lomami district where the railway had been completed: Kabinda, Tshofa, and Kanda-Kanda. With all this new territory to hunt in, the recruitment missions succeeded in overcoming the shortage of labor (see Tables 5.4, 5.5, 5.6).

Although the Maniema and Ruanda-Urundi programs were short-lived, the principle of having its own recruitment centers became established as a new company policy. Instead of importing a large number of men from many areas for short terms of work, thereafter the Union Minière concentrated on getting its labor supply for long terms from a limited area.

Smaller employers were also guaranteed a share of the available labor by a reorganized version of the BTK called the Office Central du Travail du Katanga (OCTK). It is characteristic of the government attitude toward industry that small employers received their labor allotment only after the needs of the BCK and the Union Minière had been satisfied. This policy was reflected in the composition of the OCTK's local executive committee, which consisted of two delegates from the Union Minière and one each from the CSK, the Katanga railway, and the smaller industries. Small employers thus commanded only one-fifth of the seats on the board of the organization which had been designed to protect their rights to African labor.

As of 1927 the Union Minière's recruitment problem was solved. The managers could count on labor from their own missions as well as those of the OCTK. But even then they could not afford to continue the wasteful South African model of short term service. Their labor supply was adequate only if they could persuade their employees to work for years rather than months at a time. To do this they had to make their camps more attractive.[24]

Other large employers, notably the railway, also soon found it necessary to copy the Union Minière's policy of encouraging long-term residency in the camps in order to maintain an adequate labor supply. Thus the scarcity of labor which had plagued

Table 5.4

RECRUITMENT BY THE UNION MINIERE 1926-1930, IN HUNDREDS

	MANIEMA	RUANDA URUNDI	KASAI LOMAMI	TOTAL
1925		2		2
1926		14	7	21
1927	8	5	29	42
1928	3	19	25	47
1929		17	22	39
1930		19	18	37

SOURCE: Fetter, "L.U.M.H.K., 1920-1940," p. 19.

Table 5.5

THE UNION MINIERE AFRICAN WORK FORCE

1928-1931, IN HUNDREDS

	1928	1929	1930	1930
Lomami	28	34	36	34
Other Katanga	64	60	55	38
Maniema	7	1	0	0
CONGO	99	95	91	72
RUANDA-URUNDI	6	25	41	27
NE Rhodesia	34	19	8	1
NW Rhodesia	8	13	4	0
N. RHODESIA	42	32	12	1
OTHER COLONIES	6	15	15	8
DIVERSE	1	6	4	1
TOTAL	153	173	163	109

SOURCE: Fetter, "L.U.M.H.K., 1920-1940," p. 20.

Table 5.6

THE UNION MINIERE AFRICAN WORK FORCE,

1928-1931, IN PERCENTAGE

	1928	1929	1930	1931
Lomami	18	19	22	31
Other Katanga	41	35	34	35
Maniema	5	0	0	0
CONGO	64	54	56	66
RUANDA-URUNDI	5	15	25	25
NE Rhodesia	22	11	5	1
NW Rhodesia	5	7	3	0
N. RHODESIA	27	18	8	1
OTHER COLONIES	4	9	9	7
DIVERSE	0	4	2	1
TOTAL	100	100	100	100

SOURCE: See Table 5.5.

Katanga industry ultimately resulted in the improvement of conditions for Africans living in Elisabethville's larger camps.

Similar improvements attracted Africans into the *cité indigène*. Africans there benefited from the higher wages that
smaller employers had to offer in order to compete with the
large Katanga firms. Beyond wages, the rebuilding of the *cité*
ordered by Governor General Lippens insured that Africans there
would enjoy better housing than had previously been available in
Elisabethville.

These improvements in the quality of African life in Elisabethville would not have come without the infusion of Belgian
capital into Katanga industry which occurred in the early
twenties. However, it was only after Belgian financiers had
decided to develop the Katanga mines to their full output that
they saw that the region's labor supply was inadequate. Once
this capital had been invested, however, Belgian financiers
could not afford to abandon Katanga. Lacking sufficient cheap
labor, they therefore had to spend more money on their African
work force than they had originally anticipated. This expendi-
ture, quite independent of the managers' motives, made Elisabethville more attractive to thousands of Africans.[25]

It was increased supply of capital that had ultimately stimulated the demand for an increased supply of labor. Management
might have preferred to rely on labor recruited by force or by
the pressures of the hut tax, but such labor was simply insufficient to meet expanding industrial demands. The result was
increased expenditures on labor which took two forms: at the
Union Minière, management allocated most of its disbursements to
indirect labor costs rather than to salaries. Thus the mining
company built better houses and hospitals for employees while
granting relatively small salary increases. Smaller employers,
unable to afford such amenities, attracted their labor by increasing salaries.

By the late 1920s then, Africans in Elisabethville had two
distinct choices as to the kind of urban life they wanted to live.
Some were attracted to the camps, which offered good food, housing,
and medical care, but relatively low salaries; others preferred
the higher salaries offered by smaller employers. These two environments, the camp and the *cité*, were to promote quite unlike
forms of African development in the years to come. But regard-
less of these differences and in contrast to the earlier period,
by then Elisabethville was becoming a desirable place to live
for many Africans as well as for Europeans.

Chapter 6

Life in the Boom Years

Elisabethville's society, divided as it was into distinct white and black sections, had taken on a certain permanence by the late 1920s. The first prospectors and conscripted laborers who had come to the city on the waves of the copper rush had given way to more stable settlers, Europeans and Africans alike, who had chosen to live in the city after a certain reflection. Many brought their wives and began to raise families, thus transforming the population from a pioneering society composed predominantly of men of working age to a more stable one that had a high proportion of women, children, and—eventually—old people.

As in the early days, larger employers provided housing in their camps for European employees, but the practice became less common in the 1920s. White employees objected to the dreary rows of identical wooden houses with iron roofs, each provided with servant's hut in back. Instead, they wanted to live away from the camps in the European quarter in a brick bungalow with its own garden. Given the expense of maintaining European housing, the companies gradually relented. The Union Minière, for example, allowed all Europeans to leave its camp except for production workers in the foundry.

Despite the movement of Europeans out of the camps, the work force of the large companies was demographically distinct from the rest of the white population. Union Minière employees, who constituted about 30 percent of the city's white population (see Table 6.1), were less often joined by their families than were other Europeans. In 1924, for example, the sex ratio among white copper company employees in Elisabethville was 3,900 men per thousand women, whereas the masculinity ratio in the rest of the European city was 1,700 per thousand.[1]

Table 6.1

EUROPEANS IN CAMP AND TOWN, 1921-1930

Year	Union Minière Employees and Families	Rest of Europeans	Elisabethville Total
1921	517	1,021	1,538
1922	missing	missing	1,779
1923	620	1,429	2,049
1924	713	1,726	2,439
1925	906	1,577	2,483
1926	1,003	1,645	2,648
1927	1,062	missing	missing
1928	1,018	2,101	3,119
1929	945	2,590	3,535
1930	823	2,167	2,990

SOURCES: U.M.H.K., Service Médical, "Rapports annuels," 1921-1930. (Extrapolated from Malaria Statistics.) J. Tasch, "Elisabethville d'autrefois," *Essor du Congo*, May 12, 1943.

Union Minière employees, moreover, were more likely to be
of Belgian nationality than other Europeans in Elisabethville.
Between 1924 and 1930, 82 percent of the Europeans at all Union
Minière installations were Belgians. Assuming that this ratio
applied to the Elisabethville installations where, during these
years, company employees numbered 945 staff and family, the
Elisabethville camps were comprised of 775 Belgians and 170
other Europeans. This high proportion of Belgians did not,
however, carry over to the city as a whole which, according to
European school records covering the same period, was only 58
percent Belgian. Thus, when the Union Minière employees are
subtracted from the European population of the cities as a whole,
the foreign character of the rest of the population becomes
evident. Outside of the copper camps, the city was only 46 percent Belgian, a little more than half of the percentage of
Belgians at the Union Minière.

Even among the Belgians in Elisabethville, the employees
of the Union Minière were distinct from the rest of the community
in previous occupation and geographic origin. The copper company recruited most of its staff from the coal mines of Hainaut
where it could find skilled workers. The other Belgians, most
of them government bureaucrats, came primarily from Brabant,
the province which included Brussels. These diverse hiring
patterns fostered divisions among the Belgians in Elisabethville:
those who worked outside the Union Minière tended to look down
their noses at the manual workers, at the same time envying
their higher industrial salaries.[2]

Belgians, although of such heterogeneous origin, could
adapt to Elisabethville with relative ease because they were
welcome there; foreigners had a much harder time of it. After
the troubles of Elisabethville's first decade, Belgian officials
distrusted foreign whites and tried to discourage them from
staying permanently. In 1929 the colonial government established strict rules governing immigration and even visits by
white foreigners to the Congo. At the border each foreigner
had to provide evidence of his financial solidity before he
could enter the Congo.

This unfriendly atmosphere eventually led some foreign
whites to leave the city, especially during the 1930s. During
the depression many of the oldest settlers—British South
Africans and Ashkenazic Jews with family connections in South
Africa—returned home. By contrast, the original Italian community from the Piedmont stayed, supplemented by a new wave of
foreigners—Jews of Italian nationality from the isle of Rhodes
and Greeks from the Dodecanese. The new foreign settlers were
poorer and less well-educated than the English-speakers although

they worked at the same occupations, almost all being merchants.
Thus the change in the nationality of Elisabethville's white
foreign population did not substantially alter the role of the
foreign community in the city's economy.[3]

Despite the highly segmented nature of Elisabethville's
European society, several factors surfaced during the 1920s
which gave the white community a certain cohesiveness. All
lived under Belgian rule. All were part of a miniscule white
island in a black sea.

Their sense of a common experience was reinforced by the
school system. Although there were no public schools, almost
all European children attended the two local Catholic schools
run by the Salesian Fathers and the Sisters of Charity. Both
the College St. François de Sales for boys and the Ecole Marie-
José for girls had been founded in 1911, less than a year after
Elisabethville's foundation. By the 1920s these schools were
providing a junior high education for most of the European
children in the city. As settlers' children grew older they
became part of a common subculture which surpassed the religious
and national differences which separated their parents.

Although Elisabethville was a strictly segregated society,
the changes which took place in its African community during the
1920s were remarkably similar to those which took place in its
European community. The African population was also divided
along ethnic and national lines which tended to coincide with
occupation, and employees of the Union Minière came to be
sharply differentiated from other blacks living in the city.
Despite these differences, moreover, the Africans of Elisabethville, like their European counterparts, began to share a common
local subculture.

At the end of the 1920s the greatest differentiation among
Elisabethville's thirty thousand Africans was the demographic
one between Africans working at the Union Minière camp and those
living in the *cité indigène*. The copper company had diminished
in relative importance; only 23 percent of the city's Africans
lived on company property in 1929 (see Table 5.1). Those
Africans who worked for the Union Minière, however, were more
permanently established than other Africans. Fragmentary statistics indicate that more of them lived with their wives than
did Africans working for other employers. In 1928 the sex ratio
for Africans in the Elisabethville Union Minière camps was 2,700
men per thousand women. A year later the sex ratio for Zambians
living in the Elisabethville district—most of whom worked outside of the copper industry—was 3,900 men per thousand women
(see Table 6.2). Demographically, then, Africans in the Union

Minière camps were more likely to be living with their families than Africans in the *cité*. Paradoxically, Europeans in the mining camps were less likely to be living with their families than other Europeans.

The Union Minière camps were also beginning to acquire a different ethnic composition from that of the *cité*. In the late 1920s the copper company began to replace its Zambians with Zaïrois. Thus in 1929 the camps were 37.5 percent Zambian, while the district as a whole was 44 percent Zambian (see Table 6.2). This tendency would be accentuated at the beginning of the depression when the Union Minière would fire all but a handful of its remaining Zambians.

Moreover, as indicated in the preceding chapter, the Union Minière tended to hire Zambians of a different origin than those who worked outside of the company camps. Recruiters for the copper mines worked primarily in the Fort Rosebery sub-district, which included the upper Luapula Valley, home of the Aushi people. The *cité* in Elisabethville, by contrast, tended to attract Lunda and Bena Chishinga people from the Kawambwa subdistrict in the lower Luapula valley. Thus the Union Minière camps were acquiring demographic characteristics which were quite different from those of the rest of the population of Elisabethville.[4]

The creation of a common urban culture which bridged the gap between *cité* and camp was much slower to develop among Africans than in the European settler community. Missionary schools were part of the problem. All European children attended the Catholic schools, while in the 1920s African children were served by competing Catholic and Methodist school systems. Even when the Catholics had virtually eliminated their Protestant competitors, however, strong barriers still separated the *cité* and the camps, because the European rulers of Elisabethville fostered division in the African community.

These divisions were not so much the product of a conscious policy of divide and rule; they were rather the result of company policies aimed at maximizing production. The Union Minière carefully chose its work force with an eye to getting the most out of them. It preferred workers of Belgian and Congolese nationality because it had greater control over them than over foreigners, whether white or black. The careful selection of personnel, moreover, was only one policy employed by the company in the management of the camps. Once individuals were hired by the Union Minière, they became members of a rigid hierarchy.

TABLE 6.2

AFRICAN POPULATION STATISTICS
FOR GREATER ELISABETHVILLE, 1928-29

Place	Men	Women	Children	Total
Elisabethville city.				
Union Minière camps: (Lubumbashi-Etoile- Ruashi)				
Zambians	1563	577	317	2462
Zaïrois	2612	961	528	4101
Total	4180	1538	845	6563[1]

Newly created Elisabethville district.

(Entire city-Kipushi-Rural)

	Men	Women	Children	Total
Zambians	5746	1476	1077	8301[2]
	MASCULINITY RATIO 3,900			
Zaïrois	7283	3149	2341	12,773[3]
	MASCULINITY RATIO 2,300			

1. The Zambian and Zaïrian sub-totals are extrapolated from the overall totals at a ratio of 37.5% Zambians, 62.5% Zaïrois.

2. All men either at work or looking for it.

3. Includes rural population

SOURCES: U.M.H.K., Service Main d'Oeuvre Indigène, "Rapport annuel, 1928,". J.C.C. Coxhead, "Report on Rhodesian Natives in the Katanga," October, 1929. In Zambian Archives, ZA 1/9 18/34,

Subordinate Belgian employees lived under tighter controls than anyone else in the copperbelt. Using the terminology suggested by the social psychologist Erving Goffman, they lived in a total institution. According to Goffman, a total institution is an establishment whose inhabitants sleep, play, and work under a single authority which organizes their activities according to a tight routine. "The various enforced activities," according to Goffman, "are brought together in a single rational plan purportedly designed to fulfill the official aims of the institution."[5]

In the case of the Union Minière, the official aim was the production of copper. In the first fifteen years of its existence the company had employed less rigid forms of organization, and then after 1921 had decided that the independence of its European workers lowered output. South Africans—who had constituted a high proportion of the European employees before 1920 —had been particularly troublesome, holding up production over salaries and working conditions: Belgians hired to replace them were more docile. The alternative of having to return to Europe, where unemployment was high and wages low, kept Belgian workers in line. As the company increased the proportion of Belgins on the European staff—from 44 percent in 1920 to 91 percent in 1930 —it was also increasing the likelihood of having a compliant work force.

Since Belgian subordinate employees had such a weak bargaining position, the company was able to impose draconian discipline designed to keep even the most obstreperous employees in line. Forbidden to bring their families to Africa, first-term employees lived together in company housing, ate together at the company mess, and worked together in the camps. Even their leisure hours were restricted, at least in theory, to acceptable amusements such as company clubs and football teams, which were provided as an incentive to keep them in the camps. Needless to say, many let off steam on weekends with drink and prostitutes.

Legally, Union Minière employees had fewer rights than their counterparts in Belgium. Industrial strikes and trade unions had been made illegal after the disruptions of 1919-20. Social welfare measures such as compensation for work accidents and old age pensions were voluntary, dependent upon a contribution of the worker to be matched by that of the company. Even these benefits could be lost easily, since employees who were fired or ladi off were repatriated with a loss of pension rights. Thus the lower levels of European workers lived very much at the mercy of the Union Minière.[6]

Those in the higher echelons of the Union Minière did not live under such strict discipline, but in the course of the 1920s they too became part of the great copper machine. At the beginning of the decade each of the camps was judged as an independent production unit. Directors of individual mines and the smelter, rightfully considering themselves in constant competition with one another for output, devised all sorts of schemes to promote their own operation without any concern for the company as a whole. Disregarding long term considerations, managers paid employees associated with production consistently higher salaries than those involved in maintenance. This competition between units reached its peak in 1923 during the labor shortage, when mine managers attempted to lure Africans from other camps into their own. This shortsighted strategy of pitting the managers against each other was finally abandoned when the company began to treat all installations as part of a single integrated unit of production.[7]

The integration of copper production was organized by Léon Rasson who served as director general of African operations from 1923 to 1927. Like most of the other Union Minière managers of the day, Rasson was an engineer who received his training in both chemical and electrical engineering at the School of Mines in Mons. After seventeen years in Belgium and another seven in Russia, Rasson moved to the Congo as part of the new Belgian team which replaced the Anglo-Saxons after World War I. He worked first as assistant director to Jules Cousin, whom he then replaced when the latter was promoted to the position of representative in Africa of the board of directors.[8]

As director general, Rasson created the framework for a modern line and staff organization. Previously the company had been divided into production units, notably the mines and smelter, and special departments—including the medical services; the geological service, responsible for finding new mine sites; and the research department, which developed new techniques of refining metals. Under the old system these special departments had been neglected because they did not contribute directly to company profits. Realizing that they contributed to the long-run welfare of the Union Minière, Rasson reorganized the company to favor the nonproduction departments. The director general and the heads of the camps were treated as line officers, retaining final authority in their respective spheres, but they had to consult with the heads of special departments. The latter were elevated to the status of staff officers who now disposed the authority and money necessary to be treated as equals by the line officers.

This reinforcement of the nonproduction departments made possible a final stage in Rasson's reorganization of the Union Minière. In 1926 he reorganized the Native Labor Service, which had previously been responsible for Africans only while they were in the company camps. The new department, provided with ample funds and capable leadership, also assumed responsibility for the recruitment of workers in the company's newly established labor preserves as well as for all aspects of their care and treatment in the camps.

The effect of this reorganization on Africans in the camps will be discussed below, but as far as company organization is concerned the strengthening of the Native Labor Service completed the administrative reorganization begun a few years earlier. The role of departments not directly linked to production had been defined, each department had its own set of tasks which it was expected to perform, and the central administration in Elisabethville henceforth had greater control over the allocation of resources within the company.[9]

In addition to reforming its standard operations, the Union Minière was in the process of creating a group of subsidiaries which performed services linked to the growth of the copper industry, and which were in part created to absorb profits which would otherwise have been distributed to British shareholders and the Congo government. At first they were absorbing capital rather than generating it, in contrast to the mother company, and they received close supervision from the Belgian bankers who had originally funded the Union Minière.

The chief guardians of Société Générale interests in Elisabethville from the mid-twenties onward were Jules Cousin and Edgar Sengier. Between 1923 and 1935 Cousin served as Representative in Africa of the company's board of directors. Having first arrived in Elisabethville in 1911, Cousin was an old hand at the Union Minière; his background was also archetypical of that of Belgian top management—Walloon, Catholic, and trained as an engineer. For years he was one of a handful of leaders of Elisabethville society, dominating the Union Minière by day and the settler community by night. As local head of the company responsible for Elisabethville's industrial development, Cousin considered few men his equal.

This captain of industry deferred to only two men in Elisabethville, his cousin, Edgar Sengier, managing director of the Union Minière who was eventually named to the Board of Directors of the Société Générale, and Monseigneur de Hemptinne, the head of the Catholic Church in Katanga. Of these, Sengier was almost permanently absent from the Congo after 1922. Although he had

played a key role in the Belgian takeover of the Union Minière
and was a certified engineer, he spent more of his life in European financial circles than in the copper mines. Sengier accompanied kings and colonial ministers to Africa to see that they
came away with "sound" views of the Union Minière, and he then
returned to report on his activities to the board of directors
in Brussels, to which he had been elected in 1924. Thus like
many American executives of the time, Sengier had become a liai-
son man rather than the engineer for which he had been trained.
He received enormous deference when he visited Elisabethville,
but he was seldom there to enjoy it.

Monseigneur de Hemptinne, by contrast, was almost permanently resident in Elisabethville from 1920 until his death in
1957. Like Cousin, the Monseigneur enjoyed almost unquestioned
authority by virtue of his position as head of the Benedictine
Order in Katanga as well as his autocratic personality. The
future archbishop, however, came from a background quite different from that of Cousin and Sengier. He was a French-speaker
from Ghent and scion of one of the wealthiest noble families in
Flanders.

Using his personal prestige as a springboard, the prelate
built up a power base which gave enormous authority to Benedictines. In the early 1920s most of his projects were personal,
such as management of the construction of the Elisabethville
cathedral and membership on the Katanga Subcommission for the
Protection of Natives. Having thus acquired personal influence,
he was able to help his fellow Benedictines. The prize which
the prelate sought and eventually obtained was spiritual but
with economic overtones—the evangelization of the thousands of
Africans who were leaving their homes to work on the copperbelt.[10]

Meanwhile two other religious groups stood in the Benedictines' way—the Belgian Catholic Salesian Fathers and the American Protestant Methodists. Of the two competing groups, the
older was the Salesian Order which had come to Elisabethville
in 1911. Its members ran school for both African and European
boys, responsibilities which had overtaxed their small staff and
meager resources. On the one hand, they were obliged to provide
enough classes for European boys to satisfy powerful Belgian
parents; on the other, they had to compete with the Methodists
for souls of the copperbelt's African children.

The situation came to a head in 1924 when a shortage of
funds forced Monseigneur Joseph Sak, head of the Salesian mission, to recommend the closing of the two highest grades at
their *collège* for European boys on account of their low enrol-
ments. In response parents, led by Attorney General Antoine

Sohier, insisted not only that these classes be continued even
if they enrolled only one or two students, but that a full
junior high school program be offered as well. Maintaining
these projects left the order with little money for running its
African schools.

This was a particularly bad time to be short of funds: because the Methodists were then expanding their schools, the
government expected the Catholic missions to compete with them.
In 1924 Monseigneur de Hemptinne's Benedictines took over the
Salesians' elementary schools for African boys, although the
girls' school remained in the hands of the Sisters of Charity.
In 1926 the Salesians even offered to abandon their *collège*, but
the Congo administration refused their offer. The Salesians
were allowed to keep their trade school, but they had to move it
and its 130 students out of town to a farm on the Kafubu river
where they had earlier established a minor seminary. By way of
compensation for the exile from Elisabethville, the Salesians
received ecclesiastical jurisdiction over territory in extreme
Southern Katanga around the town of Sakania, a scene of recent
religious unrest.[11]

The Benedictines assumed control of the African boys' schools
in Elisabethville at a highly opportune moment, since the Belgian
government would soon decide to subsidize schools run by Belgian
Catholic missions. The government's 1925 decision was as much
political as religious. Even former colonial minister Louis
Franck, a staunch anticlerical in Belgian politics, had long
felt that the Catholic missions were a necessary agency of social
control over Africans who had left their traditional milieu to
work in the mines. The task, according to Franck, was so delicate that it could not be shared with foreign Protestants, who
might succumb to the temptation of using the naive Africans for
their own political ends.[12]

Fear of Protestant influences also grew in the Congo itself.
In the late twenties Belgians at the Union Minière, who had previously shown no particular preference for Catholic missionaries,
joined government officials in harassing the Protestants. Their
changed attitude was due in part to fears that Protestants were
fostering African syncretic sects such as Kimbanuism and Kitawala, whose adherents were then disrupting public order in other
parts of the Congo.[13]

In fact, the Protestant schools soon proved to be no real
danger to Belgian influence in Katanga and government subsidies
enabled the Catholics to outstrip them within a short time. In
1928 there were 96 Protestant missionaries and 245 Catholics;
in Katanga the Protestants claimed 4,000 African members and

probationers, while the Catholic total was about 12,000.   In
Elisabethville 104 children attended Protestant schools, whereas
the newly created Benedictine schools alone had 495 students.[14]

Union Minière management supported education by the Benedictines because they felt that some education by the missionaries would produce better workers. Also the head of the Benedictines, Monseigneur de Hemptinne, had enunciated economic
theories consistent with the policies and practise of the company management. Traditional economy, as he described it in 1928,
made the African a poor worker. The evil lay in community
property, which deprived workers of any personal ambition or
notion of progress. The only cure for these ills, he believed,
was to put Africans to work for Europeans so that they might
become assimilated to the European way of life. A Benedictine
education would be an aid to that goal. In 1931 de Hemptinne
announced that his school should prepare stabilized Africans to
be "the humble, but necessary collaborators of the great industry into which they were born."[15]

As it happened, the Benedictines built far better schools
than any that had yet been provided in the Congo. The Methodists,
so much feared by the Belgian administration, were out of touch
with the local African community. They were losing their potential clientele—mainly workers from Northern Rhodesia and Nyasaland whose immigration to Katanga in the late 1920s was discouraged by the British government. Until 1927 the media of
instruction in the Methodist schools were Bemba and English, the
language of these foreign Africans, rather than Swahili and
French. Given this irrelevance, the Methodists left the Catholics
with little to fear.[16]

Thus between 1924 and 1927 Monseigneur de Hemptinne had
obtained for his Benedictine order two valuable franchises for
the education of Africans. Thereafter his order received subsidies from both the government and the Union Minière to run
schools for Africans. Although the amounts involved were by no
means substantial, they permitted the Benedictines to establish
an educational network which eventually included scores of
African teachers and thousands of African students. This in-
structional empire further added to Monseigneur de Hemptinne's
personal authority. He became the local expert on native
affairs, and a regular contributor to local and metropolitan
journals.

From the middle twenties onward the prelate's most important
forum was the Comité Régional du Katanga, the consultative body
which had been created just before the First World War. Super-
ficially, the *comités régionaux*, which existed in all four

provinces in the Congo, resembled the legislative councils which
the British established in their colonial empire. Both types
of assembly were composed of a mixture of government officials
and private citizens chosen to represent all sections of the
colonial population; both groups debated the important issues of
the day. The *comités régionaux*, however, differed from their
British counterparts in one important respect—legislative
councils could vote bills which became law after passing through
the appropriate channels, while the Belgian bodies were strictly
advisory. However, during the late 1920s resolutions approved
by Katanga's Comité Régional did receive a certain hearing in
Brussels because of ties between Katanga colonists and higher
officials in Brussels, but these pronouncements never had the
force of law.

Monseigneur de Hemptinne was a member of the Comité Régional
and its successor body, the Conseil de Province for nearly forty
years. Throughout his term, however, the autocratic prelate
never seemed to understand the limitations of these bodies.
Perhaps it was because he had been on the winning side too often
and had seen Comité Régional resolutions being implemented by
the colonial administration, despite the fact that such actions
were not binding. For example, his protests—supported by
others, of course—against the depopulation of rural Katanga had
been realized in the restrictions on recruitment implemented in
1926. His attacks on agricultural colonization had resulted in
the restriction of settlement. Because of these successes,
throughout his career he confused his ability to change Belgian
policy with the ability to change Belgian colonial law.[17]

Unlike the prelate, Vice Governor General Gaston Heenen
operated under no such illusions about the powers of Belgian
settlers. As part of the colonial administration, he knew all
too well where the powers of decision-making lay. Heenen had
spent most of his life in one government hierarchy or another.
Born in 1880 in Hasselt, the capital of Belgian Limburg, Heenen
had volunteered for the Belgian army at the age of sixteen.
After seven years he became an officer, spending eight years in
that capacity before his transfer to the colonial administrative
service in 1911. His rise continued during the East African
campaign of World War I, where he commanded a battalion and was
second in command of a brigade. In 1918 he became district
commissioner of Lomami district and four years later he rose to
the rank of commissioner general, second in command in Katanga
province—acting as chief executive in the absence of the vice
governor general. In 1927, after a brief term in Belgium as
head of the colonial minister's personal cabinet, he became
vice governor general of Katanga.[18]

During his six years in office, from 1927 to 1933, Hennen presided over the Katanga administration with great decisiveness, but always with an awareness of his subordination both to the governor general in Léopoldville and the Colonial Ministry in Brussels. Every April he convoked the Comité Régional to learn the opinions of its members—his district commissioners, Monseigneur de Hemptinne, Jules Cousin, and the representatives of smaller settlers—but for the rest of the year he ruled without their advice. The smaller settlers in particular, although represented by several associations, had very little input into his day-to-day decision making.

In the late 1920s Elisabethville's Belgian smallholders demonstrated the limits of their political ambitions when the question of municipal self-government on the Léopoldville model arose. In 1923 the colonial administration granted a new form of government to the town of Léopoldville, soon to become capital of the Congo. The municipality and its surroundings were designated as an urban district, separate from the other districts in its province. Representatives of the white colonists sat on a special urban council which levied local taxes and planned the district budget. This Léopoldville system served as a model for local self-government when Elisabethville settlers began to ask for a greater voice in their local government.

As early as 1925 one observer of the Elisabethville scene, former district commissioner André van Iseghem, recognized that the local settlers wanted extended political rights only if they did not have to pay for the increased taxes. The matter was fought out at the Comité Régional in 1929 when Vice Governor General Heenen offered the Elisabethville settlers an urban district on the Léopoldville model, with its own urban council to which they would choose two-thirds of the membership. Fearing increased taxes, however, the settlers on the Comité Régional refused Heenen's proposal. After much debate, they decided to request the creation of a new district around Elisabethville, whose budget—like that of rural districts—would be entirely controlled by the colonial administration. Thus, although settler representatives loudly demanded increased political powers, they were not willing to pay any additional money for such privileges.

In contrast to the situation in the Belgian colony, by the end of the 1920s white settlers in Northern Rhodesia enjoyed a larger measure of self-government than their counterparts in Elisabethville. British officials assumed that settlers ought to be brought into the government as quickly as possible, and in 1913 a handful of settlers in Lusaka had obtained an all-settler Village Management Board—more representation, which provided more popular consultation than the urban district which the

Elisabethville settlers refused in 1929. Moreover, beginning in 1924 white settlers sat on the Northern Rhodesian Legislative Council, a body which possessed law-making powers never attained by Belgian colonial representative bodies.[19]

In Katanga it was not only a question of settlers refusing more self-government because it would mean higher taxes. Katanga settlers enjoyed less self-government than their Northern Rhodesian counterparts, in part because the Belgian legal system did not allow the devolution of legislative authority, but also because of local political circumstances. In reality, neither of the most influential Belgian groups in Elisabethville—the Union Minière and the colonial administration—wanted to see increased settler representation in the local government. They feared that legislative powers would fall into the hands of downtrodden copper industry employees or foreigners who made up a majority of the rest of white population. Thus the two major Belgian organizations in Elisabethville, both of them hierarchically organized, were by no means prepared to champion the introduction of the principle of popular representation in local government. The leader of the third major Belgian organization, Monseigneur de Hemptinne, who heartily disliked the small settlers, sided with the Union Minière and the colonial government. With all these forces opposed to the expansion of settler influence, it is not surprising that the real powers of government remained in the hands of the colonial administration, which held the legal right to rule, and the Union Minière, which provided the revenue on which that administration depended.

Ordinary people in Elisabethville shared a common powerlessness, in part because they were disunited. The three major groups of Europeans in the city—mineworkers, government bureaucrats, and foreign merchants—regarded each other with mutual suspicion. In truth they had more to gain from attaching themselves to the existing power structure than from joining themselves together to oppose it. Under the Belgian regime and the prosperity brought by the Union Minière, the ordinary whites were earning a good living. Members of the African community in Elisabethville were just as fragmented as the humbler whites but for different reasons. Most had not wanted to leave their villages to work on the copperbelt, but they had been obliged to leave home by colonial fiscal policies. Of the opportunities available to Africans outside of the villages, however, Elisabethville provided the most attractive choices offering higher wages and a more exciting life.

The Union Minière—or anyone else for that matter—had not consciously embarked on a policy of making Elisabethville a desirable place for Africans. Before the labor crisis of 1923

company managers were concerned primarily with holding the cost
of labor to a bare minimum. In 1922 the company had brought in
a public health consultant from the gold mines of South Africa,
Dr. A. J. Orenstein, to recommend more efficient techniques of
running the camps. The company adopted Orenstein's suggestion
that it replace straw huts with brick dormitories. The resultant buildings, each built to house about sixty bachelors, were
inexpensive and ugly; completely barren, smelling of tar, they
resembled urinals. However, partly by following Orenstein's
suggestions, the management had reduced labor costs from 25d a
day in 1920 to 15d in 1923, and at the same time it had managed
to replace the workers' straw huts and iron shacks with permanent buildings (see Table 6.3).

The labor shortage of the mid-twenties, however, forced the
company management temporarily to abandon its economies in the
interest of obtaining a steady labor supply. The company's new
strategy was aimed at encouraging Africans to spend longer
periods at the mines by making life in the camps more attractive.
This change of approach coincided with the introduction of structural reforms in the Union Minière management, which included
the reorganizing and strengthening of the Native Labor Service
as a staff department in the new line and staff organization.

The task of this reorganization fell upon two men: Dr.
Léopold Mottoulle and Ernest Toussaint. Mottoulle had been in
Katange since the CSK administration, working at Géomines,
Forminière, and then as a military physician with the East
African expeditionary force, before joining the Union Minière.
It was during the East African campaign that Mottoulle met
Toussaint. The latter had had a varied career, going from
commerce to the army, then to the territorial service in Orein-
tale Province where he rose from territorial administrator to
district commissioner after only one term. Toussaint and
Mottoulle were capable men and experienced African hands who
fitted well into the Union Minière organization, even though
they had not had the engineering training characteristic of the
highest echelon of the Union Minière.

In 1926 Toussaint assumed control of the Native Labor Service, with Mottoulle his second in command, and immediately set
out to make it a model staff agency. During the next three
years they fired eighty out of a hundred twenty department members, replacing them mainly with agents from other company
divisions. To encourage professional pride within the service,
Toussaint and Mottoulle encouraged the study of management
techniques and rewarded diligent agents with increased salaries.

Table 6.3

UNION MINIERE TOTAL COST PER WORKER PER DAY,

1916-1932, IN FRANCS AND IN STERLING

	Outlay in Francs	Exchange Rate	Equivalent in Pence
1916	2.16	30	17
1917	2.59	30	21
1918	2.90	30	23
1919	3.12	30	25
1920	5.17	50	25
1921	4.98	52	23
1922	4.83	58	20
1923	5.30	87	15
1924	6.25	95	17
1925	8.80	101.33	21
1926	13.98	156.17	21
1927	21.75	173.65	30
1928	24.45	174.61	34
1929	28.30	174.44	39
1930	28.00	174.44	39
1931	26.30	173.82	36
1932	22.16	121.88	44
1933	14.14	120.47	28
1934	10.70	116.98	22
1935	9.76	105.12	22

SOURCES: CSK, *Rapport annuel* 1921, pp. 33-34; UMHK, Service MOI, *Rapports annuels* 1926 & 1937 in UMHK C 4. Exchange rates after 1926 come from *The Economist*'s annual tables for January.

Members of the Native Labor Service soon took on new functions within the individual camps. In the old days authority at
each plant had rested in the hands of a single line officer, the
chef de camp, who was responsible for his workers' production as
well as for their behavior and welfare. Toussaint and Mottoulle
introduced two additional staff officers: a member of the Native
Labor Service responsible for workers during their leisure hours
and a camp doctor. These two staff officers, who were less concerned with output than the line officer, tended to restrain him
from making excessive demands on his workers.

The object of the new system was to control all aspects of
employees' lives in order to maintain a steady supply of labor
and high productivity. The result was greatly increased control
over the Africans' leisure hours, along with considerably greater
outlays for their welfare. For instance, between 1926 and 1927
Union Minière expenditures on labor increased by over 40 percent
per worker. The Africans received these sums in the form of
social services. Wages accounted for less than one-fifth of
the company's labor costs, the rest being spent on recruitment,
food, lodgings, medical care and other overhead items.

The ensuing improvements in camp living conditions—including more nourishing rations and better housing—had their anticipated effect, and in 1927 the company was able to institute a
three year contract without undue resistance. Many Africans
had already recognized the advantages of longer periods in the
mines, the average term at the Lubumbashi smelter having risen
from eight months in 1921 to sixteen in 1924. Furthermore,
those who survived their first six months in the camps had a
much lower death rate than new recruits and were less inclined
to run away to the countryside, although they often deserted the
camps when offered better jobs (see chapter 5).

In keeping with the new policy, the company's improved care
of its African staff began at the recruiting stations where
future employees were selected. Africans who did not meet Union
Minière health standards were reimbursed for their trip to the
recruiting station. Those who were selected at the stations
were put on a special diet to compensate for the prevailing malnutrition; meanwhile they were taught to work in teams similar
to those at the mines, and after their training period sent by
rail to the copperbelt. Once at the camps the personnel service
encouraged the recruits to keep in touch with their families and
friends at home, since men who were not completely cut off from
their villages were less anxious to return.

As another means of keeping down the return rate, the Union
Minière adopted a plan worked out by Raoul Strythagen of the OCTK

whereby chiefs would be used to persuade young men to stay at
work for the Europeans. The chiefs received cash payments for
each man working on the copperbelt. Ostensibly these payments
formed local treasuries to be used for local projects, but in
fact they remained in the hands of the chiefs and were a continuation of the payoff system instituted in the early years of the
century by labor touts. The creation of treasuries, however,
gave the operation a legitimacy in the eyes of the colonial
government, which encouraged the emulation of the British practice of implementing native treasuries as part of the policy of
indirect rule. By 1930, thirty-nine chiefdoms in Katanga had
their own treasuries, filled largely by European employers' contributions.

But even this plan's originator, Raoul Strythagen, realized
that the chiefs' power was declining and that other influences
were to prevent the workers from returning home. Since many men
objected to going to the copperbelt because of the scarcity
there of marriageable girls, Strythagen initiated the policy of
encouraging workers to bring their wives with them. Union
Minière soon followed his lead, and in 1928 the head of the
Lomami recruitment mission told his first group of returnees
that single men would not be rehired. These efforts to "breed"
a more permanent labor supply ultimately bore fruit in 1930 when
the birthrate in the camps exceeded the deathrate for the first
time.[20]

Although a large proportion of the Africans recruited by
the Union Minière remained in the camps for long years, few
firsthand narratives have been collected which describe camp
life from the African point of view. During the academic year
1972-73 a Zaïrian undergraduate, Yogolelo Tambwe ya Kasimba, as
part of an honor's thesis, collected several graphic descriptions
of life in the Elisabethville camps from workers who had been
recruited by the short-lived Union Minière Maniema mission which
operated in southern Orientale Province from 1926 to 1928. Until
more such descriptions are collected from Africans who remained
in the camps, those collected by Yogolelo will have to be taken
as representative. Moreover, since most of the narratives were
collected from men who left the camps before 1928, they are
uncolored by later changes in camp conditions.

Bwana Muzuri Samilongo recalled the situation which awaited
Maniema workers who, after being transported five hundred miles
from their homes to the copperbelt, were placed in the Lubumbashi
preparation camp for acclimation.

The head of that camp, who was called 'Monsieur
Sikamo' was a mean white man who often beat us. . .We
spent several weeks in that Lubumbashi camp passing
our time at nothing but eating and medical examina-
tions. They divided us into work teams and sent us to
different camps. I personally was sent to Ruashi
where I worked on a team with a steam shovel.

Bwana Asani Rajabo, a co-worker, described the work conditions at Ruashi:

The drill holes chosen to hold the explosives
were dug by the capita with a borer. It was then necessary to insert the necessary number of charges,
before lighting the fuse; but since the workers often
miscounted the charges, they sometimes set them off
before everyone had left the scene and taken shelter.
That explains why we had a number of accidents at
Ruashi.

We had two work crews: on one week the first
worked from 7 a.m. to 3 p.m., the second from 3 p.m.
to 11 p.m.; the following week the morning crew worked
at night and the evening crew in the morning. No,
there was no rest period and we had nothing to eat on
the job. Only those who worked (underground) at
Kipushi received a roll called a 'kampompo' before
descending into the pit.

Another Maniema man, Bwana Lungumbu Saidi summed up his
impressions of life at the Ruashi camp:

Life at the camp was pleasant; only the food did
not suit us. . .The people from Maniema died in large
numbers, because they were not accustomed to maize
flour. Yes; we lost many of our people at Ruashi;
some died from work accidents, others, the majority,
from diarrhea. The man who had diarrhea one day died
in two or three days. All of us wanted only one
thing: to terminate our contract and return to our
country—we were so frightened by the number of people
who died each day.[21]

Taken as a whole, Yogolelo's collected accounts reveal a
tremendous ambivalence on the part of Maniema Africans to the
Union Minière camps. The workers appreciated the copious food,
good housing, and medical care; on the other hand they were worked

terribly hard and ran the constant risk of an early death. The
Maniema Africans returned home as soon as the first term expired;
some sought to remain on the copperbelt, but usually outside of
the Union Minière camps.

Camp life, away from their native environment in an alien
atmosphere, always had many drawbacks for these mine workers.
Moreover, company-imposed measures to increase productivity made
some men even more discontented with their lot. In 1928, for
example, the Union Minière abolished the ticket system for wages
and food rations. Under that system, workers received their
rations only after a day's labor had been recorded on their work
ticket; those who did not want to work on any given day were
free to remain in the camp. This system was exceedingly incon-
venient for the management, since overseers could never be sure
how many men would turn out for work. After the system was
abolished Africans were fed and paid whether they worked or not,
while their European bosses were made responsible for seeing
that they were on the job. As a result, many Union Minière
workers fled to employers who did not insist on daily work.
Others who left the mines were attracted by the higher wages to
be earned in the *cité indigène*.[22]

By the end of the 1920s the *cité* was divided into four
quarters. Largest was the independents' quarter, reserved for
those Africans who did not work for a European company on a regular basis. Next came the quarter reserved for employees of firms
large enough to own housing facilities in the *cité*, and nearby
was the quarter reserved for government employees. The smallest
quarter was the one reserved for African hawkers. In addition,
Africans could live as servants on their master's property or in
three agricultural settlements on the outskirts of town.[23]

The living standard in the *cité* proper was much lower than
that in the Union Minière camp. Although the government and
medium-sized employers had been obliged since 1921 to provide
brick houses for their employees in the *cité*, neither group had
the capital necessary to maintain their housing at the standard
prevailing in the mining camps. Self-employed Africans built
huts of whatever materials they could assemble. Health services
were primitive and most children were debilitated by malnutrition,
malaria, or intestinal parasites. The inhabitants often envied
the employees of the Union Minière for their living conditions.[24]

Why, then, did some Africans choose to live in the *cité*?
By and large, Africans chose the *cité* because they enjoyed
greater freedom there. In the mining camps men who did not
report for their shift were subject to dismissal. Camp workers

could not provide hospitality for their extended families vis-
visiting from the villages. In the *cité*, however, people were
free to act as they pleased. Men who did not like their jobs
could quit them and seek others without having to abandon their
houses. Often this house was a haven for country relatives of
the occupant. Some of the services provided by the Union
Minière for their workers, moreover, could be obtained by *cité*-
dwellers from the Benedictine and Methodist missions, which ran
schools and clinics for Africans.

     In addition to the *cité*, Africans who did not like camp
life had two other alternatives: domestic servants' quarters
and the agricultural hamlets. Most domestics lived in shacks
behind the houses of their employers so that they were available
for service at any time of the day or night. Nonetheless the
jobs had certain attractions because of the castoffs that could
be obtained from their masters, and the prestige and comfort of
living in the European section of town.

     Furthest removed from the Europeans were agricultural ham-
lets on the outskirts of town which served as a kind of halfway
house between villages and the city. Most of the inhabitants
were retired soldiers or men who had worked in the mines, who
made a living by selling their surplus crops on the European
market. Another important group were the prostitutes, who were
less frequently harassed by officials if they lived in the hamlets rather than the *cité*. Finally, the hamlets contained men
from rural areas who settled temporarily in them as farm laborers
before proceeding to the city.[25]

     The various neighborhoods in the *cité indigène* provided a
viable set of alternatives to the Union Minière camps. Frequently the choice of the *cité* meant a decision to give up
better living conditions in exchange for more personal freedom;
it also involved a decision as to what an African's relations
would be with his village of origin. Paradoxically, Union
Minière employees maintained closer ties with their former homes,
receiving free transportation to their villages at the end of
each three year term as well as upon dismissal or retirement.
Cité dwellers, on the other hand—because they were usually
illiterate and too poor to travel by any means other than on
foot—tended to lose contact with their relatives and former
neighbors. Since their employers felt no obligation to repatriate them, men who lost their jobs could remain in Elisabethville.
Hence, the situation in Elisabethville fits a distinction made
by Philip Mayer with respect to South African townspeople: camp-
dwellers were *stabilized* in that they retained important ties
with the countryside despite long-term residence in the city,
while *cité*-dwellers were becoming *urbanized*.[26]

Beyond these differences between town and camp, however, Elisabethville's Africans also shared a common experience of colonization. Very often reaction to the urban environment cut across neighborhood lines. In the course of the 1920s two clear alternatives began to open up to the Africans of Elisabethville. On the one hand, they could decide to accept European cultural influences in the same way that they had accepted urban life and tax payment. On the other, they could choose to accept only those European influences which could not be avoided while protecting themselves with institutions derived from their precolonial culture.

Those Africans who embraced European culture found the missionaries eager to enroll them in the churches. During the twenties the Methodists and Benedictines competed bitterly for the souls of Elisabethville's Africans. Both missionary groups were highly organized but small; the Benedictines in the *cité* were especially tightly organized. All activities emanated from their Mission St. Jean, where a single priest—Father Grégoire Coussement—ran the entire operation, directing schools, social clubs, and evangelization. Père Grégoire, as he was called, soon became the single most powerful man in the *cité*. His recommendation could put children into schools and men into jobs and public office. Below him, staffs of Africans taught, evangelized, and fought for favors. Europeans from both religions found it necessary to delegate everyday activities to Africans while reserving management of operations to themselves.[27]

Thus the bulk of proselytization in Elisabethville was done by African evangelists, most often men who had been converted to Christianity before coming to Elisabethville. Most of these evangelists had received little training beyond rote memorization of the catechism, Bible stories, or the lives of the saints. The real opportunities to learn about European culture were reserved for the children of this first generation of African Christians.

In the early years Christian parents sent their children to mission schools simply as a device for entry into a better paid job rather than a chance to provide a formal education for their children. In 1928 Père Grégoire complained that his fifth grade class had been abandoned because the students were being hired away as clerks. To encourage school attendance, the government and the Union Minière began offering bonuses to clerks attending night classes. Between 1928 and 1931 the company paid mothers at the camps a family allowance of ten francs a month (12 percent of their husbands' cash salary!) for keeping children healthy and sending them to school. Furthermore, a practice of paying older children for doing odd jobs for the schools in the

afternoon after class was instituted in 1930 and maintained
through the entire depression. Attendance at a mission school
seemed a clear way to increased wealth.[28]

However, not every African was willing to choose that route
to advancement. For some, the missionaries demanded too much of
a renunciation of their village past. What is more, the missionaries' resources were limited. They could provide education
for the children, but they did not have the resources necessary
to provide many social services to minister to adults. The
latter, without European financial help, often had to face problems of unemployment, illness, and death. In order to protect
themselves against a hostile urban environment, Africans in both
the camps and the *cité* relied upon closed associations similar
to the *butwa* society which had been brought to Elisabethville
before the First World War.

Veterans of the East Africa campaign had learned that
closed associations could be found in much of the territory of
East and Central Africa. This discovery gave veterans of the
campaign something in common with people who lived as much as a
thousand miles from their homes. At the end of the war, moreover,
men from Central Africa began to join closed associations which
they found in German East Africa. These new assocations were
brought back to Central Africa by veterans, who eventually
established a new network of closed associations which encompassed both rural areas and the copperbelt.

In Elisabethville this new association, called Mbeni, from
the English word "band" soon became a popular social organization.
Members of the Mbeni society frequently paraded in military
formation through the streets, dancing and singing unflattering
songs about well-known Europeans. Their officers held ranks
patterned after the military, thus perpetuating an impression
that they possessed a certain measure of the Europeans' power.

Even Africans who had not served in the war quickly reorganized their already existing closed associations on the Mbeni
model. In Elisabethville almost all African ethnic groups soon
had their equivalent of Mbeni, all of which were known collec-
tively to the Belgians as "les Belges" because of their use of
European army uniforms and titles borrowed from the colonial
administration. Their officers bore titles ranging from king
to governor general down through the entire ranks of the territorial administration.

Despite these new titles, the "Belges" bore many resem-
blances to the prewar *butwa* associations. They likewise provided services necessary in the urban environment: food sharing,

the lodging of newcomers, adiing the sick, and burying the dead.
Some groups even functioned as savings institutions which helped
members accumulate the money necessary for the bride price of
girls back in the villages.   In leadership, too, the new associations resembled their prewar counterparts.   Close relatives of
rural chiefs, who were seen as agents of the colonizers, were
specifically excluded from office.   Similarly, men who had close
ties with Europeans in the urban environment, such as foremen and
graduates of mission schools, seldom became association leaders.

This rejection of all Africans who associated with Europeans especially frightened Belgian officials.   Not surprisingly
the "Belges" dancers' parodies of administrators annoyed the
latter so much that they threatened to send leaders to jail for
their insults.   As a result the 1923-24 Subcommission for the
Protection of Natives which had so vigorously protested against
overrecruitment in rural areas, investigated the urban associations on behalf of the colonial government.   Concluding that the
associations were completely beyond the government's control and
in danger of becoming subversive, in 1924 the Subcommission
recommended that the government and missions take preventative
action against the associations.

However, the colonial lawmaking process was so cumbersome
that it took the government two years to act against the associations.   On the basis of powers delegated to the governor general, Martin Rutten finally promulgated an ordinance in February
1926 which placed all African urban organizations under the control of the provincial governments.   Thereafter such organizations were legally required to register with the colonial
adminstration and were subject to its supervision.   In practice,
however, none of the "Belges" registered and the administration
did not enforce the legislation.

The Benedictine missionaries, led by Père Grégoire, took a
more active role in fighting the associations.   Coussement's
strategy was to fight fire with fire by creating new Catholic
ethnic associations to rival the existing ones.   Between 1925
and 1930 Coussement createᵈ seven associations, all of which
duly registered with the government in compliance with Rutten's
ordinance.

All but one of Coussement's associations catered to ethnic
groups found more in the *cité* than in the camps.   These included
three Luba-ized vassals of the Luba-Katanga—the Bangobango, the
Hemba, and the Boyo; the Zela, the Lunda, and the so-called
Bemba, who were actually Bena Chishinga and Kazembe's people
from the lower Luapula.   Only the Luba-Kasai tended to live in
the Union Minière camp rather than in the *cité*.

Coussement's clubs, although providing recreation for their members just as the older organizations had done, were different in certain fundamental respects. As far as leadership was concerned, the missionaries rather than the members chose the officers; the missionaries also kept close watch on the treasuries. The leaders of the Benedictine associations were precisely those men avoided by the nonmission clubs: well-educated Africans who often had ties with ruling chiefs at home. For example, Kabongo Albert, the president of the Bena Kasai, was one of the best-educated Africans in Elisabethville, having studied at the Scheutists' teacher training school at Luluabourg. Mushitu Henri, who brought a previously existing Lunda club to the mission, was the son of the ruling Mwaant Yav and a translator at the Elisabethville court.

The clubs also performed quite different functions from the "Belges." Since they met at the mission rather than in members' houses, traditions of food-sharing and hospitality became awkward to carry out. Needless to say, the Catholic clubs also offered sparse encouragement to such activities as parodying Europeans or burying the dead according to local customs. The new clubs, however, performed important economic and social functions in that members could count on good recommendations from the missionaries when they looked for jobs and could find places for their children in the mission schools.

Despite the obvious usefulness of Coussement's clubs, the non-Catholic associations continued to flourish, particularly within the Union Minière camps. In 1928 company officials found no less than five regional associations of Africans from their Lomami recruitment mission: those representing the Kusu, the Bekalebwe, the Songye, the Bena Budiye, and the Bena Lulua (called Bena Dibeshi). In addition, the leading group of Zambians still recruited for the mines, the Aushi, had an association which was later found on the Northern Rhodesian copperbelt. Their association was called Lalela, and their dance Kalela, a society which J. C. Mitchell found in Northern Rhodesia still operating after the Second World War.

Different in origin and mode of operation, Coussement's clubs and the closed association both performed an important assimilative function for rural Africans new to the city. The purely African groups helped their members to adapt to the new urban environment through techniques grounded in village life. The Catholic associations helped their members to face many of the same problems, using the missionaries as allies. Both strategies had their weaknesses: independent African associations could not help their members in dealing with Europeans, while Coussement's groups were usually ineffective in dealing with the

ordinary problems of life. But they both helped African workers
adapt to the city.

The similarity between the two types of organization increased in the late 1920s when both groups took on the additional
function of organizing urban gangs which fought each other.
This in itself was partly a reaction to the colonial environment
in that Africans could not vent their frustrations against Europeans without running the risk of severe sanctions. Coussement's
clubs and the closed associations engaged in gang warfare that
ran across religious lines. Brawls became a weekly occurrence
and involved both Catholic and independent associations. These
fights continued until 1931 when the Benedictines gave up on
their ethnic associations and abolished them.[29]

By the end of the 1920s organized groups of Africans—
members of associations which had taken their current form in
Elisabethville—were fighting each other. This phenomenon
indicates the extent to which Africans had become acclimated to
life in the city. Instead of being captives who worked in the
city simply to satisfy their colonizers, the Africans of Elisabethville were beginning to act within an urban frame of reference. The imposition of these African patterns on at least
certain aspects of African life in Elisabethville created a
framework for present and future inhabitants of the city.

In this way the acclimatization of Africans to Elisabethville ran parallel to that of the Belgians. The latter, of
course, were more powerful than their African subjects, and the
managers at the Union Minière, the government officials, and the
Benedictines had a more profound effect on the city's development than did the African associations. Nevertheless, both
elements were essential to the city's development, because the
Belgians never had absolute control over their subjects. At
most, the Belgians could force the Africans to work, but they
could not dictate which jobs Africans should take. Neither
could they prevent Africans from organizing themselves against
the demands of colonization.

Chapter 7

Hard Times and Bright Visions, 1930-1934

The economic, social, and political foundations of Elisabethville were firmly in place at the beginning of the Great
Depression. The city served as headquarters of a thriving
copper industry which had assembled a substantial industrial
plant and a ready supply of capital. It also housed the administration of the Congo's richest province. Finally, it had
attracted a substantial number of permanent settlers, both
Africans and Europeans, who had made the city their permanent
home. Thus when the first economic storm winds reached Central
Africa in 1930 the copper capital was well braced to withstand
them. Although Elisabethville was too strong to succumb to the
economic hurricane, the gales eroded the city's most vulnerable
sections leaving only the sturdiest structures.

No observer living in 1930 could predict the effect of the
depression on the constituent elements of the city's population.
Not surprisingly some elements proved resilient in the face of
economic stress while others succumbed to it. Many African
employees of the Union Minière who had been brought to the
mining camps for what they thought would be permanent careers
had no option other than repatriation to their villages. *Cité*
Africans, by contrast, banded together for survival, and many
who wanted to remain in the city were able to stay in Elisabethville or its immediate hinterland. Partly in response to the
economic crisis, new African institutions emerged and were destroyed in rapid succession, to be quickly replaced by others.
The four short years of the depression were the most uncertain
times which the city had ever known.

The economic storm first hit the copper industry in April
1930, when a falloff in the demand for copper by the world market
forced the Union Minière to plan a long-range decrease in production. By this time the company—having become part of an inter-

national cartel, Copper Exporters, Incorporated—was no longer
in control of its output and prices. Reluctantly the management
cut back production from 120,000 tons in 1931 to 54,000 in 1932;
the amount would have been reduced again if the company had not
left the cartel in 1933.[1]

Of course these decisions to restrict production had an
immediate effect on Katanga business. In quick succession the
Union Minière, its affiliates, and other European employers cut
back their operations, leaving thousands of employees in distress. Deprived of their wages, African and European workers
had to reduce their expenditures, and the depression soon spread
to commerce and service industries. Many found themselves
trapped—no job and no hope of getting one. Reluctantly, thousands packed their bags and returned to their homes in the
Luapula Valley, South Africa, and Belgium.

The city had weathered dislocations in the copper industry
before, but never on the scale which occurred between 1930 and
1932. In those two years the Union Minière reduced its labor
force by more than two-thirds, from 16,000 to less than 5,000
Africans and from 1,800 to less than 600 Europeans. Despite
careful planning by the management, the entire industry suffered
enormously from the retrenchment. The company's largest works
at Jadotville (now Likasi), seventy miles from Elisabethville,
came to a virtual halt as the concentration works, cobalt fur-
naces, and laboratories were all shut down. Elisabethville, the
site of company headquarters, was less severely hit. Nonetheless
the Ruashi mine was closed and the local African work force
reduced from 6,765 in 1929 to 3,115 in 1934 (see Table 7.1).[2]

Other local employers culled their work force in similar
proportions. The Katanga Railway, for example, reduced the
population of its Elisabethville camp from 2,670 in 1929 to
1,957 in 1934. In the same period the African population for
the city and its immediate surroundings fell by 23 percent—from
30,000 to a little over 23,000.

Inevitably small businessmen and artisans suffered from the
cutbacks in the larger industries on which they depended. As a
result of repatriations by larger employers and the return to
South Africa of the bulk of the remaining English-speakers (Protestants and Ashkenazic Jews), the white population of Elisabethville fell by 42 percent—from 3,830 in 1930 to 2,211 in
1933. A tenth of the remaining Europeans were out of work, the
brunt of unemployment falling on foreigners of Mediterranean
origin, especially Italians from the Piedmont, Sephardic Jews
from Rhodes, and Greek Christians from other islands of the
Dodecanese. Although the Italians would ultimately be assimilated

Table 7.1

THE ELISABETHVILLE POPULATION, 1929 AND 1934

	1929	1934
Union Minière	6,765	3,115
C. F. K.	2,670	1,957
Police Urbaine	224	273
Force Publique	1,672	1,360
Total Camps	11,331	6,705
Cité Indigène	11,399	6,282
Farming Villages	1,800*	2,429
Servants & Rural	5,470*	7,689
Total Africans	30,000	23,105
Europeans	3,830(11.3%)	2,211(8.7%)
GRAND TOTAL	33,830	25,316

*Author's estimate

SOURCE: Territoire d'Elisabethville, Rapport annuel 1934, in
AP, A60 (and Table 6.3 above).

into the Belgian community, the Jews and Greeks became separate
subcastes in colonial society. During the depression the low
status of non-Belgian whites was reflected in their exclusion
from government relief funds, the meager amounts available being
reserved for Belgian nationals.[3] Needless to say, unemployed
Africans in Elisabethville expected no help from the government
or any other European agency, for that matter, and they received
none.

Most Europeans considered unemployed city Africans social
parasites and dangerous ones at that. With so much time on
their hands, such people might easily be led to theft and subversion. Early in the depression—in February 1930—the vice
governor general of Katanga promulgated an ordinance to control
the residency of Africans in urban areas. All Africans in
Elisabethville were required to obtain an internal passport.
Those known to be without work for thirty days were subject to
expulsion. This ordinance—obviously intended to discourage
urban residence by the unemployed—required a certain initiative
by the administration, which had to locate out of work Africans
before it could expel them. If an individual did not report to
the authorities, they had to spend time and effort in tracking
him down. In general the administration had neither the personnel nor the money necessary to undertake such an operation
in a regular and systematic way in a *cité* which numbered over
five thousand, and many unemployed Africans remained in Elisabethville.

The Union Minière, by contrast, had made repatriation part
and parcel of the recruitment system which it had constructed in
the late 1920s. The company guaranteed transportation from the
mines back to the recruitment centers, not only at the end of
three year contracts but also for family emergencies. Indeed,
the facilities offered workers for keeping in touch with their
families were one of the company's major selling points to
potential employees. Given this policy it required no special
effort on the part of the Union Minière to repatriate those
Africans who had been laid off because of the depression.

The management was surprised, however, by the reluctance of
so many of its employees to return to their villages. In 1931,
the year of the most substantial cutbacks, no less than three
groups of mineworkers numbering in the hundreds rioted to protest repatriation or the threat of it. Characteristically, two
of the riots took place on the outskirts of Elisabethville—one
eighteen miles away at the company's only underground mine at
Kipushi, and the other at the Ruashi mine only six miles from
the city. In both cases company officials broke up the demonstrations and sent the redundant workers home, but the Africans'

message was clear enough. Union Minière employees had become
so attached to their work that they did not want to leave it.
The effects of this realization on the company's management were
far-reaching, and a generation of employees was to suffer serious consequences from the discovery that African workers had
adjusted to the mining camps.

In contrast to the camp-dwellers, many inhabitants of the
cité indigène had not only adjusted to their surroundings, but
some of them found ways of staying in their new location. A
careful reading of the census figures shows just how successful
they were. On the face of it, the population of the *cité indigène* fell from 11,399 in 1929 to 6,282 in 1934, a decline as
substantial as that at the Union Minière. This decline, however,
was to a large degree compensated for by an increase in the
population of the rural areas surrounding the city, which rose
by 2,783 in the same period. This does not mean that only the
unaccounted-for remainder of 2,334 Africans left Elisabethville
during the worst years of the depression: the city's population
always included a substantial proportion of temporary residents.
What the figures do suggest, however, is that large numbers of
Africans did remain in or near Elisabethville despite the
efforts of the administration to dislodge them.

Those Africans who chose to remain in the city did so at
great sacrifice. Buying food was the major problem. In the
villages where agricultural lands were readily available food
could be obtained without cash. In the city, few Africans had
access to agricultural lands so most food—except for rations
provided by employers—had to be bought. Unemployed Africans
did not have the money to feed their families. Jobless married
men who chose to stay in town usually found themselves obliged
to send their families back to the villages. In 1930 alone,
one-third of the 2,000 African children in the *cité* departed
for rural areas. During those bleakest years, then, many
families were separated while the fathers tried to hang on in
the city.

The ethnic clubs, which had fostered food sharing for many
years, grew in importance for those who remained. Almost every
ethnic group in the city had a club—there were at least eighteen
such clubs in 1933—which took on the responsibility of assuring
the survival of its unemployed members. Those who had jobs or
garden plots shared their produce with their distressed brethern.
The need for these clubs did not quickly abate; in 1934 41 percent of the able-bodied men in the *cité* were still unemployed.

The role played by the clubs during this period of hardship
is remarkable: Africans in Elisabethville had created urban

institutions which enabled them withstand the economic storm. These African organizations, in fact, succeeded where their European imitators had failed. The Benedictines had dissolved their own ethnic associations in 1931 at just the moment when the nonmission organizations were performing most effectively. African initiative proved more useful than European initiative when the crunch came.[4]

One group of Africans in Elisabethville, however, faced more than a hostile economic environment; the Zambian community was subject to political harassment as well. The Belgians distrusted its members as subjects of a foreign power, and once the labor shortage of the mid-twenties was over the colonial government sought to chase the Zambians out of Belgian territory.

In the implementation of this goal, the colonial government received the enthusiastic cooperation of the Union Minière. Between 1929 and 1931 the copper company reduced the proportion of Zambians in the Elisabethville camps from 35 percent of its work force to 5 percent. Even when compared to given overall depression cutbacks, the effects of this reduction were particularly striking. The Union Minière reduced the number of Zambians in its Elisabethville camps from 2,500 to 150 in the course of two years.

Belgian administrators attempted to pursue this same policy with regard to Zambians living in the *cité indigène*. Zambians, like Zaïrois, were required to register at the new passport bureau and they were expelled if they remained unemployed for more than a month. The colonial authorities, however, took special pains to uncover unemployed "foreigners"; many Zambians left Elisabethville at this time, although a large proportion of them were replaced by other Zambian work-seekers pressed by British demands for payment of the hut tax. These crosscurrents resulted in a net decline in the British Vice Consulate of the Zambian population: in 1930-31 the British Vice Consulate in Elisabethville registered 4,480 Zambian men who left Katanga, while only 3,652 new rivals took their place. In the same two years the Zambian female population in Katanga decreased by an even greater proportion: 2,150 women left the Belgian colony, while only 1,137 arrived.[5]

Conditions of insecurity and economic distress among the local Zambians made them particularly receptive to the teachings of a millenarian movement, the Kitawala, which had existed in Central Africa since before World War I. Although this movement ultimately produced neither the end of the world nor a revolt against the colonial administration, it did have important consequences for the position of Africans in Elisabethville.

Moreover, it accentuated divisions within the Belgian colonial administration. This purely African religious phenomenon had an important effect on the colonial community as a whole.

In analyzing the millenarian phenomenon, Professor George Shepperson makes the distinction between premillenarian and postmillenarian movements. Although members of both movements believe in the approach of a thousand year period which will herald the end of the world, adherents of the former think that the Deliverer will come to inaugurate the period bringing "cataclysmic change" in the world as we know it. Members of postmillenarian movements, by contrast, believe that the millenium will come before the Messiah "as the fruit of the present Christian agencies now at work in the world and that the Second Coming or the delivering agency will occur at the end of this process." Using Shepperson's distinction, the Zambians of Elisabethville were receptive to a premillenarian movement, which historically is the more militant of the two varieties.[6]

The premillenarian movement which appeared in Elisabethville, Kitawala or Watch Tower, had been known in Central Africa since 1908. Kitawala was an offshoot of the American religious sect, Jehovah's Witnesses, which had originally preached that the world would end in 1914. Battered by European conquest and tax collection, many Central Africans were attracted to the sect, which in its original African form predicted the arrival of the millenium when all colonial governments would be destroyed and Africans would no longer be obliged to pay taxes. The movement gained wide adherence in Nyasaland (now Malawi) before the British suppressed it. Thereafter the sect in Central Africa was primarily clandestine, secretly practiced by Malawians in towns and mining camps throughout the region.

Largely cut off from the original church in the United States (which had necessarily been reorganized after the failure of the world to end in 1914), Kitawala took on a number of diverse African elements. No one local variant predominated, because the Malawians had proselytized members of widely divergent ethnic groups. In the Luapula Valley, where the movement arrived in 1924, the sect had attracted many former members of the *butwa* society. A year later it reached rural Katanga, incorporating many of the religious beliefs of the Lala people among whom it spread. Then in the towns and mining camps the movement took on a different form adapted to the prevailing ethnic diversity and the money economy.[7]

The first Kitawala evangelist in Elisabethville, Piala (known to the Europeans as Pearson Musonda), had arrived in the city in 1926. He was a Zambian from the Luapula Valley who had joined the movement at the Wankie coal mine in Southern Rhodesia. His preachings therefore contained elements of doctrine similar to those found among the sect's adherents in the industrial areas of Southern Rhodesia and South Africa. He taught that the day of judgement would soon come when American black soldiers would remove the European colonizers. Piala had gone to schools run by the London Missionary Society and the Wesleyan missions, but he opposed the missions as European-controlled. Specifically he attacked them for making excessive financial demands on their members (the practice of tithing) and for forbidding members to drink alcoholic beverages. Thus Piala was preaching against all white influences, not simply against the colonial government.

Piala made few converts before the onset of the depression, but after 1930 he began to attract a devoted following. Terrible economic conditions were undoubtedly involved in his appeal, but surprisingly few of his converts were unemployed. By and large, they were working Zambians who feared expulsion because of their nationality. Thus fear of the Belgians compounded with economic uncertainty to lead many Zambians into the underground African religious movement as it developed in Elisabethville.

This anxiety was well-grounded, given the determination of the Belgian authorities to cleanse Katanga of its Zambian inhabitants. To hide the movement from the colonial authorities, Piala did most of his preaching in secret. His followers assembled in small groups—on Sunday afternoons for prayer meetings in the *cité indigène* and in the dead of night for baptisms in the agricultural settlements on the edge of town. However, the movement lost its protective cover in November 1931 when police informers reported the existence of the sect to the colonial administration. Alarmed because the movement had escaped their attention for so long, the Belgian authorities arrested all the Watchtower members they could catch.

Belgian police records provide a detailed profile of members of the movement. Most adherents were Zambians from the Luapula Valley, although a handful of Bemba-speaking Zaïrois also joined the movement. By December 1931 Elisabethville's Kitawala included 180 members, a large membership for an urban African association but small in terms of the local Zambian community which numbered over 5,000 at the end of 1931. Had the movement continued to grow freely, the proportion of the Elisabethville community joining it would have undoubtedly increased accordingly, but it was cut short by the intervention of the Belgian police.[8]

Most of the Zambians who had joined the movement lived in the *cité* or the agricultural suburbs rather than in the industrial camps. Of the forty-nine Zambians arrested by the Belgian police in December 1931, only eight lived in the camps, four of whom worked for the Union Minière and four for the Katanga Railway. As far as the Union Minière is concerned, the reluctance of Zambian employees to join the movement is easily explained. Most of their fellow Zambians had been recently purged from the mining camps and those who were left were afraid to jeopardize their jobs.

Those Zambians outside the camps who joined the movement fell into three major categories: employees of small European enterprise, particularly shops, servants, and the self-employed. Members of the other two occupational categories, the self-employed and the servants, by contrast, provided the bulk of the 1931 movement's support. Twenty-eight of the forty-nine Zambians arrested in 1931 fell into those categories.[9]

Even before the depression, self-employed Zambians were among the most vulnerable Africans in Elisabethville. Largely as artisans, itinerant merchants, and market gardeners, they were in an anomalous situation; they earned their livelihood through the urban European economy without being directly dependent on Europeans for salaries. Instead of depending on a single employer for wages and rations, these self-employed Zambians fended for themselves much as city-dwellers do all over the world. In Elisabethville, however, such behavior on the part of Africans was deviant. The self-employed Zambians were, from an economic and social point of view, the most marginal men in the city.

In 1929 British Vice Consul J. C. C. Coxhead described the position of these itinerant merchants. Despite the fact that most of the individuals were illiterate, European merchants advanced them trade goods to sell on commission in the various urban settlements. At the end of their selling trips they returned to the individual merchants who had given them the goods. More often than not they came up short in their cash or goods and were sometimes prosecuted by the European supplier, himself not always a model of commercial morality. Thus the African hawker was in an extremely precarious position; responsible for large quantities—by African standards—of merchandise and cash, he was at the same time relatively wealthy and in constant danger of financial disaster and possible imprisonment—the town mouse of the fables.[10]

One might well ask which individuals chose such a precarious calling. A key element attracting individuals to hawking—as well as to the other occupations characteristic of Watch Tower adherents, truck farming and independent artisanry—was freedom from supervision. Individuals in these professions could earn European money without being subject to the continual surveillance of a European employer. The choice of one of these "independent" occupations in Elisabethville may well have been the result of an individual's negative attitude toward the colonizers—a resistance to European regimentation.

Moreover, such attitudes would seem to lie in the individual Watchtower member's experiences before he migrated to the city. Almost all Africans in Elisabethville in 1931 were born and had spent most of their lives in rural areas. This leads to the question of whether the preurban experiences of Zambian Watch Tower members in Elisabethville were different from those of other Zambians in the city. Here the evidence is indirect, since we do not yet have a systematic survey of Zambians in Elisabethville who did not join the sect. We do know, however, that the demographic characteristics of the Kitawala members' chiefdoms of origin were quite different from those chiefdoms on the Zambian side of the Luapula Valley as a whole. Most important, the home chiefdoms of Kitawala members were much larger than average. For members, the mean chiefdom had a population of 5,002, while the mean size of all chiefdoms in the region was 1,786. Women outnumbered men by a ratio of 1.29:1 in the average Kitawala chiefdoms and by a ratio of 1.43:1 in all Luapula chiefdoms. Paradoxically, the chiefdoms from which the Kitawalaists came had a lower rate of migration than the region as a whole. Thus Zambians who joined the sect in Elisabethville came from large chiefdoms where a fairly large proportion of the male population had not been forced to leave home in search of European employment, assuming that most men left home primarily to earn their tax money. The Kitawalists came from the minority of families, members of which were indeed forced to migrate—thus from the lowest strata of society in the Luapula Valley.[11]

On the basis of the foregoing analysis it is possible to arrive at a relatively precise description of those Zambians who joined Kitawala in Elisabethville. Economically and socially they had less to lose than anyone else in the city. They belonged to members of a persecuted nationality group in a particular economic position. However, they were largely a self-employed group over whom the Europeans had little direct economic control. They rebelled against black and white authority alike: the government, the missions, and the rural chiefs. Urbanized, detached from their rural homelands, they were the most vulnerable people in town. It is thus no wonder that they responded so enthusiastically to the Kitawala teachings.

The Belgian administration's treatment of the Kitawala cells in Elisabethville is indicative of the state of the colonial government in Katanga as it had developed through the prosperous years at the end of the 1920s. Strengthened by an unprecendented supply of copper revenues, the administration had embarked on a series of ambitious programs. Katanga officials, riding on the crest of the economic wave, had acquired a great self-confidence to go with their already proven patriotism to the motherland. The falloff in revenues occasioned by the depression had struck the colonial administration much later than it had private industry. For the whole of the Congo revenues had declined quite slowly, from 690 million francs in 1929 to 634 million in 1930 to 540 million in 1931. Thus the colonial administration was basically unshaken when Kitawala emerged openly in Elisabethville in the last quarter of 1931.[12]

The vice governor general of Katanga, Gaston Heenen, had discounted first reports of the sect and had gone on an extended home leave. Even in his absence, however, Heenen was the driving force within the Katanga administration. He had spent almost all of his African career in the province. Except in origin—his family were farmers from the Flemish province of Limburg—Heenen was the typical *Katangaleux*. He had risen through the ranks of the Belgian army from volunteer to second lieutenant before joining the colonial administration in 1911, and began his new career in rural Katanga where he remained— except for two years in the East Africa campaign—until 1921. In this first decade of African service he had demonstrated a remarkable capacity as an administrator, which was rewarded with promotions from territorial administrator to district commissioner. In 1922 he became commissioner general of Katanga, an office which brought him to Elisabethville as second in command of the provincial administration. In 1928 Heenen became vice governor general of the province.

From the moment he was first posted to Elisabethville, Heenen took a major concern in urban affairs. His greatest concern was for the welfare of urban Africans. Heenen was one of the first Belgians to realize that many of the Africans in Elisabethville had settled in the city more or less permanently. He therefore rejected the common administrative practices which left urban Africans at the mercy of their rural chiefs. Thus he opposed two prevailing colonial routines: sending Africans back to their villages after they had finished their term of labor, and governing them in the city through the chiefs' representatives. Heenen realized that a new culture was emerging in urban Katanga—a culture whose rules were different from those of the rural areas. For this reason he advocated the establishment of *centres extra-coutumiers* (CEC) in designated urban locations

where African customs would have the force of law. The colonial
administration agreed, and in 1926 declared the *cité indigène*
of Elisabethville the first *centre extra-coutumier* in the Congo.
Encouraged by this success, Heenen then advocated the devolution
of certain powers of local government to the African inhabitants
of the *centre extra-coutumier*.

Once again the colonial ministry adopted his idea, and in
1931 it promulgated a decree permitting the establishment of
institutions for African local government. The African local
government institutions envisioned by the ministry's decree
consisted of four parts: a council, a chief and his assistant, a
representative of the tutelary authority, and a supervisory
group called the *Comité protecteur*. In theory the latter two
agencies, which were European, would merely oversee the activities of the chief and council, which would be wholly African.

The council would be comprised of from five to twelve members, the exact total within this range to be decided by the
provincial authorities. The body should, however, include all
of the members of the 1926 CEC court as well as other Africans
nominated by the local district commissioner. The council's
functions were legislative and supervisory: it levied local
taxes and passed local ordinances and approved administrative
decisions of the chief of the CEC.

The chief and his assistant were to be chosen from among
the councilors, preferably from those who were judges of the
CEC court. The chief possessed extensive executive powers: the
enforcement of ordinances not specifically reserved to European
administrators, powers of police including the personal right to
incarcerate Africans for periods of up to twenty-four hours, and
the right to draft the local budget. These were wide powers to
grant to an African in 1931, hence the Colonial Ministry's
decree envisioned situations in which the administration might
grant the chief's powers to a European. Thus the governor of
the province had the right to declare an emergency during which
an agent of the colonial administration would serve as chief.
Under ordinary circumstances, however, the chief was to be an
African who would in turn be supervised by a European member of
the administration called the Representative of the Tutelary
Authority.

The 1931 decree separated the Representative of the Tutelary
Authority from the ordinary administrative hierarchy. Although
he was part of the territorial service, the representative was
appointed by and directly responsible to the governor general in
Léopoldville. His duties would include presiding over the CEC
council, authorizing the payment of funds included in the CEC's

budget, and giving assent to a limited number of the chief's administrative decisions. Hence, as defined by the decree, the representative's powers tended to encourage the exercise of power by the African whom he would supervise.

The colonial legislation also restricted the role of the *Comité protecteur* whose authority was, however, defined in extremely vague terms. Unlike the Representative of the Tutelary Authority, the six members of the *Comité protecteur* were appointed by the provincial governor in Elisabethville. By statute, three members of the *Comité protecteur* were members of the administration and three were chosen from other members of the Belgian community. The *Comité's* duties included: the right to inspect the CEC, to comment on the CEC's budget, and the preparation of an annual report on the CEC. Much of the *Comité's* later authority ultimately came from invoking a clause which empowered it to watch over the physical and moral condition of the CEC's inhabitants.

The original legislation creating Elisabethville's *centre extra-coutumier* strongly bore the imprint of its spiritual father, Gaston Heenen. And although it would fall on hard times after Heenen's departure from Katanga, it was always identified as his institution. As a result of this and other projects, Heenen and his immediate associates acquired a well-deserved reputation for promoting the rights of urban Africans. Heenen was, in fact, the leader of a liberal element in the Katanga administration which flourished in those last prosperous years before the onset of the depression.[13]

Heenen's right hand man in the administration of Elisabethville was district commissioner Auguste Verbeken. Like Heenen, Verbeken had risen through the ranks in rural Katanga whose languages and customs he knew intimately. He began his career in 1911 as *chef de poste*, the very lowest rank in the European administrative hierarchy, attaining the rank of territorial administrator in 1918 and assistant district commissioner of the Lomami district in 1925. In 1930, after three years as assistant district commissioner of Haut-Luapula district—the administrative division which included Elisabethville and the Belgian half of the Luapula Valley—Verbeken was named district commissioner of the new district of Elisabethville. This new district, which included only the city and its immediate surroundings, was an experiment in urban administration tailored to suit the projects of Vice Governor General Heenen, and Verbeken was Heenen's choice to run the new urban regime.

Like Heenen, Verbeken was devoted to the welfare of Africans, a concern which he pursued long after his departure from

the colonial administration. While still a territorial official,
he read widely in anthropology. As a result of this self-
instruction, he was later to write the first substantial biography of a local chief—the famous Msiri, founder of the Yeke
kingdom. After leaving the colonial service in 1933 Verbeken
founded *Ngonga,* the first African-language newspaper in Elisabethville. His conscience was not limited to matters of public
record. He was devoted to his mulatto son, Albert Berthier,
born to him by an African princess during his term of service in
the Lomami district. Like his superior, Heenen, Verbeken was
temperamentally committed to the promotion of African advancement;
as such he was a pillar of the liberal wing of the Katanga
administration.[14]

Not everyone in the territorial service shared the liberals'
views. Many remained convinced that urban Africans were unready
to operate the institutions which Heenen and Verbeken were con-
structing for them. Such privileges, the conservatives argued,
could prove dangerous if Africans were to fall victim to foreign
influences such as the communists and the pan-Africanists.
These suspicions intensified with the onset of the depression.
Unemployed and disgruntled Africans would surely be the targets
of outside agitators, and the liberal wing of the administration
—according to its opponents—would be far too soft to deal with
such a challenge.

In particular, the conservatives objected to Heenen's
indifference to the recently discovered Kitawala cells in Elisabethville. The vice governor general had not taken the matter
seriously enough to postpone a vacation trip to Europe. Many of
his opponents, on the other hand, felt that the movement was
extremely dangerous. They recalled an earlier outbreak of the
sect in rural Katanga which had gotten completely out of control:
in 1925-26 a Kitawala preacher called Mwana Lesa had ordered the
execution of seventy Africans before the administration even
heard of his movement. Conservatives in the Katanga government
harked back to the earlier incident to accuse Heenen of imprudent
behavior with regard to the new outbreak of Kitawala.

Among the leaders of the opposition were the officers of
the Force publique, which in the early years of the depression
had suffered more severe cutbacks than any other agency of the
colonial government. In 1930 the Force publique had expended
113.8 million francs, a figure which was reduced to 73.9 million
in 1931 and to 49.9 million in 1932. Relatively as well as
absolutely, the colonial army's share of total expenditures fell
from 15.9 to 8.7 percent of colonial spending. Officers of the
Force publique thus had good reason to fear that the colony's
defenses were being disproportionately sacrificed in the name of

economy. These fears made them the natural allies of those who
sought to strengthen the country's military, and by the same
token alienated them from officials such as Gaston Heenen who
appeared to be equally careless in the face of subversion.

A few days after the vice governor general's departure in
September 1931 his enemies sent an anonymous memorandum to his
interim replacement, L.-J. Postiaux, suggesting action against
both Kitawala and other subversive movements. To the conservatives, the basic problem was one of security. They asserted
that even the territorial administration might be infiltrated
by communists, warning that the magistracy might be too conscious
of legal constraints to act effectively against Kitawala and
other similar movements. The authors of the memorandum therefore suggested that Postiaux create a secret intelligence committee of four or five members responsible to the governor alone.
This select group would take security matters in hand.

The arguments advanced by the Katanga administration's
conservatives struck a responsive chord with official thinking
in Léopoldville. The governor general's staff had been troubled
by independent African religious movements since 1921, when the
Protestant-related Kimbanguist sect broke out among the Kongo
people. Equally troubled by Kitawala, officials in the colonial
capital were already preparing strong measures to deal with subversion when Postiaux received the memorandum from Heenen's
opponents. The process had begun in 1929 when Governor General
Auguste Tilkens established a counterespionage service as part
of the Force publique. In the same year the administration had
tightened restrictions on African movements in cities after dark
and on the sale to Africans of alcoholic beverages.

None of these measures having succeeded in curbing the
African sects, security-minded conservatives began calling for
more effective action. In response the governor of Léopoldville-
Kasai province in October 1931 established a secret committee
which was, in fact, much along the lines of the one suggested by
the Katanga conservatives. Given this initiative by the heads
of two of the Congo's four provinces, the governor general felt
obliged to create a new Congo-wide counterespionage service
which would include secret committees similar to those proposed
by the governor of Katanga and to those already established in
Léopoldville-Kasai.[15]

Acting Governor Postiaux, hence reinforced in his get-tough
policy, proceeded to act against the members of Kitawala. In
three raids conducted during the week before Christmas of 1931
Katanga soldiers and police arrested sixty of the hundred and
eighty known members of the movement in and around Elisabethville.

Following their existent Congo judicial procedures, the Zambian members were deported, some only after a few months in jail, while the Zaïrian members were sent to distant detention camps. Thus under Postiaux's leadership, the administration temporarily broke the back of the Kitawala movement. Later development would prove that the government had not acted effectively, but for the moment the conservatives in the Katanga administration had carried the day.

When Vice Governor General Heenen returned to Elisabethville in March 1932 he found it impossible to reverse the measures which his replacement had taken. There was no denying the necessity of suppressing Kitawala; neither could he dissolve the new security apparatus. At most he could import a new direction to the counterespionage service, making it subject to normal judicial procedures and less paranoid about African behavior.

District Commissioner Verbeken played an important role in the dissemination of Heenen's plays for redirecting the intelligence service. In June 1932 he sent a circular letter to his territorial administrators describing Heenen's goals for the counterespionage service. According to Verbeken, administrators should obtain most of their information directly, relying on a knowledge of local languages and individuals rather than through an elaborate spy network. On the basis of this personal familiarity with the local Africans, an administrator would then be able to evaluate critically the reports of paid informers. For Verbeken as for Heenen, no spy network could ever be as valuable as the confidence of the administered peoples.[16]

In the matters of Kitawala and counterespionage, then, Heenen and his allies were able to reestablish their influence in the Katanga administration. Other matters which arose, however, were not dispatched so quickly. Moreover, henceforth Katanga's liberal establishment would lose its élan. And as new problems arose Heenen and his friends would find it increasingly difficult to cope with them.

Needless to say, the sad state of the depression economy was at the root of most of the administration's difficulties. As layoffs followed layoffs, previously secure sections of the Belgian community began to feel the economic pinch, blaming the government for not coming to their aid. Belgian settlers, led by local newspaper editors and Monseigneur de Hemptinne, became restive. Desperate, they began to look for ways to force the government to intervene. At the annual meeting of the *Comité régional* held back in April 1931 they had already demanded the right to debate the provincial budget, a topic formerly reserved to the administration. At the next meeting a year later they

went a step further and passed a resolution urging the government to spend one hundred million francs on a public works program to promote the economic recovery of Katanga.[17]

The efforts of the settlers to obtain government financial
help came at a particularly inopportune time. The Congo government was on the brink of bankruptcy. Receipts from all sources
fell from 542 million francs in 1931 to 387 million in 1932. To
make matters worse, colonial companies which had obtained
government guarantees on their dividends were requesting unprecedented amounts from the colonial treasury. For the year 1933
the government anticipated paying colonial investors 105 million
francs. After three years of budget deficits these new demands
pushed the government into a fiscal crisis. The colonial
government had proposed a budget for operating expenses and
dividend guarantees of 725 million francs for 1933, but could
anticipate receipts of only half that amount. Thus of the money
that was expected, almost a third was already pledged to colonial investors.

Administrators in Brussels and Léopoldville, far from
adding to Katanga's budget, were looking for ways to cut back
expenditures. One strategy which they devised was to identify
and reduce the duplication of services. Each of the four provinces had its own administration which included not only the
territorial service but also a series of specialized departments.
In 1932 Governor General Tilkens ordered the elimination of the
territorial administration directly under the governor general
and his staff.

This reorganization resulted in some savings but not nearly
enough to restore the colonial budget to equilibrium. In
November 1932 Colonial Minister Paul Tschoffen called for massive aid from the metropolitan government. In view of the
Belgian taxpayer's notorious reluctance to spend money on the
Congo, this was indeed an act of desperation. This time Belgian
parliamentarians responded with uncharacteristic charity, voting
direct annual subsidies of 165 million francs for a period of
three years as well as a colonial lottery whose proceeds would
further supplement the colonial budget. In return, the metropolitan legislators demanded further cutbacks in administrative
costs for the colony. In response Colonial Minister Tschoffen
and Governor General Tilkens continued along the lines which
they had already established: maintaining the central administration as much as possible, while reducing expenditures on the
provinces. This policy fell particularly heavily on Katanga.

In 1932 Tschoffen and Tilkens had redrawn provincial boundaries, depriving Katanga of the Lomami district which had become

the Union Minière's principal source of labor. The final blow
fell in May 1933 when the Colonial Ministry decreed a general
administrative reorganization. Symbolically, the old provinces
were deprived of their names—all provinces were henceforth to
be designated by the name of their capital city. The vice
governors general were downgraded to provincial commissioners,
with the supervision of district commissioners as their main
task. Services which had formerly been administered in the
provinces were transferred to the cabinet of the governor
general, while the *comités régionaux* were reduced to provincial
councils with strictly limited membership.[18]

These structural reforms were accompanied by administrative economies which further cut back European personnel and
services. Until then the government had reduced only specialized departments while sparing the territorial administration.
Henceforth, even the latter was fair game; the average number of
territorial agents in Katanga fell by 18 percent, from 81 in
1933 to 66.5 in 1934. The economies had affected the colonial
bureaucracy at all its levels, threatening the privileged position of Katanga among the provinces and also boding a severe
decline in the efficiency of rural administration in all parts
of the Congo.

Administrators and settlers alike were stunned by the
severity of these measures. All four vice governors general
soon resigned from office rather than continue under the new
regime. Heenen left Katanga administration in September 1933
accompanied by two of the most important members of the liberal
wing of the administration: District Commissioner Auguste
Verbeken and Chief Justice Antoine Sohier of the Katanga Appeal
Court, who retired in 1934.

Enraged by the reorganization, settlers in Elisabethville
seriously considered seceding from the Congo. Leaders of the
community—including Monseigneur de Hemptinne, who had recently
become a bishop, and Jean Sépulchre, founder and editor of
Elisabethville's largest newspaper, *Essor du Congo*—tried to
convince Heenen "to take over the reins of an autonomous government and declare the independence of Katanga." Heenen briefly
considered the possibility but ultimately refused to head the
movement, which then evaporated for lack of support.

Heenen's subsequent thoughts on the matter, confided to the
British consul general during their homeward journey to Europe,
shed much light on the political situation in Katanga as well as
on his own plans. Heenen was not concerned with Elisabethville
politics where local leaders had no real power. He had Belgian
ambitions. Thus, he considered his retirement only as a temporary

140

setback in a career which he hoped would lead him to the
governor generalship or to the colonial portfolio—which indeed
he would eventually hold.

Heenen's reasoning suggests once again the degree to which
decisions affecting Elisabethville were determined by metropolitan considerations. The Europeans of Elisabethville, even
though they discussed secession from the Congo, did not possess
a discrete national identity. They were Belgian colonists whose
major concern when making vital decisions was the repercussion
such decisions were likely to have on their situation in Belgium.
As in earlier times, the link with Europe proved far stronger
than any local ties.[19]

The failure of this first Katanga sucession movement paved
the way for a reconciliation between the colonial hierarchy and
the settler community. To gain popular support, Governor General Tilkens bypassed the local leadership, appealing directly
to the poorer members of the European community. During a visit
to Elisabethville in December of 1933 he promised them long-
needed aid: relief for unemployed Europeans, incentives to
large companies to hire European workers in Africa, and help for
European farmers. He established a *bureau* of European labor
composed of delegates of large industries, the small settlers,
the government, and the OCTK. Before its termination in the
late thirties, this organization found jobs in the larger companies for many of the white unemployed and gave relief payments
to others. As an additional benefit and in order to compensate
for the closing of the upper classes of the Salesian high school,
the Congo administration opened a vocational school staffed by
employees of the large companies. The school became popular
as an institution of adult education and remained so even after
the Salesians reopened their upper level classes in 1936.[20]
Thus the Europeans who managed to survive the first four years
of the depression ultimately received government aid. They had
weathered the economic storm and became part of the postdepres-
sion community.

The economic crisis had played strange tricks on Elisabethville society, destroying groups which had appeared strong while
preserving groups which had seemed vulnerable. In the city's
European community two disparate groups, the liberal wing of the
administration and the English-speaking merchants, had suffered
the greatest losses. Most English-speakers, although longtime
residents, had recognized the futility of remaining in Belgian
territory and had moved south to the Rhodesias and South Africa.

Paradoxically, many of their former enemies in the Belgian
administration left at the same time. A sizeable proportion of

those patriotic Belgians who had defended the Congo against
settlers from the south had ultimately become members of the
progressive wing of the administration, men who believed in
improving conditions for Africans in Elisabethville. For them,
the Belgian nationality of the Congo could best be protected by
a more satisfied and hence more loyal African citizenry. By the
mid-thirties, however, the times had turned against them.
Budgetary reductions had made it henceforth impossible for
administrators to have the same intimate knowledge of Africans
which they had previously possessed. Moreover, future administrators would be overworked, spending more and more of their
time on the completion of bureaucratic forms rather than on the
administration of Africans.

As with the European community, important elements had
been eliminated from Elisabethville's African community. The
Union Minière had fired most of its Rwandese workers, who in
1930 had been the largest single ethnic group in the camps.
Despite their longer service, the company had also fired most
of its Zambians. What remained was a work force that was predominantly Kasaian, with a preponderance of workers from the
territory of Kabinda. Demographically as well as ethnically,
the work force that remained in the camps had been substantially
transformed. Where the camps had formerly contained a high
proportion of bachelors, most of the inhabitants were now
married. In the company as a whole the proportion of married
employees doubled, from 32.6 percent in 1929 to 65.3 percent in
1936. The Union Minière's African labor department had finally
obtained a largely stabilized labor force.[21]

Similar ethnic and demographic changes were taking place in
the *cité indigène*. Unfavorable economic conditions, potentiated
by Belgian persecution, persuaded many foreigners to leave the
cité. The proportion of Zambians there declined from about 40
percent of the *cité* population in 1929 to less than a third in
1942.[22] Surprisingly, those Zambians who stayed showed an increasing tendency to bring in their families from the villages.
From 1929 to 1946 the ratio of women to men in the *cité* had
risen from about 400 per thousand to 630. Thus the ratio between the sexes in the *cité*, like that in the Union Minière
camps, was more evenly balanced after the depression than it had
been before.

One can only suggest the explanation for this phenomenon.
The difficulty of remaining the city during the early thirties
had forced many Africans to rethink their attitudes toward
urban life. On the other hand many former city dwellers who
had returned to rural areas found life in their villages much
harder than they had remembered. Indeed, conditions in rural

areas may well have deteriorated as a result of the overrecruitment of the twenties. Thus many former city dwellers, disappointed by the villages, decided to return to the city and
brought their families with them.

Whatever the causes, Elisabethville emerged from the
depression more firmly rooted than it had been before. Most
Africans and Europeans who had withstood the storm were now
permanent residents. The stabilization of the city's population,
however, also had disadvantages from the African's standpoint.
Safe in the knowledge that workers were very unlikely to flee to
the countryside, employers could treat their workers less well
than they had done during the labor shortages of the 1920s.
The supply of labor also affected those poor whites committed to
living in Elisabethville; they had less leverage than formerly
with the managerial elite which ran the city's industry.

The late thirties would see a tightening of the screws on
almost everyone, both economically and in other ways. Residents
of Elisabethville were less independent than they had been previously. This was a phenomenon striking both Europeans and
Africans. Most obvious, the province of Katanga had lost much
of its autonomy as a result of the Tschoffen-Tilkens reorganization. Africans, too, were beginning to lose what little chance
they had for independent behavior. With the creation of the
secret police, African organizations found themselves under
increased Belgian surveillance. As the decade progressed,
liberty—always a comparative term—suffered in Elisabethville
as it did in many other parts of the world.

Chapter 8

In the Grip of the Autocrats, 1933-1940

1933 was a pivotal year for Elisabethville's Africans.   In
that year the two major Belgian agencies in Elisabethville, the
Union Minière and the colonial government, both adopted a more
authoritarian line toward Africans within their respective jurisdictions, although for different reasons.   Union Minière's managers tightened the screws on their African work force in order
to increase profits, while the colonial administrators did so
in the name of public order.   By the late 1930s, moreover, both
policies seemed to have succeeded, in that profits rose and
overt resistance—however feeble—to the colonial regime declined.
As far as Elisabethville was concerned, this success was more
apparent than real.   Under the placid surface discontent was
building up which would manifest itself during and after the
Second World War.   In those last prewar years, however, the
Europeans who ran the city had little inkling of any resistance
to their new policies.

Physically the city changed relatively little in the last
years of the 1930s.   Except for a few projects, including an
imposing new headquarters for the Union Minière on the edge of
the European city and some public buildings in the *cité indigène,*
little new construction was undertaken.   Since there was a
housing surplus by the mid-thirties, newly arriving Europeans
and Africans alike simply moved into unoccupied buildings which
had been abandoned at the beginning of the depression.   The
housing surplus is explained by population date.   Twenty-six
thousand people lived in Elisabethville in 1940, still less than
a decade earlier, although the population had grown steadily
since 1934.   Nor had one section of town grown at the expense
of any others.   Europeans still numbered about 10 percent of the
population; the combined population of the African work camps
was equal to that of the *cité.*

The major changes which took place in the late thirties
were organizational ones which could not be measured by changes
in the city's skyline. However, several important developments
did occur in provincial government and in the Union Minière
which would have a great effect on the lives of the city's
African inhabitants. These changes came in part because the
powerful copper company no longer faced the problem of finding
constant new sources of African labor.

The local managers of the Union Minière had discovered
their new power over their African employees two years before
they were able to take advantage of it. In 1931 the company's
management had been surprised by the resentment shown by Africans who were being repatriated from the mining camps. At that
time, however, the European bosses were in no position to derive
immediate benefit from their employees' attachment to camp life.
Retrenchment being the order of the day, the managers' main task
was to maintain a skeleton force which could be fleshed out when
economic conditions improved.[1]

The tide began to turn in 1933, when the Union Minière was
able to increase production from a low point of 54,064 tons in
1932 to 66,596 tons. This output, although small in comparison
to the peak years of the late twenties, signalled the Brussels
management's intention to revive production. Plans were drawn
up for further expansion in 1934, a year in which copper output
was to reach 110,085 tons, almost as much as it had been in 1928.[2]

Management attitudes toward African labor, however, had
changed considerably from those which had prevailed during the
earlier production boom. In the late twenties, still fearful
of another labor crisis, the company had treated Africans with
considerable circumspection. Such fears had been largely dispelled by the antirepatriation riots of 1931 and were to be completely allayed by the increasingly firm alliance between the
government and the copper industry which finally would be welded
in the late 1930s.

The relationship between the Belgian government and the
copper industry, it will be remembered, was as old as the Union
Minière. Between 1906—the year of the company's foundation—
and 1926, the government had intervened on behalf of the company both politically and financially on half a dozen occasions.
During the boom of the late 1920s, however, the power relationship between the two parties had been reversed, as the colonial
government became increasingly dependent on the copper industry
for revenue. Calculated conservatively, the Union Minière was
responsible for 18 percent of colonial receipts in 1926 and 24
percent in 1930. With the decline in other revenues at the

beginning of the depression, the mining industry's contribution
to the colonial budget reached a high of 32 percent in 1932.
During three years of intensive metropolitan subsidies to the
colonial treasury from 1933 to 1935, the industry's contribution
declined to an average of 13 percent, but with the end of the
metropolitan grants in 1936 the copper company's contribution
regained its earlier importance. Thus between 1936 and 1940 the
Union Minière generated an average of 25 percent of the total
colonial revenues.

Such an important contributor to the colonial exchequer
could hardly be ignored by colonial officials. No evidence has
yet appeared for the existence of a formal agreement on the
part of the colonial administration to compensate the Union
Minière for its contributions to the treasury, but administrators proved willing to help the company on a number of occasions.
Their greatest services were in the recruitment and maintenance
of the company's labor supply.

In the late thirties, when the Union Minière needed help in
recruitment, it called upon the provincial government of the
newly created province of Lusambo, better known as Kasai. Although the province itself was created in 1932, the area included
in its boundaries had long been a source of labor for the mines.
Beginning in the late 1920s most of the company's Zaïrian recruits came from the old Lomami District, now renamed Sankuru.
After the depression the district still was a principal source
of mineworkers, providing over two-thirds of the 3,099 men
which the Union Minière engaged between 1935 and 1941. This
recruitment depended on close cooperation between the company
and the highest levels of the provincial administration. Between July 1937 and June 1938 the province's chief executive,
Provincial Commissioner Wauters, authorized Union Minière labor
contract engagements while forbidding all other recruitment in
the province.

The chief executive of what was left of Katanga, then
called Elisabethville province, was similarly helpful. Although
the provincial commissioner could not give the company a recruitment monopoly, he did partition the Kabongo territory—from
which the copper company was obtaining a third of its new
recruits—between the Union Minière and the tin company, Géomines.

Government officials also helped the company maintain its
labor force in the mining camps. During the late 1920s the
Union Minière had instituted the stabilized labor policy, predi-
cated on the assumption that workers who lived in company camps
with their wives would work in the copper industry for longer
periods of time than single men living away from their families.

Thus the company's personnel department had begun encouraging
young bachelors to bring wives to the camps. To promote marriages, the company had started in 1931 to furnish bride-wealth
payments to bachelors who had found eligible girls. At this
point, however, the company's pro-nuptial policy had run into
another obstacle: traditionally, marriages were arranged only
after protracted discussions on the terms of the marriage contract between the family of the groom and the family of the
bride.

To overcome this sticking point the territorial administrator at Kanda-Kanda, located in the heart of the Union Minière's
recruitment region, found a way to help the company marry off
its bachelors. The colonial official cleverly suggested that
he, rather than the grooms' families, could take care of the
negotiations. Accordingly, a new procedure developed whereby
the worker brought his request for his intended's hand to the
head of his mining camp who then wrote to the administrator of
the man's home territory. Thus marriages in the camps between
Africans were arranged through two European intermediaries.
The system became very popular, and the number of marriages
thereby arranged rose from 133 in 1935 to 243 in 1938.

The Union Minière's marriage brokerage system had extremely
damaging psychological implications for the Africans who became
its clients. Most important, it fostered increased feelings of
helplessness in that African men thus married realized that they
depended on their employer not only for wages, food, and housing,
but for love and family as well. Complementarily, the system
reinforced feelings of paternalism on the part of European
supervisors. The directors of the personnel service, Toussaint
and Mottoulle, expressed these feelings succinctly in instructions issued to their European staff in 1938: "the blacks have
the souls of children," went the memo, "and the company must act
as their guardians."

The Union Minière's paternalism had financial rewards in
the form of higher productivity. Africans who were scientifically nourished, well-housed, and married stayed on the job
longer and worked harder while they were there. The effect of
these labor stabilization policies grew over time. At the end
of 1940, 78 percent of the workers at the Lubumbashi camp had
more than three years' experience while 37 percent had worked
for the company for more than nine years. As a consequence of
the longer terms of employment, workers became seasoned to the
camp, enjoying better health than new recruits. The deathrate
at the camp as a whole fell from twenty per thousand in 1928 to
less than two per thousand in 1939, despite enormous cuts in
medical service during the early thirties. By the outbreak of

the Second World War, the Union Minière supervisors had achieved
their goal of a stabilized labor force.[3]

As professional managers, company officials were also concerned with cutting costs. Their problem was to devise economies which would not lower production. At the depth of the
depression they had been remarkably successful, reducing total
African labor costs by half—from three shillings and eight
pence per worker per day in 1932 to one shilling and ten pence
per day in 1935. Despite the severity of these reductions,
managers continued to look for ways of economizing. In the
opinion of the African personnel service only two expenditures
could be further reduced without cutting back on productivity:
food costs and expenditures for education for the children of
workers.

Throughout the remainder of the decade members of the Union
Minière's provisioning department found a number of ways to
effect small savings on the food rations issued to African employees. First they began replacing meat with equally nutritious
fish. This raised no objections from workers as long as the fish
was fresh; most Africans had eaten fish as their principal
source of protein before coming to the mines. In 1936, however,
the provisioning department began supplying smoked fish, and
this caused resentment. Africans did not object to smoked fish
as such, but they did resent the company's practice of giving
only 700 grams of it for every kilogram of meat in the normal
meat ration. As far as the company was concerned the lesser
quantity of smoked was the nutritional equivalent of the greater
quantity of fresh fish, but the Africans saw only that they were
getting smaller amounts of food in their rations. By 1940 more
than 40 percent of the protein ration was fish, most of it
smoked, and workers were understandably resentful of their diminished rations.

The company also economized on the rations given workers'
wives. The company had originally provided wives with the
same variety of rations as their husbands, albeit in slightly
smaller quantities. During the 1930s, however, the company
eliminated fruit and vegetables from the wives' rations, assigning them garden plots instead. The rationale for this change
was moral as well as economic in that managers felt that wives
in the camps had been unnecessarily idle. Reasoning that idle-
ness would lead to promiscuity and promiscuity to disputes which
would lower production, the personnel department gave the women
garden plots to keep them busy while their husbands were at work.
Unfortunately, the soil in these plots was soon exhausted, and
the company did not provide new plots or fertilizers. Thus the
wives had been deprived of their rations without receiving any

compensation. Both the smoked fish and the garden plots would
return to haunt the company during the African strike of 1941.[4]

The effects of economies in the schools provided for Africans
were felt even sooner. Early in the depression the personnel
department had criticized the schools run in the camps by the
Benedictine Fathers as "bookish," since these schools were not
directed sufficiently at training good laborers. Following cuts
in the educational budget, the schools did not train scholars
either. In 1938 only eight of the 419 school-aged children at
the Lubumbashi camps were receiving postprimary training. The
consequences of this policy became apparent in May 1941 when
tests given to African clerks revealed that they could scarcely
add, or write and speak French.

From the mid-thirties onwards company officials realized
that these economies in education were costing the company in
lost services, but they still refused to build an effective education system in the camps. Either consciously or unconsciously,
they preferred not to create a group of educated Africans who
might challenge the company's authority. High level managers
however, such as Dr. Léopold Mottoulle, assistant director of
the personnel department, recognized the indirect costs of
paternalism. In 1934 he estimabed that only 5 percent of the
Union Minière's African employees were performing tasks previously reserved to Europeans. In contrast, some 63 percent of
the BCK railway African staff were in jobs formerly held by
Europeans. The railroad company had trained over 2,000 of its
employees at special trade schools during terms ranging from
five weeks to eighteen months. In the thirties the Union Minière
opposed such schools despite their demonstrated success, pre-
ferring not to raise their workers' horizons.[5]

Characteristically, the mining company rewarded its workers
for long service and loyalty rather than for technical or managerial skills. The device by which the Union Minière allocated
power to some of its African employees clearly demonstrated how
company management encouraged these nonintellectual qualities.
In 1934 the personnel department created an elite rank called
Main d'oeuvre indigène/spécialisée (specialized native labor
force; MOI/S). The rank of MOI/S carried with it a number of per-
quisites, including better housing and higher wages, and many
Africans aspired to attain it. The means of selection of the
MOI/S and the duties which its titularies performed, however,
fostered passivity rather than leadership.

The selection of the MOI/S was entirely in the hands of the
European chief of each of the African residential camps, and no
single set of qualifications was established for the position.

Qualifications did make a difference as far as salaries for
production work were concerned, but not for this "elite" status.
Thus the would-be MOI/S had to find some way of ingratiating
himself with his white headman. Some tried fawning servility
while others resorted to black magic. One popular technique
was to throw a ritually slaughtered chicken at the white chief's
house. Given the social distance between the personnel department and the African miners, this method was as effective an
influence as any other, particularly if the white man could find
out which African wanted the job badly enough to sacrifice a
Sunday dinner!

Once selected for the job, the MOI/s had few opportunities
for exercising leadership over their fellow employees. In
theory, they were supposed to serve as models of behavior for
their coworkers; in practice, their main duties were to convey
managerial directives to the other workers and to report
trouble-makers to the *chef de camp* at their weekly meeings with
him. Thus the men promoted to the rank of MOI/S were expected
to conform to a very passive model, in no way operating as
leaders of their fellow Africans.[6]

Less than a hundred miles from the nearest Union Minière
camp, British companies on the Northern Rhodesian copperbelt
were fostering a substantially different African leadership.
Many of the patterns for development in what is now Zambia were
established at the Roan Antelope Mine at Luanshya. Compared
with Union Minière establishments in Elisabethville, Luanshya
operations were recent, exploitable deposits having been discovered only in 1926 and the town built next to the mining camp
in 1930.

African labor at the Roan Antelope mine fell under the
jurisdiction of F. Spearpoint, the compound manager—the British
equivalent of a Belgian *chef de camp*. Like his Belgian counterparts, Spearpoint realized the need for an organized group of
Africans to serve as intermediaries between himself and the
mass of African workers. At first he relied on the mine's
African police force, but he found these men more concerned
with bolstering their own authority than in communicating
workers' grievances. Thus the policemen tried to prevent
workers with complaints from reaching the compound manager,
reasoning that such complaints would only annoy him.

Frustrated by these obstructions, Spearpoint created a new
group to serve as a channel of communications between himself
and the workers. In 1931, after clearing his innovation with
the various ethnic groups working at the mine, Spearpoint established a council of ten tribal elders. Instead of choosing them

himself, he allowed the members of each ethnic group at the
mine to elect its own representative. This selection procedure
could not have been further from that employed at the Union
Minière. Afrians who were elected to the council had the confidence on the one hand that Spearpoint was willing to listen to
them, and on the other that they had the support of their constituents.

The tribal elders had two sets of responsibilities. As a
group they attended council meetings where they reported grievances and received managerial directives, much the same as their
counterparts at the Union Minière. In addition, however, the
tribal elders performed many of the functions of rural chiefs.
They received extra rations and larger houses much like their
counterparts in the Congo but they were expected to use their
special facilities to lodge and feed newcomers to the mining
camp. They also acted as judges for their constituents in petty
cases, mostly of a domestic character.

This authority both enhanced the status of the elders and
insulated the mass of Africans from the European management of
the mine. One might also infer that it saved the British managers considerable amounts of time and money which they might
otherwise have spent in deciding cases or in lodging newcomers
fresh from the villages. Whatever the company's aims, the
devolution of economic and judicial authority to the tribal
elders prevented the creation of an atmosphere of paternalism at
the Roan Antelope Mine. Unlike the Union Minière Africans, the
Roan workers developed a sense of their independence from
European authority.[7]

The contrast between the two varieties of mining camp under-
lines the managerial objectives of the Union Minière's personnel
department. The Belgian company was interested in its employees
beyond their time on the job. By regulating off-the-job aspects
of its employees' lives, the company hoped to maximize production. In the 1930s the Union Minière was creating a total institution for African employees comparable to that which it had
created for its European employees a decade earlier. Despite
external differences, the basic model was the same: complete
control of employees' lives in order to increase copper output.
The process had taken somewhat longer with the African staff,
largely because of the earlier shortage of African labor. Now
that African workers were eagerly seeking long term jobs in the
mines, the company could enclose them in a total institution
like that built for their European coworkers.

The new system which developed was even harder on Africans
than the total institution in which Europeans had lived. Most

of the white employees of the Union Minière were Belgian citizens who, at least theoretically, could protest company abuses
in Belgian courts. The African employees, by contrast, were
members of a conquered race, a colonized people who had only
those rights which the Belgians chose to give them. In addition,
their total institution was to be much longer-lasting than that
constructed for Europeans.

During the late thirties, as a matter of fact, the company
began to ease its controls on European workers. The major step
in that direction taken by the Union Minière was to agree to
hire European workers already living in Katanga. During the
twenties the company had kept its white workers in check by
preventing them from developing roots in Africa. Few local
Europeans were hired because they were potentially too independent. The threat of firing was far more serious to a man who
risked being sent back to Belgium than it was to a man who had
his own home and friends in Elisabethville.

By 1933, of course, the considerations which had once mili-
tated against hiring Europeans in Elisabethville had diminished
in importance. Local Europeans long out of work could not
afford to annoy any potential employer. The Europeans left in
Elisabethville, moreover, were Belgians and Italians, rather
than the South Africans who had caused the Union Minière so much
trouble after the First World War. Thus the company risked
little in hiring the local settlers.

On the contrary, the Union Minière stood to gain from the
points of view of public relations and economy. For very little
cost the company could gain the gratitude of the colonial
government and the white community for putting unemployed Europeans to work. These settlers cost the company less than agents
hired in Europe, since they did not require an expensive voyage
at the beginning and end of their contract. Furthermore, the
company did not have to house them in camps until they found
permanent housing. Lower cost was probably the deciding factor
in the company's decision to change its hiring policy, and between 1937 and 1939 it hired locally one-third of its new white
personnel.[8]

Thus Europeans at the Union Minière in 1940 found themselves somewhat less under company control than they had been
a decade earlier. Yet the Africans felt the full weight of the
company and were now inmates of an oppressive total institution.
The changes in the treatment of its subordinate European and
African staff were not the result of substantial shifts in the
direction of policy. They were simply new methods of obtaining
the Union Minière's permanent goal of maximizing profit, implemented by a local management little changed from the late twenties.

The colonial government at Elisabethville, by contrast, had undergone enormous changes in both top personnel and policy. The liberal wing of the administration, represented by Vice Governor General Gaston Heenen, District Commissioner Auguste Verbeken, and the great jurist, Antoine Sohier, had gone into retirement. Their successors not only opposed many of their policies, but they were much less adept at carrying on the daily functions of government. Perhaps no group of administrators could have maintained effective government after the budget cuts which hit the province in 1932-33, but the records left by the new rulers of Katanga show them to have been reactionary and incompetent, irrespective of the available funds.

The leader of this new regime was Heenen's successor, Amour Maron, who held the office of provincial commissioner for the Province of Elisabethville. It is undoubtedly significant that in 1933 the Colonial Ministry abolished both the name of Katanga and the title of vice governor general. At any rate, Maron was the man for the reduced job. An educated Walloon from rural Namur, Maron had completed a degree in commerce at the University of Louvain before entering the colonial service in 1912. For the next twenty years he held a variety of administrative posts, primarily in the province of Congo-Kasai. In 1932, after a brief term as acting head of that province, Maron transferred to Katanga as commissioner general, second in command and heir apparent to Gaston Heenen.

Maron's views about Africans could not have been further from those of his predecessor. He was particularly distrustful of educated Africans. At the last meeting of the *Comité régional* in April 1933, he disclosed an almost classical prejudice against them. For him, they were "semi-civilized" and "subject to excesses." Worse, if not carefully controlled they might become "a class of malcontents, a logical source for recruitment of the leaders and sowers of subversive ideas." Thus Maron was particularly inept in dealing with the more literate Africans in Elisabethville.[9]

Like the provincial commissioner, his second in command, Charles Dupont, had some knowledge of the Congo but little experience in Katanga. Born to a prominent Brussels family in 1889, Dupont studied law at the University of Brussels. He entered the colonial magistracy in 1914, spending most of the next seven years in the western part of the colony. In 1922 he spent a few months as head of colonial minister Franck's personal cabinet, but he soon resigned from the post to take a job with Huiléries du Congo belge, a subsidiary of Lever Brothers, which ran a chain of oil palm plantations in the western Congo. Before

his retirement from the plantation company in 1931 he was named
to the Commission for the Protection of Natives in Brussels.
This renewed contact with the administration prepared the way
for his reentry into government service, and at the end of 1933
Dupont became principal district commissioner at Elisabethville.

Dupont's particular blindspot complemented that of Maron.
The district commissioner distrusted rural chiefs. He defined
his position most clearly in a report which he wrote in February
1935 after investigating an outbreak of Kitawala in rural south-
western Katanga. Although Dupont reluctantly concluded that
the movement caused little immediate harm, he nonetheless recommended preventative measures. Characteristically, he proposed
the creation of a secret police network of Africans attached to
district commissioner, a network which would be entirely unknown
to the commissioner's European subordinates. Beyond this cir-
cumvention of colonial authority, Dupont also proposed to over-
ride existing African political institutions. He thought that
"the black representative of the colonial authority ought to be
imposed on the collectivity. Customs have nothing to do with
his function as invested chief." This position was anathema to
the advocates of indirect rule and to the chiefs themselves.
Dupont's solution to the problem, moreover, ran contrary to
Maron's position regarding educated Africans. The district
commissioner felt that "only literate natives, educated in the
missions and having proved their attachment to the European
regime, should be invested as chiefs." Thus the two leading
members of the new administration distrusted complementary sections of the African population.[10]

Maron's other close collaborator, Paul van Arenberg, in
contrast to Maron and Dupont, by reputation was a great friend
of the Africans. Van Arenberg was a dynamo of energy who burned
himself out at an early age. Like Dupont, he had studied law
at the University of Brussels where he had graduated with high
honors. In 1926 he went to Elisabethville as a substitute
magistrate, rising to the rank of chief prosecutor in 1935. He
was a good friend of Father Grégoire Coussement, energetic head
of the Benedictine mission in the *cité indigène*. Van Arenberg
took an active role in mission activities, serving as scout-
master to Coussement's black scout troop and as an advisor to
the club which Coussement had founded for *évolués*. Thus van
Arenberg inspired greater confidence on the part of Africans
than either Maron or Dupont and, as events would show, was ultimately more dangerous to them.[11]

Van Arenberg, like the other members of Maron's new regime,
was committed to a hard line in dealing with African dissidence,
and none of them shrank from using the new security apparatus

which had been created during the Kitawala outbreak of 1931.
Dominating these activities was the secret committee to which
Maron appointed Dupont as chairman, van Arenberg, and Father
Coussement; these three men constituted the high command in
Maron's battle against subversion.

The new team received its first test at the end of the
rainy season in 1934 when the Elisabethville police discovered
another outbreak of Kitawala. In contrast to the situation in
1931, the administration was ready for action. Once the essential information was collected, the police captured all known
Kitawala members in a single predawn raid on May 7th. Within
eight days the government prepared an expulsion ordinance for
forty Zambians who were hurried across the Luapula into British
territory. All this went smoothly, and the members of the
secret committee congratulated themselves on their tough-minded
handling of the sect. After a few months, however, they learned
that they had acted with undue haste. In October the Belgian
territorial administrator in the Luapula Valley reported that
eighteen of the forty expulsees had not been members of the sect
at all, but had been falsely accused by African detectives on
the Elisabethville police force whom the authorities had believed
without question.

Even in light of this evidence of overreaction, however,
the secret committee could look back on the 1934 raid as a
success. Although Kitawala would henceforth appear in many
parts of the Congo, the movement never again became important
in Elisabethville. For members of the sect there were many
safer places in Central Africa.[12]

Having successfully employed the powers of the colonial
government to extirpate Kitawala in Elisabethville, Maron and
his friends set about to deal with other problems of urban
administration. As far as they were concerned the greatest
challenge to their authority was the institution for partial
urban government for Africans, the *Centre extra-coutumier* (CEC).
None of them approved of the principle of devolving authority
to Africans, but they could not directly abolish government
agencies which had been established by their liberal predecessors. Maron and his minions therefore spent considerable time
and effort trying to subvert the institutions without attacking
them directly. Actually these men were continuing a demolition
already begun.

During the last years of the previous regime Vice Governor
General Heenen had not implemented the decree for African urban
government as he had originally envisioned it. The Colonial
Ministry had issued the decree empowering the provincial govern-

ments to establish the CECs in November 1931 during Heenen's home leave in Belgium. But when Heenen returned to Elisabeth-ville four months later he found that the conservatives, using the Kitawala outbreak as an excuse, had completely changed the direction of the administration's policies toward Africans. In the brief time he had left in office Heenen thus had to modify his plans for the CEC to meet the new political reality, and when he used his administrative powers to create the new insti-tution in August 1932 he had no choice but to forego a central element in his project, the African chief. The accordance with Article 16 of the ministry's enabling legislation, he declared a state of emergency and named a European territorial agent as chief of the new CEC. Thus when Heenen left office in September 1933, the only African component of the CEC that was functioning was the African council.

Heenen's successors went to a considerable effort to des-troy the CEC. Using the provincial commissioner's power to appoint the members of the *Comité Protecteur*, Maron packed the supervisory body with individuals opposed to African self-government. Furthermore, he secured the appointment to the post of representative of the Tutelary Authority of L. Laurent, Territorial Administrator, who proved an enthusiastic collabor-ator in sabotaging the CEC.

During the mid-thirties the main strategy of Maron and his associates was designed to prevent the emergence of African leadership on the CEC council and in its two executive positions. The administration's first target was the CEC council which, according to the 1931 statute, had real powers of local legis-lation and taxation. To undercut the council, Maron and his men began a process of tinkering with its membership. When Maron took office in 1933 the administration reduced the coun-cil's membership from twelve to five carefully chosen educated Africans who were presumably amenable to the administration's suggestions. When these councilors proved uncooperative, the government increased the the number of councilors to twelve, then reduced it to eight, then increased it again to ten. These frequent and arbitrary changes of membership were very destruc-tive of the council's original legislative function. Councilors came to see themselves as "yes-men" rather than as representa-tives of their various communities. By 1940 the job had become so unimportant that it could no longer attract competent candi-dates; four of the ten councilors could not even write their own names.[13]

While Maron was undermining the council, he was also fight-ing a rearguard, and ultimately unsuccessful, action to prevent the appointment of an African chief of the CEC. The provincial

commissioner preferred that the job remain in European hands,
but he found himself under pressure from higher authorities.
In June 1934 the Colonial Ministry informed him that it was
legally impossible to keep the CEC government functioning without an African executive. To avoid inconsistency the ministry
advised him either to appoint a chief or to repeal Heenen's
ordinance of 1932 which had created the Elisabethville CEC.
This Maron was unprepared to do, given the enthusiasm which
local Africans had shown for the CEC. He persevered through
inaction until June 1936, when Governor General Pierre Ryckmans
ordered him outright to appoint an African chief and an assistant chief for the CEC. Even then Maron delayed the installa-
tion of the new chief until July 1937. Thus he had held off
the appointment of a chief for nearly four years.[14]

    Once the chief had been appointed, Maron turned to yet
another strategy: destruction of the CEC by amalgamating it
with the European section of town through the establishment of a
new administrative unit which would be dominated by the settlers.
In 1939 he got the European community to endorse the old project
of an Urban District designed to become an institution of European local government. Although his superiors in Léopoldville
and Brussels welcomed a project by which Elisabethville would
obtain its own city government, paid for by local taxes, they
persisted in their refusal to allow the destruction of the CEC's
government. The Colonial Ministry authorized the creation of a
new Urban District, with members appointed by the Provincial
Commissioner to a city council but the new statute excluded the
CEC from its boundaries, attaching the African quarter to the
rural territory of Sakania. Once again the CEC was saved, but
this time only temporarily. In 1944 agents of the Europeans'
Urban District literally invaded the CEC building, evicting the
CEC staff and installing their own African Population Bureau.
Then when the offices of CEC chief and subchief became vacant,
the administration refused to fill them. All that was left was
a token CEC council which had been deprived of all real authority.
Heenen's project for African self-government had finally been
destroyed, this time with the acquiescence of the colonial
hierarchy.

    Ironically, the European agency which effectively replaced
the CEC—the Elisabethville Urban District—gave the local settlers less self-government than they wanted since its powers
were strictly limited to local affairs. It was, however, a step
forward from the lowpoint of settler representation which
occurred in 1933 during the great governmental reorganization.
At that time the Colonial Ministry had removed all settlers from
Katanga's quasi-legislative body, the Regional Committee. The
exclusion of settlers from the Provincial Council, which replaced

the Regional Committee in 1934, moved settlers to form private
groups which could represent their interests to the provincial
government. Most of these groups proved ephemeral, being little
more than vehicles for the political ambitions of colonial
journalists; but one group, the *Fédération des Groupements et
Associations du Katanga,* did organize on a large scale. The
new settler association would play an important role in the
policies of the Urban District and many years later in Katanga
Secession. In the late thirties, however, its main significance
was in rallying Europeans against the CEC.[15]

African government could not survive in the presence of any
organized European competition. The whole idea of an African
government in the CEC, moreover, was something of an anomaly.
Nowhere else in settler Africa had Africans obtained representative institutions before similar institutions were granted to
the European settler community. Across the border in Northern
Rhodesia, to take one example, Europeans had sat on Village
Management Boards and in the Legislative Council long before
Africans had ever received such representation. There the Europeans obtained seats first and Africans fought long and hard to
obtain the same representation.[16]

Returning to the case of Elisabethville, neither Africans
nor Europeans obtained elected self-government during the
thirties. As in the 1920s, the Colonial Ministry was not prepared to share its lawmaking powers with anyone. Moreover, the
ministry would not authorize even municipal elections until
1957, only three years before independence.

In Northern Rhodesia, by contrast, the elective principle
was established for Africans in the 1930s, paradoxically in the
mines more than in the towns. In 1931 the management of the
Roan Antelope mine at Luahshya took the lead in encouraging
Africans to elect their own tribal elders. In the towns, the
Northern Rhodesian government appointed tribal elders upon the
recommendation of rural chiefs. In 1938 the town and mine
governments in Luanshya were amalgamated into a single body,
the Advisory Committee. Thus in Luanshya at least, a single
body represented all of the Africans from one urban area.[17]

In Elisabethville the administration of Africans in the
camps would be kept strictly separate from that of Africans in
the city until 1957. Indeed, instead of leading the government
toward greater African representation, the Union Minière was
providing the example for greater repression without representation. Of course, no one in Maron's administration proposed
to treat the Africans of Elisabethville as members of a single
community either. Government and industry had reached a

consensus quite different from the one developing in Northern
Rhodesia. Leading whites in the copperbelt believed that more
liberal policies from an earlier period would be attenuated and
Africans brought to heel.

The autocratic policies of the Europeans in power provoked
a variety of responses from Africans in Elisabethville. At the
beginning of Maron's regime, Africans sought to protect their
interests through urban associations of a type traditionally
successful in helping blacks cope with earlier problems of
survival in the city. When these associations proved unequal
to the task, many Africans turned to the Roman Catholic missions.
In the presence of determined opposition from the provincial
administration, however, none of these groups succeeded very
well.

The decline of the urban associations had begun in 1933
just before the departure of the liberal wing of the Katanga
administration. It started with the controversy over public
dancing. European ballroom dancing had become popular with
Africans in the early thirties and several of the ethnic clubs
had opened their own dance halls. Reports of "immoral behavior"
at these halls reached the leaders of European opinion, and
early in 1933 the archbishop, Monseigneur de Hemptinne, and the
assistant director of the Union Minière's Personnel Department,
Dr. Mottoulle, formally complained to provincial authorities.
District Commissioner Auguste Verbeken investigated the matter,
finding no impropriety in the operation of the dance halls; but
he felt obliged to take action against them nonetheless. In
April 1933 Verbeken announced that the alcoholic licenses of
these establishments would be allowed to expire, adding however
that ballroom dancing would be continued at the new CEC hall.

After Verbeken's resignation from the administration, the
new representative of the Tutelary Authority for the CEC, L.
Laurent, carried matters a step further. In 1934 he issued an
order requiring all African associations which used the community dance hall to hold their regular meetings in the CEC building as well. Henceforth the formerly independent ethnic associations held their meetings in a single room, one after the
other, under European supervision. Furthermore, Laurent forbade
certain organizations whose membership was primarily foreign
from meeting at the CEC hall. This ruling effectively barred
all foreign clubs from public social gatherings, since they
could neither obtain liquor licenses nor use the dance facilities at the CEC[18]

Among these clubs, a major target of the Europeans' wrath
was the *Association Franco-Belge,* a group ostensibly limited to

Africans originally from French territory but whose membership
also included those Zaïrois who had learned the French language.
The knowledge of the colonizers' language gave the leaders of
the association great confidence in dealing with the authorities.
In 1931 they were the only African group outside of those
founded by the Benedictine mission to register officially with
colonial authorities. However, their confidence was perhaps
misplaced. Even Verbeken was a bit distrustful of the association, characterizing its members as "rather cultivated, exces-
sively pretentious, often highly paid." Fitting this image very
well was the Franco-Belge's president, Mustapha, a railway
engineer. Despite this African's off-putting demeanor and
foreign origin, Verbeken nonetheless invited him to serve as one
of three speakers at the dedication of the new CEC building in
1933.

Not surprisingly, the club fell into difficult times under
the Maron regime. The representative of the Tutelary Authority,
Laurent, saw the prestige of an association of "foreign Africans"
as a threat to Belgian authority. Thus he banned the Association Franco-Belge, together with the Malawians' club, the Tonga
Special Committee, from using the CEC building. This ruling,
in effect from 1934 to 1937, destroyed the two foreign associations as leaders of Elisabethville's African community.[19]

Zaïrian ethnic associations, although escaping the ban
inflicted on the foreign clubs, also fell on hard times. During
the twenties and early thirties these associations had performed
the important functions of organizing the distribution of food
and finding housing for their members, thus helping hundreds of
Africans to survive in a hostile urban environment. This function ran counter to the aims of the Maron administration which
did not want Africans to remain in Elisabethville unless they
were employed.

A further source of tension between the Zaïrian associations and the new regime occurred over the *Centre extra-coutumier.*
The new local governmental district had its own budget, funds of
which were allocated by the CEC council and chief. Thus representation on the council, which also had the right to select the
chief, meant real political power and it is hardly surprising
that the leaders of the already influential ethnic associations
sought positions in the newly established body. In response
Maron and his associates, being particularly reluctant to grant
any additional power to the ethnic associations, raised as many
barriers as possible to their representation in the council.

The first CEC council, installed while Gaston Heenen was
still chief executive, had already posed a set of problems for

the leaders of the ethnic associations. The twelve man council
appointed in 1932 had consisted of eight judges (appointed under
the urban courts law of 1926) plus four other members selected
by District Commissioner Verbeken. These judges came from a
social background substantially different from that of the
association presidents. The former were men with ties to rural
chiefs; they had often acquired a knowledge of French and had
proved their political loyalty to the colonial administration.
The latter, by contrast, were commoners who had been informally
chosen as club leaders by their neighbors in the *cité* without any
reference to their loyalty to the colonial administration. When
members of the various ethnic associations learned in 1932 that
Africans other than CEC judges would be named to the CEC council,
many sought to have their leaders appointed. In cases where
their old presidents seemed too far from the Belgian's idea of a
proper African leader, the clubs quickly elected new officers.

All this proved of no avail when Maron installed his regime
at the end of 1933. The CEC council was reduced to five, and
Maron's regime appointed Africans who had close ties to the
Catholic missions to serve on it. The ethnic associations obtained no representation on the CEC council then or, for that
matter, any time before the Second World War. Moreover, the
ethnic clubs' general influence in the *cité* was to show a general demise after the mid-thirties.[20]

By the end of the decade the heads of the declining ethnic
associations had long since realized that the Maron regime had
no intention of allowing them to exercise any political power
within the CEC. However, failure to gain political influence
was not the only cause for the clubs' decline. With recovery
from the depression, the associations had lost many of their
economic functions. Long time residents could now obtain food
and shelter without having to rely on the associations. Gradually the clubs fragmented and diminished in size to the point
that they became informal agencies through which a few people
from the same village could share their resources until they
obtained permanent jobs.

Thus the ethnic associations gradually lost their importance
in Elisabethville's African community. Their decline, however,
should not detract from the crucial role which they played
during the first twenty-five years of the city's existence. The
ethnic associations performed a vital acculturative function
during the city's formative years, facilitating the survival of
rural Africans in an essentially hostile urban environment. As
conditions improved in the city, however, most Africans found it
possible to live without these associations and the institutions
subsequently had atrophied by the eve of World War II.

During the same period the influence of the Catholic missions increased among Elisabethville's Africans. The missions catered to the Africans' more spiritual needs, but most important, they provided education, which was the key to advancement in colonial society. Under devoutly Catholic colonizers like the Belgians, moreover, a Catholic education was a surer way to advancement than a Protestant one.

Paradoxically, more Africans living in Elisabethville in the 1930s had received their education outside of the city than in it. Most of the best educated Africans in the city had gone to schools run by the Scheut Fathers in the province of Lusambo (Kasai). In 1935 the Scheutists taught a hundred thousand children in their primary schools and over five hundred in post primary schools. In addition, they sent thirty-three young African men to major seminaries, the only higher education then available to Zaïrois. (See Table 8.1) Compared with the Scheut Fathers of Kasai, the Benedictines of Katanga provided inferior and less extensive facilities. The latter's primary schools reached only half of Elisabethville's school-aged African children, while between 1932 and 1938 enrollment in post-primary classes was limited to forty-three per year.[21]

Since there were so few opportunities for African education in Elisabethville, the Benedictine schools—especially the *Ecole St. Boniface*, successor to the School for Clerks-in-Training—were extremely popular. Many rural students came to live with relatives in the *cité* in order to attend St. Boniface. Well-informed parents sent their children to the Benedictines because the Fathers had access to an increasing number of jobs, both with the government and the Union Minière. The most desirable of these posts—apart from the chiefship of the CEC—were the clerkships at the Elisabethville European courts, positions first open to Africans as an economy measure during the depression. Other mission school graduates became teachers in the Benedictine primary schools, but these jobs were unpopular on account of the low salaries attached to them.[22]

Most graduates were far from happy with their new jobs since they were underpaid and subject to the same restrictions as the rest of the African population. In his annual report for 1937 Provincial Commissioner Maron wrote that educated Africans' salaries were "rarely in harmony with their needs, their training, or the cost of living." Having failed to achieve either high salaries or status, the *évolués* became restive. Most frequently they vented their frustrations after work in drunkenness, gambling, and brawling.[23]

Table 8.1

CATEGORIES OF EDUCATED AFRICANS AT BENEDICTINE

AND SCHEUT MISSIONS, 1936-1945

Of the six Catholic orders serving in Katanga, these two
were the most important: the Scheutists, who served the Kasai
labor reservoir; and the Benedictines who ministered to Elisabethville and the other industrial centers.

The following statistics have been grouped according to the
level of instruction. The category "Higher" includes African
priests, lay brothers, nuns, and students at major seminaries.
Middle schools are broken down between *écoles moyennes* (junior
high schools), minor seminaries, professional schools, and normal
schools. Elementary schools include both kindergarten and elementary schools. The number of African teachers is listed
separately, since they received varying degrees of instruction.

Table 8.1 con't.

	1935 Scheut	1939 Scheut	1945 Scheut
HIGHER (Grands Séminaires)	33	56	92
Ecole Moyenne	75	353	326
Petit Séminaire	78	84	111
Ecole Professionelle	0	161	82
Ecole Normale	360	356	517
MIDDLE	513	954	1,036
LOWER (Ecoles Primaires)	104,853	111,254	123,515
TEACHERS	2,992	3,850	3,983
	Benedictine	Benedictine	Benedictine
HIGHER (Grands Séminaires)	0	0	1
Ecole Moyenne	20*	28*	119*
Petit Séminaire	18	11	50
Ecole Professionelle	179	550	564
Ecole Normale	31	43	35
MIDDLE	248	632	768
LOWER (Ecoles Primaires)	19,775	21,730	21,433
TEACHERS	593	609	582

* The figures for écoles moyennes are taken from the Congo *Rapports annuels*, 1935, 1938, and 1939-45 rather than from the *Statisques annuels catholique, Congo belge et Ruanda-Urundi*, 1935, 1939, 1945, which seem to include the whole population of St. Boniface, rather than just the junior high school students.

SOURCE: *Statisques annuels catholiques, Congo belge et Ruanda-Urundi*, 1935, 1939, 1945.

The Benedictine Fathers were by no means insensitive to
the problems of their former students. In addition to finding
them jobs, the missionaries also felt a certain responsibility
for their welfare during leisure hours. As early as 1924 Father
Grégoire Coussement, head of the mission in the *cité*, had formed
a boy scout troop. By 1929 the mission also ran a soccer club,
a savings club, and two proselytization societies. Central to
his planning at that time, however, were the mission's Catholic
imitations of the ethnic associations; but after the ethnically-
based antirepatriation demonstrations in 1931 he replaced them
with a new set of mission clubs, this time based on occupation—
for African merchants, farmers, and *évolués*. [24]

The club for *évolués*, the *Cercle St. Benoît*, began with the
support of the most influential members of Elisabethville's
European community. Two of its earliest sponsors were Attorney
General Paul van Arenberg and District Commissioner Auguste
Verbeken. In 1932 the latter directed a play which he had
written especially for the club; quite unconventionally the
cast included both European and African actors.

The presence of these influential Europeans at the *Cercle*
attracted many of the best-educated Africans in Elisabethville.
Most of the first group of CEC councilors were members. To
reinforce the position of this new Catholic élite, two lay
Catholic social workers founded a club for the wives of *Cercle
St. Benoît* members. [25]

Under the Maron regime, however, the *Cercle*, like so many
other African organizations in Elisabethville, lost its white
support. Maron distrusted educated Africans and had no intention
of giving them any political power or any real influence. Nor
did he approve of a club composed of ambitious Africans, regard-
less of their missionary connection. A CEC council packed with
mission club *évolués* was no more acceptable to him than any
other CEC council.

The distance between the Maron administration and its
predecessors was accentuated, moreover, by the continued presence
of Auguste Verbeken. After a few months in Belgium, the former
district commissioner returned to the city as a private citizen,
hoping to implement a long-cherished project to create a newspaper in language for Africans. Verbeken invested all of his
savings and energy into the newspaper, which he called *Ngonga*.
Needless to say, the idea of an independent African newspaper
was unwelcome to the new administration, to the Union Minière,
and to the archibishop, Monseigneur de Hemptinne, who did all
they could to sabotage it.

The first issue of *Ngonga* appeared in June of 1934 and almost immediately became a bone of contention between the white sponsors and the African members of the *Cercle St. Benoît*. They disagreed not so much on the content of its articles—which was exceedingly bland—but on the principle of its very existence. The Europeans heartily disapproved of a newspaper whose columns were open to letters of complaint by Africans and whose assistant editor, Makonga Bonaventure, was also an African.

Thus Father Coussement and Attorney General van Arenberg, sponsors of the *Cercle St. Benoît* and members of Maron's high command, attacked the newspaper and its publisher, Verbeken. Most of the Africans had fond memories of Verbeken as district commissioner and they sprang to the defense of his journal. Tensions within the *Cercle* increased as *Ngonga* began to fail for lack of advertising—the main source of which was, of course, the white business community. Interested *évolués* became angry with their sponsors for not helping Verbeken, and the situation reached a climax when he ran out of money and closed the newspaper. It had been in print for only eleven months. To add fuel to an already hot controversy, at that point someone told the Africans in the *Cercle St. Benoît* that their sponsors, van Arenberg and Coussement, were also leaders of the local secret police. Disheartened by this enormous breach of their confidence, most of the *évolués* left the *Cercle*.[26]

This scandal ended Father Coussement's usefulness to the Benedictines in Elisabethville, and in 1936 the order wisely transferred him to the remote Kasenga mission on the Luapula. Before he left, however, he was able to use his influence with the administration on behalf of one of his most loyal protégés. Under orders from the governor general and the Colonial Ministry to stop stalling and appoint a chief of the CEC, the Maron administration sought Coussement's advice; he recommended the loyal President of the *Cercle St. Benoît*, Kabongo Albert, for the post. Kabongo got the appointment before his powerful patron left Elisabethville.

The new chief had long been one of Coussement's favorites. A product of the Scheut Fathers' schools in Kasai, he was better educated than the Benedictines' own alumni. In 1931 Coussement had put him in charge of the most advanced class available to Africans at the Ecole St. Boniface, the seventh grade. Thus at the time of his appointment Kabongo had as much authority as any African could then possess in Elisabethville: he was the teacher of the highest grade in the school system and president of the mission's *évolué* club.

In theory at least, his new post would yield him even more influence. However, Kabongo's career as the only African ever to hold the office of chief of the CEC would not be a happy one. Despite his connections to the Benedictine Mission, Kabongo held an office the very existence of which was opposed by most of the European community. Once in office he encountered constant harassment from the missions, the government, and the Union Minière. Pressure from these quarters ultimately broke Kabongo's spirit, and in 1943 he suffered a nervous breakdown and resigned from the chieftainship after almost seven years of holding the difficult job.

In a broader perspective, Kabongo was not simply the victim of the Maron regime's hostility to the *Centre extra-coutumier;* he was destroyed by a wider coalition made up of the government, the missions, and industry. This coalition is well-known to scholars of Zaïrian affairs: Crawford Young, in his widely respected *Politics in the Congo,* refers to it as that "trinity of power" which underlay Belgian rule.[27]

In Elisabethville, however, this colonial trinity was not solidified into its final form until the 1930s. Until that time both the government and the Union Minière were unwilling or unable to exercise the kind of power over Africans which these two agencies ultimately came to wield. The Union Minière did not completely tighten its grip on its work force until 1933 when it was sure of their submission and the company's own economic future. Moreover, until the administrative reforms of 1933 Katanga's provincial administration had been moving slowly in the direction of greater representation in the governing institutions for Africans. Only the Catholic missions, which had cemented their position of power by virtue of the De Jonghe accords of 1925-26, enjoyed unquestioned authority in their own domain before the Great Depression. Thus the colonial trinity was of relatively recent origin.

This is not to say that life for Africans in Elisabethville before the establishment of the colonial trinity had been a bed of roses. Nor were there fundamental changes for the worse in the alternatives available to Africans after the establishment of the colonial trinity. By the mid-thirties each of the three major groups—the government, missions, and industry—simply wielded more power than heretofore in its own area, cooperating with the others when necessary to keep European dominance total. The forces weighing on Africans in Elisabethville, however, went beyond mere operating arrangements between different groups of European colonizers.

Africans who went to Elisabethville in 1936 did so for
basically the same reasons that their fathers had gone in 1911.
They left their homes in order to earn money to pay the colonial
hut tax. The major change affecting their choice was in the
relative conditions in city and countryside. The villages of
Central Africa were progressively impoverished by the continuous
removal of able-bodied men, while life for Africans in the city
became somewhat better as death rates fell, brick houses were
built, and food supplies became more reliable. An African
worker in the 1930s, unlike his father a generation earlier, was
likely to find the urban environment a little less miserable
than the home village.

Once an African had decided to stay in the city, two clear
choices had emerged as to the kind of life he might lead. He
could live in the camps in relative security or in the *cité* in
comparative freedom. In either case his situation was better
than during Elisabethville's earlier years when men usually had
left their families in the villages. Both of the urban milieux,
moreover, had real advantages over village life. A man could
come home to his family after work, and his family, by rural
standards, would be reasonably well-fed and sheltered. Elisabethville was by no means a paradise, but life there possessed
a security and comfort unavailable in rural areas.

In the 1930s Africans in Elisabethville were by no means
unconscious of the disadvantages of both urban alternatives.
Many at the Union Minière would resentfully remember the diminished meat and vegetable rations when they went on strike
against the mining company in 1941. *Evolués* would recall the
treachery of their mission friends, Coussement and van Arenberg,
when they joined the Luluabourg mutiny in 1944. Other resent-
ments would lie still further below the surface. Elisabethville
was only a place of refuge against the worst blows of colonization, which fell with greatest impact on the impoverished rural
areas of Central Africa.

Chapter 9

Conclusions: Elisabethville in Its Wider Perspective

        Within the brief space of thirty years Elisabethville grew
from a mining camp into a colonial city housing thirty thousand
permanent residents.   European imposed urban institutions had
come to the African savanna to stay.   This phenomenon of urbanization in outlying non-European rural areas was both unique and
universal: the form which Elisabethville took was the result of
the particular forces which influenced that city, but the process
of Europeans founding new industrial cities was taking place on
hundreds of sites throughout the Third World at the same time.
The unique developments in Elisabethville, then, throw a certain
light on the more general phenomenon of urbanization in the colonized world of the early twentieth century.

        Between 1910 and 1940 the city of Elisabethville went through
two major phases: the period of formation between 1910 and 1920
and the period of consolidation from 1920 until 1940.   The initial phase, which lasted only ten years, was absolutely critical
to the city's survival; moreover, events in those years determined
much about the direction of Elisabethville's future development.
In that brief period Belgian administrators made the city Belgian, purging it of British influence; and the bankers and engineers who dominated the Union Minière made the copper industry
profitable.

        The most important event in the first period of the city's
development was the establishment of the Belgian colonial regime
in Katanga.   This was not simply a matter of a handful of administrators choosing the city as the headquarters of a new province.
The new Belgian regime was laying the groundwork for the transformation of an entire geographic region.   European technology
brought the mineral-rich soils of Katanga into industrial production; but even more important, the administration brought the
inhabitants of the region to the mines through the use of force.

One might argue that British administrators in Northeastern Rhodesia actually collected the taxes which forced most of the early copper workers to go to the mines, but it was the Belgian local administration which promoted recruitment in Katanga and fostered the development of the mining industry which paid the Africans their salaries. Belgian administrators in Katanga aided the mining industry not so much because they were operating in the interests of distant capitalists, but because they saw their own interests as tied to the development of their territory's market economy. Without an export industry the colony would not have been able to collect adequate tax revenue and the administrators would have lost their jobs.

During this first period in the development of Elisabethville, the major collaboration between government and industry took place in Europe rather than in Africa. The national governments of Belgium, and, less successfully, of Germany played an important role in the capital formation of the copper industry. Belgian leaders, acting out of nationalistic rather than economic motives, encouraged their citizens to work for and invest in the Union Minière. They considered the Congo a part of the national heritage left to the Belgian state by Léopold II—a heritage that might be lost if the most promising industry were allowed to remain in the hands of foreign capitalists—namely the British. Thus the Belgian government was willing to set aside long cherished canons of fiscal responsibility and even wartime alliances in order to help the Union Minière become once and forever Belgian.

Officials in Brussels communicated sentiments about the urgency of making the copper industry Belgian to their subordinates in Elisabethville. As a result, members of the Katanga administration felt free to deal harshly with foreigners in the mining industry as well as in other occupations. These patriotic sentiments, present from the first days of Elisabethville's existence, ultimately resulted in the persecution of English-speaking missionaries, trade unionists, and managers at the Union Minière between 1917 and 1920.

These struggles among Europeans had relatively little effect on Africans working in the city during the first decade of its existence. Although administrative measures regulating hygiene ultimately made the city a safer place to live, few of the Africans who worked there before 1920 chose to stay on a permanent basis. For the most part they remained in Elisabethville just long enough to earn the money demanded by Europeans and then returned to their villages, but the social institutions of these Africans who spent only a brief time in the city left a permanent mark on its later development. The *butwa* associations

formed by members of recruitment gangs became the models for the
more permanent urban African associations of the 1920s.

Africans played a more important role in the developments
which occurred during the second period of the city's history
which lasted from 1920 until the fall of Belgium in 1940, but—
as in the earlier period—Europeans dominated the action. This
second phase was characterized by the consolidation of the colonial trinity—missions, government, and corporations. Moreover, between the two world wars, the city—and, in fact, the
entire Belgian colonial system—took on the characteristics it
was to maintain until Congolese independence in 1960.

During the interwar period, the Union Minière underwent two
important developments: the reconstruction of its recruitment
system and the rationalization of its operational structure.
Between 1923 and 1927 Léon Rasson reorganized the company's
African operations, transforming a series of competing production units into a single integrated organization. This brought
individual managers under greater company control, since their
performance was subsequently judged on the basis of their contribution to the company as a whole rather than on the success
of their individual division.

At the same time that the company's structure was being
reorganized, its labor system was also being completely over-
hauled. For the first years of its existence the Union Minière
had followed the South African model of labor recruitment, relying on unskilled workers for short terms of service. In the
mid-twenties this labor system proved unsatisfactory in the
Congo because of the sparsity of the population living within
easy reach of the mines. The Union Minière thereupon developed
the stabilized labor system by which it encouraged Africans to
stay at the mines for long periods of time. Not only did the
company acquire a guaranteed labor force, but productivity increased as a function of length of residence in the mining camps.

Until the Great Depression, many managers still doubted the
efficacy of the stabilization policy in obtaining the loyalty of
the African work force, but in 1931 some Africans rioted when
threatened by repatriation to their home villages. Following
this display of attachment to the camps, company managers tightened their grip on their African employees, eventually enclosing
them in a total institution which had many of the attributes of
a prison or army barracks.

By the end of the 1930s the Union Minière had become a
formidable organization, with power concentrated in the hands of
a few key managers. The company's rigid social hierarchy was

reflected in the society of Elisabethville. The city became
clearly segmented along lines followed by the company itself:
town and camp; black and white; executive and employee.

Along with the political and economic transformation of the
Congo, the Belgians also introduced their religion to the Africans. Like the Union Minière, the Catholic Church was hierarchically organized and socially stratified, so the two institutions as they existed in Elisabethville had much in common.
During the interwar period, however, organized Christianity in
the city also underwent important changes. Most important,
Monseigneur de Hemptinne and his Benedictine Order effectively
eliminated all Protestant and Catholic competition. Having
gained a clear field for evangelization by 1925, de Hemptinne
then entered into a series of agreements with the Belgian government and the Union Minière which gave his order spiritual hegemony over the Africans in Elisabethville. Thereafter, the Benedictines operated nearly all social services and education in
both the *cité indigène* and the Union Minière camp. This Benedictine monopoly, it might be added, was not really in the interest
of the local Africans; in the absence of competition, the Fathers
probably provided fewer facilities than they would have done had
there been other missionaries for the community.

Seen from an institutional standpoint, it is also significant that Monseigneur de Hemptinne had to deal separately with
the Union Minière and the colonial government in order to gain
spiritual hegemony over Elisabethville's Africans. By the late
twenties the separate jurisdictions of the company and the administration were clearly defined. Government police and soldiers
stayed out of the camps leaving law enforcement to the company.

Thus the members of the colonial trinity had defined their
respective spheres in Elisabethville and, for that matter, in
all of industrial Katanga: the Benedictines provided social
services and education for Africans both inside and outside the
camps; the Union Minière maintained a firm hold on the Africans
living inside the camps; and the government regulated Africans
living outside the camps. We have here the beginnings of control
by Crawford Young's colonial trinity, a control to be thoroughly
consolidated during the thirties.

In the last years before the depression, however, the government was not in complete agreement with the leaders of the
Union Minière and the Benedictine Order. The latter were more
authoritarian than the eight year liberal regime led by Vice
Governor General Heenen. They were particularly suspicious of
Heenen's *Centre extra-coutumier*, an institution designed to share
governmental authority with Africans in the *cité*. The leaders

of the company and missions found Heenen's successor, Amour
Maron, more to their liking. He shared their lack of confidence
in the ability of Africans to govern themselves, and together
the administration, missions, and company effectively destroyed
Heenen's *Centre extra-coutumier*. A consensus on how Elisabethville ought to be run developed in the late 1930s between the
three elements in the colonial trinity. At that time, it might
be added, the colonial administration was the weakest of the
three institutions, since it lacked the economic power of the
Union Minière and the strong leadership of the Benedictines.

During this second phase in Elisabethville's history, while
Europeans were consolidating their authority, a number of Africans decided to make the city their permanent home. Between
1918 and 1930 the city's African population rose from seven
thousand to thirty thousand (15 percent a year), although a
sizeable proportion of these inhabitants lived in the city only
temporarily. The process of urbanization was a slow one: many
returned to their villages several times before deciding to
remain in the city.

By the end of the 1920s Africans who opted for urban life
had a choice between two social environments in Elisabethville:
the camps and the *cité*. In the former they could live in security and in greater comfort than any other Africans living south
of the rain forest, but in exchange they had to work hard and to
live within increasingly oppressive social constraints. In the
latter most lived less comfortably but more independently.
During their leisure hours, they could participate in their own
voluntary associations which—like the earlier *butwa* society—
had been adapted from rural areas to meet urban conditions.

The situation of Africans in both *cité* and camps worsened
during the 1930s, partly because of the economic crunch and
partly because both the Union Minière and the colonial administration tightened the screws. As a result many Africans might
have returned to their villages had not life in rural areas
been even harder than in Elisabethville. The only Africans to
make some advancement in the 1930s were those who collaborated
most closely with the Europeans. Africans chosen for the new
specialized labor force (MOI/S) at the Union Minière profited
materially and socially as a result of their services in helping
keep the mass of workers under control. Similarly, those Africans most closely attached to the missions got the best jobs.

Even Africans who seemed to have "made it" through cooperation with their European masters had their illusions dispelled
in 1935 when they learned that their best "friends" were part of
the secret police. In 1940 few of the 26,000 Africans living in

Elisabethville had great cause for optimism about their future
in the city. Conditions there were better than those in rural
areas; one could obtain relative comfort but only but dint of
hard work, obedience, and collaboration with the Europeans.

This pessimistic prognosis about Elisabethville's future
was borne out by the experience of Elisabethville's inhabitants
in the years between 1940 and 1976. In recent times the city
has passed through four distinct phases: the upheavals which
accompanied the Second World War; the relatively prosperous
period from 1945 to 1957; the years from 1957 to 1965 which saw
the devolution of political power to Africans; and the domination of the Mobutu regime.

World War II had a great demographic and political impact
on Elisabethville: its population expanded rapidly and was frequently in a ferment. Most of these changes affected Africans
more profoundly than Europeans. The Belgian colonial war effort,
with its unrestrained recruitment and its heavy quotas on agricultural production, made rural conditions worse than they had
ever been before, and Africans moved to the city by the thousands. Between 1940 and 1945 Elisabethville's African population rose from 26,000 to 65,000, a growth rate of 18 percent a
year—the highest in the city's history.

In the city Africans began demonstrating a militance
which the Belgians had not anticipated. In 1941 employees of
the Union Minière struck in protest against gradual decline in
their standard of living which had begun in the 1930s and accelerated in the early months of the war. The company broke the
strike only after calling in the colonial army which fired on the
strikers, killing seventy of them. In 1943 black noncommis-
sioned officers of that same colonial army brought members of
the city's African elite into conspiracy against the Belgians.
The conspirators at Elisabethville were poorly organized and
easily disarmed, but their revolt marked the first protest of
the city's more educated Africans against the colonial regime.
Even though these wartime activities did not dislodge the colonial trinity, they did show that Africans would resist when
sufficiently provoked.

During the war turbulence also hit Elisabethville's European community, but here again not with sufficient force to
dislodge the colonial trinity. In 1940, after the fall of Belgium to the Germans, influential settlers led by Monseigneur de
Hemptinne initiated a movement to take the Congo out of the war,
but they were overruled by the governor general and the European
officers of the colonial army. A white trade union movement
which flourished from 1941 to 1945 made substantial gains in

response to its demands for higher salaries and political representation for white mine workers, only to lose most of its
power after the war. The trinity was shaken, but it hung on.

Then between 1945 and 1957 the colonial trinity regained
firm control over the city. European settlers, although lacking
in political power, enjoyed a prosperity generated by the expansion of the Union Minière and its affiliates. Moreover the
white population, which rose from five to thirteen thousand in
this period, developed a sense of community and permanence which
was reflected in the appearance of the city. Wide avenues, posh
residential quarters, and thriving night clubs even gave it
something of the reputation of a cultural center. In 1956 the
colonial government authorized the construction of a university—
attended primarily by the white population, of course.

Africans shared in the prosperity, in part because the
Union Minière was doing well and also thanks to legislation
enacted after the war. Workers in the *cité* and camps alike
enjoyed relatively good wages and a standard of living which
was considerably higher than that obtained by most of their
fellow countrymen. For once in the city's history, Africans
migrated to Elisabethville because of the pull of improved conditions there. In this period the city's African population
grew from 70,000 to 170,000, a rate of approximately 8 percent
a year. To house the new migrants the Belgian administration
authorized the construction of three new residential quarters
for Africans which were substantially better than the old *cité*.

The political atmosphere also became somewhat more liberal.
The Belgian government, as part of a general reform of the
colonial administration, began to plan for a new urban government which would have an African input. Even the Union Minière
granted concessions, allowing certain African employees the
right to live outside of the company camp. Thus, although
Africans were still barred from positions of responsibility in
government and industry, institutions were created which would
accommodate their later entry. In 1957, for example, the
Benedictines began offering a complete program in secondary
education leading to high school-leaving certificates equivalent
to those given in Belgium. All things considered, in 1957 both
Africans and Europeans had reason to be optimistic about the
future. Eight short years later, however, their expectations
would be sharply altered.

In response to international pressures to decolonize, and
to internal divisions in Belgian politics, a reluctant Colonial
Ministry in 1957 initiated what it thought would be a gradual
devolution of power to Africans. Within three years, however,

the Zaïrois had precipitously obtained their independence. As
is well-known, Elisabethville—as capital of Katanga—played an
important role in these events.

Between 1957 and 1961, Europeans in Elisabethville continued to fill a more important role in the city's politics than
did Africans. Although both racial communities participated in
the first municipal elections which were held in 1957, the Union
Minière and, to a lesser extent, organized white settlers, attempted to maintain their privileged position by paying off all
potential African leaders. Eventually they threw their support
behind a secessionist movement which made Katanga a neocoloni-
alist state entirely independent of the rest of the country.
Between 1960 and 1962 these two European groups ardently supported the regime of Moïse Tshombe, a control which was opposed
with equal fervor by the Congo's central government and by the
United Nations which sponsored an invasion of Katanga in August
1961.

This invasion brought the question of Katanga secession
directly to the African inhabitants of Elisabethville. The
local black community was sharply divided in its attitude toward
the United Nations armed forces. Africans of Kasaian origin
tended to side in the struggle with the United Nations, while
those from Katanga tended to support the secessionist regime
whose black leaders were mostly Katangese. This division provoked serious fighting between the two African groups, and the
United Nations commanders ultimately felt it necessary to send
the Kasaians back to Kasai for their own safety. Thus thousands
of Kasaians, many of them born in Elisabethville, were shipped
back to villages they had never seen before, and the city was
deprived of many of its best-educated Africans.

The situation began to stabilize in 1962 with the extinc-
tion of the secessionist government and the departure of United
Nations troops. For the next three years, a reorganized central
government ruled the country under the leadership of various
civilian politicians including Moïse Tshombe, the former secessionist. The end of the fighting brought peace and stability to
Elisabethville. Although a few Europeans left because they preferred not to live under African rule, the majority remained,
enjoying unexpected prosperity. Former residents from Kasai and
Katangese seeking jobs flocked to the city. Despite all the
troubles, the city's total population rose from 170,000 in 1957
to a quarter of a million in 1965—an overall rate of 5 percent
a year.

The most recent phase of Elisabethville's history began in
November 1965 when General Mobutu Sese Seko gained control of

the Congo's central government, a control he continued to hold
in 1976. As president the general initiated a program to give
Africans control of the country as well as to develop national
unity. Symbolically, he changed the name of the city to the
name used by its African inhabitants, Lubumbashi, while renaming
the country Zaire. He also introduced a new leadership based on
educated Africans and the national army. Officeholders were
transferred from the home regions to distant parts of the country in order to instill a sense of national identity. In pur-
suit of this same goal, he introduced the apparatus of a totali-
tarian state: single party, arbitrary arrests, sycophant press.

Despite these idealistic reforms, the country deteriorated
under Mobutu's rule. In part, the general inherited the legacy
of Belgian rule which had discouraged African political development and had created a general atmosphere of repression. Thus
many government officials were underqualified for the jobs which
they held, seeing them as simply an opportunity to embezzle from
the public coffers. Following the example of higher officials,
policemen, civil servants, and school teachers were also corrup-
ted. Their salaries frequently unpaid, these lower officials
began to extort money from the local population.

By 1973 Mobutu had gained sufficient power to dispense with
the European community. He therefore ordered the expulsion of
almost all Europeans who were neither aid personnel nor employees
of the copper industry. At the Union Minière Europeans remained
in control although Africans obtained titular authority. The
Union Minière, now nationalized, underwent two changes of name
and lost its monopoly of copper mining and smelting in the area
but continued its profitable operations.

The presence of jobs in the copper industry and the government continued to attract Africans to the city from rural areas.
Between 1965 and 1975 the population rose from approximately
250,000 to 400,000, a growth rate of about 5 percent a year.
Many Kasaians returned to the city, but an equal number of migrants arrived from Katanga, most of them moving into new quarters in houses constructed from bricks made of clay found in the
local ant hills. Thus the city's inhabitants were relying on
construction techniques introduced by the first white settlers.
Paradoxically, the old European quarter, except for a few government high-rise office buildings, deteriorated while these
new African quarters were being built.

In summary, the city in 1976 was much as it had always been
for Africans, not very pleasant but better than the surrounding
countryside—a place where an individual could earn a better
living than in his village. Beginning in 1960 the city's imme-

diate hinterland had undergone an almost continuous deterioration. Roads, first unsafe because of military conditions, were
allowed to disintegrate. Farmers who lived away from the rail-
line could no longer send their crops to market; neither could
they import consumer goods.

Given this dreary but consistent evaluation of Elisabethville's history, we can now try to test the applicability to that
story of certain theories of urbanization which have been developed in recent times. In the last thirty-five years, the theory
of urbanization has undergone substantial changes. Social scientists led by Robert Redfield, in attempting to understand the
differences between the behavior of individuals in rural and
urban areas, devised a single model to account for the differences between city people and country people. Redfield coined
the expression "folk-urban continuum," defending the theory that
rural and urban areas were at opposite ends of a single spectrum
of behavior with rural people being particularistic, less in
touch with the outside world, governed by their traditions and
their kinship relations, while urban people were at the opposite
end of the continuum in every one of these respects.

In the course of time other social scientists began to cri-
ticize this theory on several grounds. Reinhard Bendix pointed
out the danger of characterizing social behavior on a single continuum rather than allowing for diverse forms of development in
different circumstances. Other social scientists began to suggest the existence of different types of cities and different
types of rural backgrounds.

In one of the most highly developed of these discussions,
T. G. McGee has defined three distinct types of cities: the
modern industrial city, the preindustrial city, and the colonial
city. The modern industrial city is the city as it now exists in
Europe and North America: a densely populated area which serves
as a center for government, manufacturing, and commerce. The
preindustrial city, its earlier counterpart, was much smaller
than the cities of today and served as a center for government
and religion. As McGee defines it, the colonial city, in contrast
to the other two, is modern in origin and does not perform all of
the functions of the industrial city. Instead of producing manufactured goods and stimulating commerce, it is the outpost of a
foreign power and its industry is mainly oriented toward the
export of materials to its foreign metropolis. Beyond this division of cities into three types, he suggests that cities can be
characterized according to their demography: those whose population grows mainly through migration and those whose population
grows mainly through natural increase.

If this classification were not complicated enough, McGee argues that cities also owe their differences to the sort of hinterland which they serve. These rural areas fall into three more types: farming areas, peasant areas, and folk areas. In farming areas, the inhabitants possess a high rate of literacy and are integrally tied to a market economy. Peasants, by contrast, belong to a market economy but are illiterate, while the "folk" are both illiterate and uninvolved in a market economy.

All in all, McGee gives us three kinds of rural areas and three kinds of cities categorized according to their functions; and two kinds of cities distinguished by their demographic characteristics—a total of eighteen possible urban types. From the earlier oversimplification of the explanations for urban development, we have gone to extreme complexity. Indeed, Elisabethville has a place in McGee's system; in the period under study Elisabethville was a colonial city which grew mainly by migration of people from a "folk" culture. These conclusions, however, could have been reached without any detailed study of the city at all and, what is more important, they do not show the city to be different from almost any other city in colonial Africa.[1]

Urban geographers led by Walter Stöhr have proposed a more elegant typology which fits our case much better, since it can be used to describe and explain Elisabethville's growth in comparison with other cities. Stöhr, in summarizing the literature, suggests that cities should be seen in their relationship to their hinterlands and that the regions comprised by the cities and their hinterlands fall into two basic types: the sector model and the export-base model.

The sector model, used by many of the established African urban geographers including Akin Mabogunje, assumes that a city's development is induced by local conditions. This theory, according to Stöhr,

> explains the development of a region from subsistence
> economy to more advanced stages of development through
> specialization of agricultural activities and the for-
> mation of an intraregional transport system which per-
> mits the exchange of products between different loca-
> tions. This specialization leads to higher productivity
> and creates a surplus which can pay for transport and
> marketing of products . . . At some stage, certain
> regional activities will become competitive on the
> national or international market and will thereby
> create an additional export base for the region which
> may accelerate its development relative to the other
> [regions].

Thus the cities are the natural outgrowth of the economic development of the region. The exchange of goods and services at the
local level leads to the creation of increasingly large centers
with the ultimate result that the region comprises a pyramidal
network of urban centers. This situation characterizes the
urban development of Western Europe, the United States, and
China, but not of colonial Central Africa. Except for other
copper towns and minor administrative centers, Elisabethville
did not develop in conjunction with its hinterland. Instead,
the city took labor and food from its surrounding region and
gave little in return.

More appropriate to the case in hand is what Stöhr called
the export-base theory (externally induced development).

Export-base theory explains the development of a region
through external demand for its natural resources (or
skills). As a response to this outside demand, export
activities . . . will emerge . . . In an undeveloped
region, penetration lines from outside are first established to facilitate the export of products out of the
region and the movement of labor and capital equipment
into the region. The settlement pattern, as well as
administrative and economic institutions, will emerge
so as to facilitate these export-base functions. Cities
will form in the natural resource areas (*mining towns*,
central places for agricultural or tourist areas) and
at trans-shipment points . . . Their relative growth
rate will depend on the access to outside markets and
the magnitude of the resources of their hinterland.
They will essentially be oriented towards and dominated
by factors outside the region or country.

The export-base theory sheds light on much of the development of Elisabethville both internally and in its relationship
to its hinterland. Most of the investment attracted by the city
has been intended to promote the export of raw materials rather
than the development of the region. Most of the copper industry's profits went back to Belgium in the form of dividends,
salaries, and taxes rather than being invested in the development of Elisabethville's hinterland.

In theory, the city's export-base economy could have promoted regional development, but in practice it did not. The
precolonial economy of Central Africa was not strong enough to
resist the demands made upon it by the colonial economy. In
reality, a weak sectoral economy existed before the introduction
of the colonial export economy. According to Stöhr, the earlier
of the two patterns in any given area should have prevailed over

the later, but the case of colonial Africa departs from Stöhr's
model in that precolonial sectoral economy was completely
swamped by the colonial export-base economy.[2]

This model of economic development attributes a particularly
important role to the colonial government. The Belgian administration aided colonial companies to develop industries which
exported most of their profits along with their raw materials,
while being itself exploitative in that it sent money to Belgium
to pay for colonial pensions and supplies purchased at prices
above those prevailing on the world market. Thus, the colonial
government promoted an unequal exchange of resources between the
colony and the mother country.

Paradoxically, this unbalanced flow of resources took place
while European officials were calling on colonies to live within
their own means. The application of classical accounting procedures thus forced the Congolese government to run the colony
on what was left after the money had been shipped back to Belgium. This left the government to run on a shoestring.

Even after the expansion of the 1920s, the Belgian Congo
was relatively poorly endowed in comparison with other African
colonies. The mining industry and agricultural industries such
as palm oil production provided the colony with revenues which
were about the same as those of French West Africa and one-third
less than those of British West Africa.[3]

The paucity of funds available to the Belgian regime reduced the scope of governmental activity. Once the Belgians had
allocated money to the central government of the Congo and to
the provincial governments, little was left for local government.
F. Grévisse has shown that over half of the revenues of Elisabethville's *Centre extra-coutumier* came from local taxes on
single women and African beer. The Belgians applied the principle that local government for Africans should be supported by
taxes on urban Africans rather than allocating general revenues
to the city.[4] Thus the Belgians established a policy of meeting
the budgetary needs of the colonial administration rather than
assuring the welfare of the Africans they were administering.

Belgians thought of the allocation of colonial resources
strictly in terms of European money. The budget had to run on
it, and no agency of the government could hope for money from
the government unless it demonstrated that it was operating in
the Belgian national interest or that it was bringing money into
the colony. Urban administration suffered first, but in 1933
the provincial government of Katanga also underwent severe cutbacks because officials in Brussels and Léopoldville were able

to argue that a strong provincial government was no longer necessary to insure that Katanga remain Belgian.

All this explains the procedure by which Belgians allocated
resources within their own governmental structure, but it does
not show how they dealt with strictly African economic activities. In chapter one, the author introduced Bohannan and Dalton's notion of a multicentric economy to account for the differences between African and European economic behavior.
Furthermore, we have shown how the European economy became
parasitic on the African economy, drawing out labor which had
not previously been for sale. Not only were Africans forced to
sell their labor to Europeans, however, but they were forced to
do so in an unfavorable market, in which wages were driven down
by African competition for available European money.

Bohannon and Dalton's model of the colonial economy allows
for a duality accepted by most economists between the western-
ized sector and the so-called traditional sectors, but does not
presuppose that rural areas were paralyzed in some precolonial
stupor. Rather it attributes rural underdevelopment at least in
part to the removal of labor from the rural economy. Thus rural
areas were not simply fixed at some "primitive" stage of economic development, but were really worse off than they had been
before the Europeans arrived. The city, where rural labor was
employed, had grown at the expense of the rural areas.

The conclusion that Africans were pushed out of the countryside rather than pulled toward the city does not mean that they
did not adapt as well as they could to urban life. Indeed, as
Professor Elliott Skinner has shown in a recent study of
Ouagadougou, one of the main characteristics of urban Africans
is "the ingenuity with which they use the available choices
open to them."[5] In absolute terms, however, life for Africans
in colonial Elisabethville was never satisfactory. Most people
lived from day to day, letting out their frustrations in drink,
sex, and petty theft.

Perhaps it was their children who kept them in the city.
Medical facilities there were far superior to those in rural
areas and a far greater percentage of children survived to
adulthood in the cities than in the countryside. Those children
who did survive, moreover, had a better chance of attending a
mission school than did children in the country. By 1945
approximately half of the school-aged children in town were in
school.[6] And so an African who spent his day in some menial
and degrading job could return home to his family where he could
dream about the advancement of his children. For most Africans
in Elisabethville, the city was far more attractive in the future
than it was in actuality.

And yet, for most Africans, that tomorrow never came. Even when the Belgians left, conditions for the average Zaïrois did not take a turn for the better. Elisabethville, and for that matter, the whole colonial regime had been built for the colonizers, not the colonized. African education and political freedom were restricted—all in the interests of keeping the regime running smoothly. Is it any wonder that the governmental machinery broke down when there were no longer Belgians to run it?

Abbreviations of Archives Cited in Notes

AP   Affaires Politiques, Lubumbashi

AR   Archives du Royaume, Bruxelles

Ar Rég   Archives Régionales du Shaba, Lubumbashi

MC   Archives du Ministère des Colonies—now administered by the Ministère des Affaires Estrangères, Bruxelles

MRAC   Musée Royal de l'Afrique Centrale, Tervuren

PR   Palais Royale, Bruxelles

PRO   Public Records Office, London

RE   Archives Régionales de l'Education Nationale, Lubumbashi

ZA   Zambian National Archives, Lusaka

NOTES

NOTES: CHAPTER 1

1. On the foundation of Elisabethville, see the report of
J. Tasch's speech in *Essor du Congo*, June 12, 1945; R. Grauwet,
"Souvenirs coloniaux," pp. 106-7, typescript at Musée Royal de
l'Afrique Centrale, Tervuren, Belgium.

2. On Msiri, see August Verbeken, *Msiri, roi du Garen-
ganze* (Bruxelles, 1956). On Kasongo Niembo, see Henri Seghaert,
Un terme au Congo belge. Notes sur la vie coloniale, 1916-1918
(Bruxelles, 1948), pp. 159-60.

3. John S. Furnivall, *Colonial Policy and Practice: A
Comparative Study of Burma and Netherlands India* (Cambridge,
1948), p. 33.

4. Cyril Ehrlich, "Building and Caretaking: Economic
Policy in British Tropical Africa, 1890-1960," *Economic History
Review*, (1973):649-67.

5. For the latest account of the finances of the Congo
Free State, see Mutwale-Muyimbe, *Les source publiques de finance-
ment de l'Etat Indépendant du Congo, 1885-1907* (Bruxelles: Les
Cahiers du CEDAF 5/1973).

6. On the increased importance of company contributions to
the colonial budget in the 1920s, see Bruce Fetter, "L'Union
Minière du Haut-Katanga, 1920-1940: La naissance d'une sous-
culture totalitaire," *Les Cahiers du CEDAF*, 6 (1973):7-10.

7. For an earlier version of this argument and a review of
the economic literature, see Marvin Miracle and Bruce Fetter,
"Labor-Supply Functions in Africa," *Economic Development and
Culture Change*, 18 (1970):240-351; idem., "Two Causal Models of
African Economic Conduct: A Reply," ibid., 21 (1972):171-73.

8. Richard Gray and David Birmingham, *Pre-Colonial
African Trade: Essays on Trade in Central and Eastern Africa
before 1900* (London, 1970), p. 4.

9. Paul Bohannan and George Dalton (eds.), *Markets in
Africa* (Evanston, 1962), pp. 1-7.

10. For a discussion of Hoselits's distinction when applied to Africa, see Akin Mabogunje, *Urbanization in Nigeria* (London, 1968), pp. 21-22.

NOTES: CHAPTER 2

1. J. Stengers, "Léopold II et la fixation des frontières du Congo," *Le Flambeau*, 46 (1963):153-97.

2. R. J. Cornet, *Katanga* (Bruxelles, 1946), pp. 55-95, 186-91; L. Gann, *A History of Northern Rhodesia: Early Days to 1953* (London, 1964), pp. 56-64.

3. J. Stengers, *Belgique et Congo: l'Elaboration de la Charte Coloniale* (Bruxelles, 1963), p. 32; H. Feis, *Europe, the World's Banker 1870-1914* (New York, 1965), p. 137.

4. P. Joye and R. Lewin, *Les trusts au Congo* (Bruxelles, 1961), pp. 19-22.

5. R. J. Cornet, *Terre Katangaise* (Bruxelles, 1950), pp. 21-27, 35-36; Gann, *Northern Rhodesia*, pp. 56-64; Cornet, *Katanga*, pp. 183-203.

6. H. Delvaux, "L'occupation du Katanga," *Essor du Congo*, September 28, 1936; Cornet, *Terre Katangaise*, pp. 54-55, 61; E. Verdick, *Les premiers jours au Katanga* (Bruxelles, 1952), p. 78.

7. Stengers, *Belgique et Congo*, pp. 206-10.

8. Ibid., p. 41.

9. Gann, *Northern Rhodesia*, pp. 119-20; S. E. Katzenellen-hagen, "The Building of the Benguela Railway and the Related Railway and Economic Development of Northern Rhodesia and Katanga, 1900-1913," Ph.D. thesis, Oxford, 1970, pp. 7-44, 52.

10. Katzenellenhagen, "Benguela Railway," pp. 44-65, con-tains the best narrative, but see C. Terlinden et al., *Comité Spécial du Katanga 1900-1950* (Bruxelles, 1950), pp. 25-32, 54-56.

11. Terlinden, *CSK*, pp. 31-69. On the magistracy in other parts of the Congo, see H. Anet, *En énclaireur: voyage d'étude du Congo Belge* (Bruxelles, 1913), p. 223; on the Katanga magis-tracy, see H. Rolin, *Les vices de l'administration du Katanga: les remèdes* (Bruxelles, 1911), pp. 21-22.

12. The character of the CSK administration can be gauged
from two documents in the Zambian National Archieves: Commandant Weyns to Administrator, Northern Rhodesia, August 12, 1902,
ZA BS 1/86 I; H. T. Hannington to Administrator, Northeastern
Rhodesia, October 6, 1904. Also excerpts from the diary of Mr.
Pirie, a Scottish geologist, in R. Williams to Sir E. Grey,
June 22, 1906, in the Public Records Office, London (PRO), FO
367/32. For CSK profits, see *CSK 1900-1925* (Bruxelles, 1927),
pp. 98-99.

13. Terlinden, *CSK*, pp. 24-32, 54-56.

14. *Union Minière du Haut-Katanga, 1906-1956* (Bruxelles,
1956), pp. 67-86; R. R. Sharp, *Early Days in Katanga* (Bulawayo,
1956).

15. S. J. S. Cookey, *Great Britian and the Congo Question
1885-1913* (London, 1968), pp. 81, 94-98, 140-44, 174-75, 264.

16. *Compagnie du Chemin de Fer du Bas-Congo au Katanga,
1906-1956* (Bruxelles, 1956), pp. 13, 40-43; *UMHK 1906-1956,*
pp. 12-16, 65-74.

17. Muyimbwe, *Sources publiques*, pp. 36-38; Feis, *Europe,
the World's Banker*, pp. 39-43.

18. Joye and Lewin, *Les trusts*, p. 226; Muyimbwe, *Sources
publiques*, pp. 46-49.

19. Stengers, *Belgique et Congo*, pp. 197-200.

20. Muyimbwe, *Sources publiques*, pp. 46-49.

21. Stengers, *Belgique et Congo*, p. 60.

22. Gann, *Northern Rhodesia*, pp. 56-58.

23. Stengers, *Belgique et Congo*, p. 47.

24. Ibid., pp. 206-12.

25. Joye and Lewin, *Les trusts*, p. 224.

NOTES: CHAPTER 3

1. Sharp, *Early Days in Katanga,* pp. 108-10.

2. *UMHK*, p. 87; F. V. Olsen, "L'historique des troupes du
Katanga pendant la period 1910 jusqu'à l'offensive en A.O.A.

pendant la Première Guerre Mondiale," *CSK Congrès Scientifique* (Elisabethville, 1950), 7:42-49; F. van der Elst, *Le Katanga. Son administration, sa législation* (Bruxelles, 1931), pp. 64-65.

3. Sharp, *Early Days in Katanga*, pp. 111-12; Jean du Terril (pseudonym of Antoine Sohier), "A l'aurore du Katanga," *Etoile du Congo*, June 30, 1923; CSK, *Rapport annuel 1920*, p. 38.

4. F. Grévisse, *Le Centre extra-coutumier d'Elisabethville*, Institut Royal Colonial Belge, Section des Sciences morales et politiques, Mémoires, Collection in -8°, Tome XXI (Bruxelles, 1951), pp. 3-5; A. Yav, "Vocabulaire de Ville d'Elisabethville" (Elisabethville, mimeo., 1965).

5. R. Legrand and B. Thoreau, *Les bénédictins au Katanga* (Loppem-les-Bruges, 1935), pp. 63-67; R. Goldseller to Vice Governor General Wangermée, July 26, 1912, Archives Régionales de l'Education Nationale, Lumbumbashi (RE); Africa No. 1, Cd. 6606; HMSO (London, 1913), p. 9; Sohier, "Aurore Katanga," *Etoile du Congo*, August 11, 1923.

6. Sohier, "Aurore Katanga," *Etoile du Congo*, August 11, 1923.

7. European population figures for the years 1911 (1,132) and 1912 (955) are provided in CSK, *Rapport annuel 1920*, p. 38, which are slightly different from those broken down by nationality in *Journal du Katanga* on which Table 3.1 is based.

8. Bruce Fetter, "Immigrants to Elisabethville: Their Origins and Aims," *African Urban Notes*, 3, 2 (1968):18-19. Information on the Germans comes from "Note d'une commission de contrôle postal sur la situation du Congo belge depuis la guerre," in Archives du Royaume (AR), Bruxelles, Fonds de Broqueville, p. 421.

9. Bruce Fetter, "African Associations in Elisabethville, 1910-35: Their Origins and Development," *Etudes d'histoire africaine*, 6 (1974).

10. On food, see *Rapport Agr. Kat. 1911-12*, p. 16, *Reseignements de l'Office Colonial 1912*, p. 267; Territorial Administrator Tytgat to A. Boulty, March 8, 1919, in Affaires Politiques, Lubumbashi (AP) 110, MOI T-M. On objections to regular work at the Union Minière, see van Iseghem to VGG (de Meulemeester), November 22, 1916, AP 12, Chefferies; Acting District Commissioner to VGG, August 20, 1915, in AP 20, Dist. H-L.

11. E. Weberg, "L'évolution des exploitations minières," UMHK, *Evolution des techniques et des activitiés sociales* (Bruxelles, 1956), pp. 71-91; E. Toussaint, "Mémorandum," July 7, 1942, in Gécamines, Lubumbashi, Personnel Archives, UMHK, p. 65.

12. Médecin Provincial Polidori to VGG, Katanga, January 30, 1911, in Archives du Ministère des Colonies—now administered by the Ministère des Affaires Etrangères—(MC) H 833/22; A. Pearson and R. Mouchet, *The Practical Hygiene of Native Compounds in Tropical Africa* (London, 1923).

13. *Le mouvement géographique*, May 18, 1913; Congo, *Rapport aux chambres, 1918*, p. 101.

14. Fetter, "African Associations."

15. On Malawian education, see J. van Velsen, "The Missionary Factor among the Lakeside Tonga of Nyasaland," *Rhodes-Livingstone Journal*, No. 27 (1959):1-21. On the restrictions on migration to South Africa, see F. E. Sanderson, "The Development of Labour Migration from Nyasaland, 1891-1914, *Journal of African History*, 2 (1961):267-68; J. E. Springer, *Pioneering in the Congo* ([New York and Cincinnati] 1916), pp. 8-10, 261-62.

16. Miracle and Fetter, "Labor-Supply Functions in Africa."

17. Fetter, "Immigrants to Elisabethville," pp. 23-26.

18. M. Gelfand, *Northern Rhodesia in the Days of the Charter* (Oxford, 1961), pp. 94-99, summarizes recruitment for Southern Rhodesia but is not always reliable. On the competition between Southern Rhodesia and Katanga, see D. E. Brodie (Secretary of the BSA Company) to L. P. Beaufort (Acting Administrator of Northeastern Rhodesia), February 12, 1910, in ZA 3/3/2, No. 9.

19. Gelfand, *Northern Rhodesia,* pp. 103-4.

20. Undersecretary Colonial Office to Undersecretary Foreign Office, November 10, 1913, in PRO, FO 371-1730.

21. Cookey, *Britain and the Congo Question*, pp. 26-27, 211-12, 275-76.

22. Albert I to M. Schollaert, May 11, 1910, in Palais Royal, Bruxelles, (PR) Cabinet du Roi Albert I, II B 7 bis; Vice Consul Beak to Consul Thesinger, February 8, 1910, in PRO, FO 367/166.

23. Stengers, *Belgique et Congo*, pp. 177-86, 202-3, 206-12.

24. The latest discussion of British plots appears in Cookey, *Britain and the Congo Question*, pp. 254-56, 272-73. On the reaction of the Belgian government, see the note by P. Orts of May 3, 1910, in PR, Cabinet du Roi Albert I, II B 7 bis.

25. On the contacts between the king and Grey, see Albert I, "Note pour le Ministre des Affaires Etrangères," June 9, 1910, in PR, Cabinet du Roi Albert I, II B 7 bis; and minutes by Grey on telegram from G. Beak, October 19, 1910, in PRO, FO 367/215.

26. On Belgian fears, see Sohier, "Aurore Katanga," *Etoile du Congo*, August 26, September 1, 1923; R. Asmis, *Aus den Archiven des belgischen Kolonialministeriums* (Berlin, 1918), pp. 1-5. Lord Crewe's refusal to invade is communicated in a telegram from the High Commissioner for Southern Africa (Lord Herbert Gladstone) to the Governor of Northeastern Rhodesia (L. A. Wallace), October 29, 1910, in ZA, NWR 3/6 (old filing system).

27. Stengers, *Belgique et Congo*, pp. 13-17.

28. Ibid., pp. 107, 136-139.

29. Joye and Lewin, *Les trusts*, pp. 237-41; S. H. Frankel, *Capital Investment in Africa* (London, 1938), p. 409; "Note justificative au projet de convention annexe," in AR, de Broqueville, p. 346.

30. Katzenellenbogen, "Benguela Railway," pp. 44-65, contains the best narrative; but see also Terlinden, *CSK*, pp. 24-32, 54-56.

31. *UMHK 1906-1956*, pp. 107-8.

32. "Questions financières coloniales," May 18, 1914, in AR, de Broqueville, p. 343.

33. On the commission, see *UMHK 1906-1956*, pp. 103-8; E. van der Straeten, *Jules Cousin, pionnier, chef d'entreprise et homme du bien (1884-1965)*, ARSOM, Classe des Sciences Morales et Politiques, NS 38 2 (Bruxelles, 1969), pp. 9-10. On Williams's debts, J. Renkin, "Augmentation de capital de la société UMHK," May 1912, AR, de Broqueville, p. 347.

34. UMHK, *Evolution des techniques*, p. 294.

35. Renkin, "Augmentation de capital," AR, de Broqueville, p. 347; Terlinden, *CSK*, pp. 60-61.

36. Sohier, "Augore Katanta," *Le Foyer*, 14 (January 15, 1924).

37. For the general Belgian attitude, see A. DeBauw to van Iseghem, Musée Royal de l'Afrique Centrale, Tervuren (MRAC), Fond André van Iseghem (AvI); December 20, 1910, P. Forthomme, *La véritable signification du Katanga pour la Belgique* (Bruxelles, 1911, p. 33; A. Lodewyck, *Katanga en Zuid-Afrika* (Gent, 1911), pp. 25-26; CSK *Rapport annuel 1920*, pp. 28-29. On *La Pastorale*, see E. Leplae, *Exploitation d'un ferme au Katanga et dans les régions élevées du Congo belge* (Bruxelles, 1921), pp. 17-18. Leplae's scheme is covered by R. J. Cornet, *Les phares verts* (Bruxelles, 1965), pp. 125-34, to which should be added Leplae's description in *Echo de la Bourse* reprinted by *Essor du Congo*, August 8, 1936; *Rapport Agricole du Congo Belge*, 6 (1915):89. On government undercapitalization, see van der Elst, *Katanga*, p. 95. The magistrate G. van der Kerken, in *Les sociétés bantoues au Congo belge et les problèmes de la politique indigène* (Bruxelles, n.d. [ca. 1920]), p. 204, estimates that Leplae's scheme cost eight million gold francs.

38. On the background of Catholic activities in industrial Katanga, see Mgr. de Hemptinne, "Discours prononcé aux fêtes jubilaires de l'enseignement officiel de 14 juin 1952 à Elisabethville," *Cahiers de St. André*, 9 (1953):40-42; *Mémorial de Salésiens* (Elisabethville, 1952), pp. 7-9. On the Sisters of Charity, see *Cahiers de St. André*, 1 (1938):233, and their report to the provincial department of education, South Katanga, April 1966 (RE). On the Benedictines, see Legrand and Thoreau, *Bénédictins*; Congo, *Rapport annuel 1910*, p. 72. On government aid, see Renkin to VGG, November 22, 1911, and February 28, 1913; Chef de Cabinet Denyn to VGG, September 30, 1915—all in RE; Congo, *Rapport annuel 1915*, pp. 18-19. On DeDecker's life, E. G., "D. Idesbald DeDecker," *Cahiers de St. André*, 13, (1956):80-83.

39. R. Lemarchand, *Political Awakening in the Belgian Congo* (Berkeley and Los Angeles, 1964), pp. 57-62.

40. Association des Licenciés sortis de l'Université de Liège, *Le Katanga: Province Belge* (Liège, 1911), p. 42; Rolin *Les vices*, p. 27.

41. The number of government officials in Katanga comes from the Congo, *Rapport annuel 1910*, ibid., *1922*. On the choice of territorial officials, see van der Elst, *Katanga*, p. 113. On the problems of training officials, see Rolin, *Les Vices*, pp.

21-22. Van Iseghem's evaluation comes from his letter to General
Donny, April 8, 1914, in MRAC, AvI. On the syndicate of
government employees, see *Essor du Congo*, February 2, 1934,
and *Journal du Katanga*, February 3, 1914; A. Sohier, "L'organization de la Magistrature Congolaise," *Revue de Droit et de
Juridiction Katangaise*, 2 (1925):43-44.

42. The names of Wangermée's council members appear in
Journal Administratif du Katanga, 1913, p. 173.

43. Note by Administrateur R. Marchal, September 23, 1940,
in AP A 36, B 6 bis.

44. Dom Marc de Montpellier d'Annevoie, *Deux ans au
Katanga* (Bruxelles, 1921), p. 117; F. Harfeld, *Méntalities
indigènes du Katanga* (Bruxelles, 1913), pp. 24-25; *Journal du
Katanga*, August 13, 1912; J. M. Springer, *I Love the Trail*
(Nashville, 1952), p. 95; J. Tasch, "La capitale du Katanga,"
Essor du Congo, July 12, 1928.

NOTES: CHAPTER 4

1. Springer, *Pioneering in the Congo*, p. 253.

2. Bruce Fetter, "Central Africa 1914: German Schemes and
British Designs," Académie Royale des Sciences d'Outremer,
Bulletin des Séances (1972), pp. 541-49.

3. J. Atkin, "Official Regulation of British Overseas
Investment, 1914-1931," *Economic History Review*, 23 (1971):
324-35.

4. The original agreement between the Chancellor of the
Exchequer, Reginal McKenna, and Renkin was signed on July 4,
1916, PRO,FO 371/2638; for subsequent complications, see PRO,
FO 371/2852. On the use of German track to complete the line,
see G. Moulaert, *La campagne au Tanganika (1916-1917)* (bruxelles,
1934), p. 186.

5. Bans on African consumption of European food can be
found in the *Journal Administratif du Katanga*, 1917-20;
Ordonnance-lois No. 13 du 20 juin 1917, No. 24 du 17 octobre 1917,
No. 00/4 du 13 septembre 1917, No. 11 du 27 février 1920, 20
decembre 1920. Bans on the export of African food crops are contained in ibid., No 00/4 du 1 mai 1918, No. 2 du 20 janvier
1919, No. 25 du 11 novembre 1919. Confiscation appears in ibid.,
No. 00/1 du 21 juin 1918, No. 13 du mars 1920 which was abrogated
30 juin 1920.

6. Undated (November or December 1916) Annexe aux instructions BTK, No. 23, *Journal du Katanga,* July 10, 1915.

7. P. Ferraris, *Une excursion au Katanga (Congo belge)* (Liege, 1918), pp. 50-52; UNHK, Service Médical, *Rapport annuel 1921.*

8. Fetter, "Immigrants," pp. 24-25.

9. Kawambwa and Fort Rosebery subdistrict notebooks, National Archives of Zambia, Lusaka (ZA).

10. Gelfand, *Northern Rhodesia,* p. 104; M. A. B. Denton-Thompson, "Native Labour in the Katanga. Annual Report for the Year Ending 31st March 1917," Henry Lambert, Colonial Undersecretary, to R. Graham, Foreign Undersecretary, August 31, 1917, both in PRO, FO 369/917.

11. E. Muller, *Les troupes du Katanga et les campagnes d'Afrique 1914-1918* (Bruxelles, 1935), 1:60-61; 139-44; C. Hordern and H. F. Stacke, *Military Operations in East Africa, History of the Great War Based on Official Documents by Direction of the Historical Section of the Committee on Imperial Defence* (London, 1941), 1:186-87; M. Luwel, "La Force Publique à Tabora et à Saio," *Africa-Tervuren,* 12 (1966):55.

12. F. Dellicour, "Rutten," *Biographie belge d'outremer,* 6:714-21; Représentant du CSK Weyns to Administrator, Northeastern Rhodesia, Codrington, August 12, 1902, in ZA. BS 1/86 I; L. Dieu, *Dans la brousse congolaise* (Liège, 1946), pp. 277-29.

13. E. C. Hartzler, *Brief History of Methodist Missionary Work in the Southern Congo during the First Fifty Years* (Elisabethville, 1960), pp. 9-27; de Rennette de Villiers Perwin to GG, March 31, 1917, and de Rennette to Renkin, August 1, 1917 and January 5, 1918, both in Department of Education, Katanga Province; Kambale Munzambo, "L'Ecole Professionelle de la Kafubu tenue par les pères Salésiens (1912-1950), Thèse de Licence, UNAZA, Lubumbashi, 1973, p. 33.

14. On Horner's relations with the Belgians, see van der Straeten, *Jules Cousin,* p. 12; J. G. Watson to A. A. Thompson, April 15, 1916, in PRO, FO 371/2600; Horner to G. Velge, May 6, 1916, in R. Williams to Sir W. Langley, June 7, 1916, in FO 371/2634.

15. O. Louwers, *Codes et lois du Congo belge* (Bruxelles, 1914), pp. 795-96, 405-6.

16. No single narrative of these events has been published.
On Rutten's mission, see F. Dellicour, "Martin Rutten,"
Bulletin de l'IRCB, 8 (1) (1946):209. On conditions at the
mines, see A. Boigelot, "Réponse à M. le Représentant du
Conseil d'Administration de l'Union Minière," *Comité Régional*
3, Annexe 14 (April 22, 1921). On the emergency recruitment
see UNHK, *Evolution des techniques*, p. 283.

17. On the American offer, see Renkin to Albert I, September 13, 1917, in Palais Royal, Brussels, Fonds dit du Havre,
Questions Coloniales-Congo. Sengier described his mission in
Comité Régional 3 Annexe 10 (April 19, 1921). On his background, see *Essor du Congo*, February 7, 1936.

18. A. Boigelot, *Rapport sur l'hygiène des travailleurs
noire période de mai 1918 à mai 1919* (Bruxelles, 1920), p. 51;
CSK, *Rapport annuel 1920*, p. 26; *Journal Administratif du
Katanga 1919*, pp. 157-73.

19. On the use of Africans, see L. Scraeyen to Lambert
Jadot, September 25, 1915, in R. Williams to Sir W. Langley,
November 8, 1915, in PRO, FO 371/2283. On early conditions for
Europeans, see Gann, *Northern Rhodesia*, p. 173; idem, *A History
of Rhodesia* (New York, 1969), 1:266; *Journal du Katanga*, January
16 and March 12, 1912; and *Comité Régional*, 1 (April 7, 1919):
46-47.

20. UMHK, *Evolution des Techniques*,, pp. 300-1; *Rapport
officiel du coût de la vie au Katanga* (Elisabethville, 1919),
esp. pp. 8, 20-21. On the services provided by the companies,
see also CSK, *Rapport annuel 1920*, pp. 36-44. On the persecution of British merchants, see Vice Consul Denton Thompson to
Undersecretary Foreign Office, April 15 and May 14, 1920, and
Acting Attorney General A. Sohier to VGG M. Rutten, May 15,
1920, in Ambassador Villiers (Brussels) to Lord Curzon, August
3, 1920, all in FO 371/3650.

21. Two conflicting versions of the last strike can be
found in UMHK, *Evolution des techniques*, pp. 301-2, and the
first chapter of A. Corneille (pseudonym A. Poortman), *Le
syndicalism au Katanga* (Elisabethville, 1945); see also P.
Dufrénoy, "Syndicalisme colonial," *Vétérans Coloniaux*, 18
(September, 1946):9-21, and Congo, *Rapport annuel 1920*, pp.
46-47. On the increased percentage of Belgians in the work
force, see UMHK, *Evolution des techniques*, p. 284.

22. J. Comhaire, "Lubumbashi et Nairobi: Etude comparée
de leur évolution," *Revue française des sciences politiques*
(1972), pp. 56-57; *Comités régionaux:* 1 (April 2, 1919):8-9;

genda 1925, 1; J. de Boelpaepe, "Participation des colons belges
à l'administration de la Colonie," *Congrès colonial*, 1
(Bruxelles, 1921):308.

23. On government holdings in the Union Minière and on the
company's first dividends, see *UMHK 1906-1956*, pp. 68-72, 107-8,
128-30. On the settlers' project, see C. Young, *Politics in
the Congo* (Princeton, 1965), pp. 483-84n, and Lemarchand,
Political Awakening, p. 60.

NOTES: CHAPTER 5

1. Maurice Lippens, *Notes sur le gouvernement du Congo*,
1921-1922 (Gand, 1923).

2. Legrand and Thoreau, *Les bénédictins*, pp. 136-38; A.
Auffray, *En pleine brousse équatoriale: Histoire de la Mission
salésienne du Katanga (Préfecture apostolique du Laupula
supérieure)* (Turin, 1926), pp. 53-55.

3. Grévisse, *Le CEC*, pp. 5-6. On the South African urban
policy which was pioneered in Durban, M. W. Swanson, "Reflec-
tions on the Urgan History of South Africa: Some Problems and
Possibilities," *African Urban Notes*, 4, 3 (1969):30-40.

4. CSK, *Rapport Annuel 1923*, p. 69. The specific require-
ments for new African housing in the *cité* were outlined in
Ordonnane No. 3 du 6 février in *Journal Administratif du Katanga
1922*, p. 47.

5. *Hansard*, 5th Ser., March 19, 1918; ibid., May 13, 1918.

6. Gaddis Smith, "The British Government and the Disposi-
tion of the German Colonies in Africa, 1914-1918," in P. Gifford
and W. R. Louis, *Britain and Germany in Africa* (New Haven, 1967),
p. 283.

7. Atkin, "Official Regulation of British Overseas Investment," pp. 324-25.

8. *The Economist*, 92 (1921):198-99; ibid., 100 (1925):542.

9. *UMHK*, pp. 130-33. J. de Geest, "La stratégie de la
Société Générale dans le secteur des non-ferreux," *La revue
nouvelle*, 56 (1972):365.

10. Ch. d'Ydewalle, "Trois grandes entreprises," *Revue
coloniale belge*, 257 (1956):460; L. Franck to the Belgian

Parliament, June 16, 1922; J. Stengers, *Combien le Congo a-t-il coûté à la Belgique?*, ARSC Classe des Sciences Morales et Politiques, Mémoires in 8°, NS 10, 1(1957):87-97.

11. *UMHK*, pp. 150-54; Stengers, *Le Congo combien?*, pp. 12-14.

12. R. Asmis, *Der Belgisch Kongo nach dem Weltkriege* (Leipzig, 1920), p. 54; *The Economist*, 100 (1925):622; A. D. Chandler, Jr., *Strategy and Structure: Chapters in the History of the Industrial Enterprise* (Cambridge, Mass., 1962), pp. 326-30.

13. Fetter, "L'UMHK," pp. 12-14. Much of the material presented in this chapter was first discussed in this work, albeit in a different light.

14. UMHK, Service Medical, *Rapports annuels 1921-1924*.

15. Much of the following discussion is documented in Fetter, "L'UMHK," pp. 12-21.

16. Gann, *Northern Rhodesia*, p. 23n.

17. Contract between Robert Williams and Co. and the Northern Rhodesia Administration, February 1, 1919, in ZA, 1/9 19/5 (old filing system).

18. Miracle and Fetter, "Labor Supply Functions," pp. 246n, 247n; *Comité Régional*, 7 (1925):156; Congo, *Rapports aux Chambres*, 1915-1924.

19. C. W. G. Walker, "Notes of a conversation between Sir Edward Grigg and Monsieur Jaspar," June 18, 1927, in ZA, B/1/1/A 1599 (old filing system); BCK, Division Nord, Règlement (n.p., 1925), p. 17.

20. Chalux (Roger de Châtelux), *Un an au Congo belge* (Bruxelles, 1925), p. 195.

21. *Journal Administratif du Katanga*, 1924, p. 97.

22. CSK, *Rapport annuel 1924*, pp. 66-67; Fetter, "L'UMHK," p. 23.

23. Kawambwa Sub-District Notebook, pp. 387-88, in ZA, KSG 3/11, Fort Rosebery Sub-District Annual Reports, ZA, KDF 6/13.

24. *Journal Administratif du Katanga*, 1918, pp. 90-91; Fetter, "L'UMHK," pp. 15-21.

25. Fetter, "L'UMHK," pp. 21-25.

NOTES: CHAPTER 6

1. *Essor du Congo,* May 12, 1943; UMHK, Service Médical, *Rapport annuel 1924*; "Le développement d'Elisabethville," *Le mouvement géographique,* October 16, 1921.

2. UMHK, *Evolution des techniques,* p. 88; Fetter, "Immigrants," p. 21.

3. *Essor du Congo,* August 24, 1929; J. Sohier, *Quelques traits de la physionomie de la population européenne d'Elisabethville* (Bruxelles: IRCB, 1953), pp. 65-68.

4. J. C. C. Coxhead, "Report on Rhodesian Natives in the Katanga," October, 1929, in ZA, ZA 1/9 18/34.

5. Erving Goffman, *Asylums: Essays on the Social Situation of Mental Patients and Other Inmates* (Garden City, N. Y., 1961), pp. 5-12. For all attempts to apply Goffman's notions to the entire institution of slavery, see G. M. Fredrickson and C. Lasch, "Resistance to Slavery," *Civil War History,* 13 (1967): 315-29.

6. Fetter, "L'UMHK," pp. 10-12.

7. *Essor colonial et maritime,* October 6, 1923; interview with E. Toussaint, October 4, 1966.

8. Chalux, *Un an au Congo belge,* p. 347.

9. Chandler, *Strategy and Structure,* pp. 286-89; UMHK, *Evolution des techniques, passim.*

10. P. de Smet, "Hommage au Camarade J. Cousin," *Lovania,* 15 (1949):194-201; E. van der Straeten, "Sengier," *Biographie belge d'outremer,* 7, 1:429-37. L. A. Petillon, "de Hemptinne," ibid., 7, 1:291-99.

11. Dossiers: "Ecole St. Boniface," "Ecole St. François de Sales," "Ecole officielle de la Kafubu," RE.

12. R. Anstey, *King Leopold's Legacy* (London, 1966), p. 89; Hostelet, *L'oeuvre civilisatrice de la Belgique au Congo, de 1885 à 1945* (Bruxelles, ARSC, 1954), 1:282-83.

13. Order of the Director General, August 9, 1927, in UMHK, B7.

14. Figures on the number of missionaries come from Congo, *Rapport annuel 1928*; those for the number of proselytes, from Legrand and Thoreau, *Bénédictins*, pp. 146-47, and *Foreign Mission Report* 1928, p. 170. For school enrollments, see dom G. Coussement, "Rapport sur les écoles desservies par la Mission Bénédictine dans le territoire d'Elisabethville," February 2, 1927, in RE, Ecole Industrielle; W. F. Shields, report of January 31, 1927, in RE, Installations Missions Etrangères; dom P. Legrand, report of January 1927, in RE, Ecole St. Boniface.

15. *Essor du Congo*, July 12, 1928; Courrier d'Afrique, March 7, 1931.

16. *Journal of the Congo Mission Conference*, July 1927.

17. *Comités Régionaux*: 5 (1923):58; 7 (1925):156-57, 8 (1926):207-9.

18. *Essor du Congo*, March 8, 1953; J. van der Straeten, "Heenen," *Biographie belge d'outremer*, 6:463-69.

19. Young, *Politics of the Congo*, p. 107. A. van Iseghem, untitled article in *Bulletin de la Chambre de Commerce d'Elisabethville*, 2 (1925):10; *Comité Régional*, 10 (1929):140-82; Gann, *Northern Rhodesia*, pp. 141, 237.

20. Fetter, "L'UMHK," pp. 21-25.

21. Yogolelo Tambwe ya Kasimba, "Mission de recrutement de travailleurs de l'UMHK au Kivu Maniema (1926-1928)," Thèse de license, Département d'Histoire, Université Nationale du Zaïre, 1973, pp. 88, 102, 105-6.

22. Réunion Direction Génefale, Service Médical, May 11, 1929, UMHK, C8, *1931 Labor Commission*, 47.

23. District Elisabethville, "Rapport annuel, 1930," AP, A 3.

24. Dr. H. Staudt, "Note au sujet de l'inspection médicale de l'école pour garçons noirs à Elisabethville," February 27, 1930, in RE, "Ecole St. Boniface."

25. Grévisse, *Le CEC*, pp. 151-66; CSK, *Rapport annuel*, 1924, pp. 31-32.

26. See J. A. Taylor and D. V. Lehmann, *Christians of the Copperbelt: The Growth of the Church in Northern Rhodesia*

(London, 1961), p. 301; P. Mayer, *Townsmen or Tribesmen* (Cape Town, 1961), pp. 4-5, 9; J. Berg, "Mombasa between Two Worlds; A Study of Urban Transition, 1940-1914," Ph.D. dissertation, Madison, Wisconsin, 1969, pp. 1-20.

27. *Cahiers de St. André*, 14 (August 1957):74.

28. Fetter, "L'UMHK," pp. 25-28.

29. Fetter, "African Associations," pp. 205-23.

NOTES: CHAPTER 7

1. Tanganyika Concessions, Ltd., *Annual Reports*, 1932, 1933; W. Y. Elliott et al., *International Control in Non-Ferrous Metals* (New York, 1937), pp. 459-86, cited in Katzenellenbogen, "Benguela Railway," p. 334. See also Congo, *Rapports annuels 1931, 1932*; *UMHK*, pp. 171-73.

2. Fetter, "L'UMHK," pp. 29-37.

3. Sohier, *Quelques traits*, pp. 65-68; A. Chapelier, *Elisabethville: Rapport aux chambres 1931*, p. 200; *Essor du Congo*, January 16, 1934.

4. Fetter, "African Associations," pp. 215-16.

5. H. Y. Willis, "Reports of the Inspector of Rhodesian Natives, 1931-33," in ZA, ZA 1/9, 18/34.

6. G. Shepperson, "The Comparative Study of Millenarian Movements," in S. Thrupp, *Millenial Dreams in Action: Comparative Studies in Society and History Supplement*, vol. 2 (The Hague, 1962), pp. 44-45.

7. Fetter, "African Associations," p. 218. Sholto Cross "Jehovah's Witnesses and Socio-Economic Change in the Luapula Province," presented to the Political Science Workshop, University of Zambia, August 1972.

8. Cross, "Jehovah's Witnesses"; Acting Governor Postiaux, "Note au sujet de la secte Kitawala," Elisabethville, le 31 décembre 1931, in Archives Régionales du Shaba, Lubumbashi (Ar Rég), dossier Kitawala; H. Y. Willis, "Notes of the Kitawala Movement," January 9, 1932, in ZA, ZA 1/15/M 1.

9. Bruce Fetter, "Zambian Watchtower at Elisabethville, 1931-1934. An Analysis of Personal and Aggregate Data,"

presented to the annual meeting of the African Studies Association, 1974.

    10. Coxhead, "Report on Rhodesian Natives," in ZA, ZA 1/9 18/34.

    11. Fetter, "Zambian Watchtower," op. cit.

    12. Idem., "L'UMHK," p. 31.

    13. Van der Straeten, "Heenen," pp. 463-69; J. Magotte, *Les centres extra-coutumiers* (Dison-Verviers, 1938), p. 24; Grevisse, *Le CEC*, pp. 19-25, 35-38, 46.

    14. M. Walraet, "Verbeken," in *Biographie belge d'outremer*, 6:1050-54; *Essor du Congo*,, March 8, 1953; interview with A. Berthier, May 1966.

    15. "Note secrète remise à Monsieur Postiaux, Gouverneur du Katanga," September 16, 1931; Lettre circulaire du GG Tilkins à tous les Gouverneurs de Province et Procureurs Généraux relative au service de renseignements, October 10, 1929; Postiaux to Tilkins, November 10, 1931—all in Ar Rég, dossier Kitawala.

    16. "Rapport de synthèse Kitawala," Colonial sûreté, 1954, pp. 126-29, Archieves sous-régionales de Kalemie, copy in the author's possession.

    17. *Comités Régionaux*: 12 (1931), p. 98; 13 (1932), pp. 86-87.

    18. Fetter, "L'UMHK," pp. 30-31; *Agence économique et financière*, May 15, 1933.

    19. Province du Katanga, *Rapport annuel 1933*; Province Elisabethville, *Rapport annuel 1934*; Consul General Harold Swan to Ambassador Neville Bland (Brussels), December 8, 1933, in PRO, FO 371/17287; van der Straeten, "Heenen," pp. 463-69.

    20. For promises made by Tilkens during his trip to Elisabethville, see *Essor du Congo*, December 1, 1933; ibid., April 15, 1939; *Le Soir*, December 1, 5, 1933; ibid., March 6, 1934; *Courrier d'Afrique*, February 16, 1934. On the schools, see *Essor du Congo*, March 9, 1936; ibid., April 14, 1939; dossier, "Ecole Industrielle," in RE.

    21. Fetter, "L'UMHK," pp. 32-33; "Note pour M. le commissaire provincial . . . Lusambo," March 11, 1938, in UMHK, B5; UMHK, Service Médical, *Rapports annuels 1929, 1937*.

22. The ethnic census of 1942 provided in Fetter, "Immigrants," seriously underestimates the proportion of Zambians in Elisabethville. To the 16 percent Bemba known to the administration must be added 85 percent of the Africans who identified themselves as Aushi and Tabwa. Thus the proportion of Zambians in the CEC was approximately one-third.

23. Coxhead, "Report on Rhodesian Natives," ZA, ZA 1/9, 18/34; *Essor du Congo*, February 1, 1936.

NOTES: CHAPTER 8

1. Territoire d'Elisabethville, *Rapport annuel 1940*, AP, A 60.

2. UMHK, *1964 Monograph*, p. 19.

3. Fetter, "L'UMHK," pp. 28-37.

4. Tableaux 13 and 14 bix in D/510 of August 1940 in UMHK A 6; note 673/D 900 of September 9, 1940, in ibid., A 1.

5. Fetter, "L'UMHK," p. 37, n; L. Mottoulle, *Contribution à l'étude du déterminisme fonctionnel de l'industrie dans l'éducation de l'indigène congolais* (Bruxelles: IRCB, 1934), pp. 27-29.

6. Fetter, "L'UMHK," p. 34.

7. A. L. Epstein, *Politics in an Urban African Community* (Manchester, 1958), pp. 1-47.

8. *Dépêche coloniale belge*, October 29, 1939; *Essor du Congo*, April 22, 1939.

9. A. Engels, "Maron," *Biographie belge d'outremer*, 6:691-94; *Comité Régional 13*, April 27, 1933, pp. 220-21.

10. A. Engels, "Dupont," *Biographie belge d'outremer*, 4:259-62; *Essor du Congo*, October 25, 1938; C. Dupont, "Note analytique sur le mouvement Kitawala dans les territoires de Jadotville et de Malanga district du Lualaba," February 26, 1935, in Ar Rég, Dossier Kitawala.

11. *Essor du Congo*, September 15-16, 1944.

12. Commissaire de la Police Urbaine Charlier to Commissaire de district, Haut-Katanga, May 15, 1934; Administrateur

Territorial van Huffel, Rapport trimestriel Sûreté Publique,
IIIe trimestre 1934, in Ar Rég, Dossier Kitawala.

13.   Grévisse, *Le CEC*, pp. 10-19, 34-50; Province Elisa-
bethville, *Rapport annuel 1935*, 117 in AP, A 1; F. Grévisse,
"CEC Provision budgetaire, 1940," in Bureau de l'Etat Civil,
Lubumbashi.

14.   Grévisse, *Le CEC*, pp. 10-19, 34-36; minute by Maron
on Service AIMO, *Rapport annuel*, June 22, 1936, in AP, A 60.

15.   Lemarchand, *Political Awakening*, pp. 82-85; Grévisse,
Le CEC, pp. 39-42, 74-89; R. Marchal, annex to the projected
budget for the CEC for 1941, December 18, 1940, in Bureau de
l'Etat Civil, Lubumbashi; *Conseil de Province 1939*, p. 36;
Ryckmans to Maron, October 30, 1940, in dossier BAE, 1941,
Archives de la Zone de Lubumbashi.

16.   Gann, *Northern Rhodesia*, passim.

17.   Epstein, *Politics in Urban African Communities*, pp.
26-47.

18.   Malira Kubuya-Namulemba, "Les associations féminines
de Lubumbashi (1920-1950)," Mémoire de Licence, Département
d'Histoire, UNAZA, Lubumbashi, 1973.

19.   District Elisabethville, *Rapport annuel 1931*, pp.
11-12; *Essor du Congo*, July 4, 1933.

20.   Territoire Elisabethville, *Rapport annuel 1934*, in AP,
A 60; *Conseil de province 1937*, p. 37; District Commissioner
Ziegler de Ziegleck to A. Kabongo, May 4, 1937, in Security
Files, Bureau de l'Etat Civil, Lubumbashi.

21.   District Haut-Katanga, *Conseil du District*, June 8,
1944, in Ap, A 107; dom (later Mgr.) F. Cornelis, "L'instruction
et l'éducation de la population indigène masculine d'Elisabethville," *Congrès scientifique*, 1:357; *Comité Régional*, 14 (April
27, 1933):217.

22.   Province Elisabethville, *Rapport annuel 1937*, in AP,
A 1.

23.   *Conseil de Province 1938*, pp. 105-6.

24.   *Cahiers de St. André*, 3 (1946):267-70; ibid., 14
(1957):74-75.

25. Legrand and Thoreau, *Bénédictins,* pp. 151-52; *Essor du Congo,* November 22, 1932; ibid., October 19, 1933; G. Dutillieu, "Activités complémentaires," *Problèmes sociaux congolais,* 44 (1959):97-98.

26. Information on the activities of Coussement and van Arenberg with the secret committee was given in confidence by both Europeans and Africans, *Cahiers de St. André* (1957), pp. 71-80.

27. Young, *Politics in the Congo,* p. 10.

NOTES: CHAPTER 9

1. T. G. McGee, *The Urbanization Process in the Third World: Explorations in Search of a Theory* (London, 1971).

2. Walter B. Stöhr, *Interurban Systems and Regional Development,* Commission on College Geography Resource Paper No. 26 (Washington, D.C.: Association of American Geographers, 1974), pp. 11-12; see also Richard M. Morse, "Trends and Issues in Latin American Urban Research, 1965-1970," *Latin American Research Review,* 6 (1971), 1:13-52, 2:19-75—especially 2:45-50. Two colleagues introduced the author to the relevant literature: Professor David Buck of the History Department and Professor Lutz Holzner of the Geography Department, University of Wisconsin-Milwaukee.

3. R. L. Buell, *The Native Problem in Africa* (Cambridge, Mass., 1928), 1:941.

4. Grévisse, *Le CEC,* pp. 77-80.

5. Elliott P. Skinner, *African Urban Life: The Transformation of Ouagadougou* (Princeton, 1974), p. 446.

6. Cornelis, "L'instruction et l'education de la population indigene masculine d'Elisabethville," p. 357.

BIBLIOGRAPHIC NOTE: For bibliographic material, see Bruce Fetter, "Elisabethville," *African Urban Notes,* Bibliographical Supplement No. 7, June 1968.

INDEX